The American Congress

By

Roland Young

Harper & Brothers, Publishers, New York

THE AMERICAN CONGRESS

M-G

Library of Congress catalog card number: 58-5081

CONTENTS

PREFACE

The study of legislatures offers a provocative challenge to everyone whose interest has been drawn to a close examination of politics and of political institutions. The challenge has several sides, including the development of legislative theory, the promotion of research, and the transmission of our political heritage to the oncoming generations. The transmission of our political heritage—that is, teaching students to think about the problems of governing—is often emphasized at considerable length, with many officials being so impressed by its need that they see to it that the subject is studied in heavy doses. Here we may enter a caveat, not on the purpose but on the possible limitations of such study. The transmission of our political heritage may indeed be necessary for the survival of our culture, but the process may be sterile as well as misleading if the material to be handed on is not subjected to occasional analysis and a theoretical interpretation of its meaning.

Legislatures in modern times have a less sure place in our political thought than they had, say, a hundred years ago. The separation of legal authority into three distinct spheres may not in fact be followed by a corresponding separation of functions actually performed or of influence exerted. During the last century the world has seen newly created and undeveloped states attempting to gain the benefits of freedom through legislatures, only to have the government usurped by the man with a gun. It has also seen other types of states, more modern in the sense of scientific advancement and more fully developed economically, substitute dictatorship for constitutional legislatures. Even in those parts of the world which have remained solidly constitutional in principle, the functions of the legislature are by no means or surely not always clear. However, the ability of many legislatures to resolve conflict, to create a pattern of legal order, to establish responsibility, and to promote or create areas of freedom, would seem to indicate that they have functions to perform which can neither be suspended nor neglected in a constitutional democracy.

Legislative theories do not develop by themselves, as if wishing would make them so, and in the case of Congress, at least, there is an open opportunity for developing useful legislative theory—for theory that will guide as well as explain—which utilizes the benefits of empirical research. Unfortunately for those who want a quick or easy answer, the dynamics of the legislative process do not relinquish their secrets readily. The complexity of the process combined with the manageability or at least the observability of its operations, make the use of a variety of research methods especially suitable. Similarly, the inquiry should attract a wide number of investigators whose interests range, say, from public policy formation to the behavior of political leaders under conditions of stress and strain.

The present volume attempts to place the various facets of the legislative process into a framework which will reveal the functional interrelation of its various parts. In doing so, it also indicates some areas where our knowledge is incomplete as well as the absence of broadly accepted standards for governing the behavior of the members concerned. Whatever values this approach may have, it is of course not the only approach possible, and other methods of investigation may offer additional clues to the perpetual problem of resolving conflict and establishing order and stability in society. A Research Guide has been appended to the body of the text to serve as an introduction to legislative documents and studies as well as to suggest additional topics for research.

I owe a debt to various colleagues who, through comment and conversation, have contributed to the preparation of this manuscript. My thanks go to Professor Ralph K. Huitt, for his helpful and perspicacious comments on the manuscript; to Robert Strodel and David

K. Marvin ,for assistance in preparing the Research Guide; and to Charles S. Huneman, Richard C. Snyder, and David Apter, who perform so well the functional role of academic provocateurs.

Evanston, Illinois   R. Y.
December, 1957

The American Congress

CHAPTER 1

The Requirements of a Legislature

AN ATTEMPT IS MADE IN THIS BOOK TO DEVELOP A framework of ideas for examining the part played by Congress in the American system of government and for taking a fresh view of the expectations of its performance we may rightly hold. Congress has many strengths which are not always recognized (and not always used), but its basic function may at times be overlooked because of the continual pressure of new problems, the turnover in membership, and the passage of time. Even at the risk of emphasizing the obvious, there may nevertheless be some value in restating the requirements of Congress—the requirements which it must fulfill if it is to be a Congress—and later to discuss in more detail how Congress goes about fulfilling these several requirements. The essential requirement for Congress is that of establishing a basic legal pattern of order for society. This in turn leads to the additional requirements for creating an autonomous legislative organization to make policy and for establishing continuing relations with the government bureaucracy and with the society which is governed.

1

FIRST REQUIREMENT: ESTABLISHMENT OF ORDER

We may begin our inquiry into the legislative process by introducing initially the broad assumption that all of our lives are lived under some pattern of order, that everything we do is not the result of random chance, that there is no built-in mechanism either in ourselves or in what we vaguely call society which provides automatic adjustments of conflict or which gives instinctive or intuitive answers to issues of choice. We must perforce establish controls over our own personal lives; controls over the physical environment; controls over the possible conflict between individuals and groups; and controls in the sense of giving direction and anticipating need. Other than for the individual (who has his own nervous system), these controls over the environment and society and other individuals are culturally created, and the institutions which exercise these controls are the product of man. To use a rather bookish expression, but one which points up the interrelation of individuals in society, we can say that the purposes of life are achieved through a large variety of systems of action—and that the word "system" is used in the sense that the actions of the people directly involved in the system are functionally interrelated. What one person does affects another in some meaningful and often productive fashion.

Further, we can postulate various categories of systems of action, based on their complexity, their significance for or value to other systems of action, and the meaning of the system to those immediately involved. We can think, for instance, of the whole transportation system of the nation: Visibly complex, it is composed of many lesser identifiable parts; its activities may have considerable effect on other systems of action within specific areas which are immediately dependent on the successful operation of the transportation system. We can cite another example of a system of action, less terrestrial in scope but which is nevertheless complex and interrelated with other activities —the distribution of milk in an urban area. The patterns of action here involved reach out into the milksheds in the hinterland area and terminate on the thousands of doorsteps where milk is delivered. Or we can pick still another example of a system of action which is confined to relatively few people; it is complex not in the sense of having a vast administrative network but in the interplay of thought and personality and procedures; and its actions may in turn have considerable effect on others—that is, Congress.

We may assume further that the various systems of action (and not only those mentioned) require some control in order that they can operate effectively as a system. Internal controls will be needed to give direction to the system; external controls will be needed to prevent or adjust possible conflict with other systems of action. The Western world has developed to a high degree various types of governmental authority whose function it is to establish controls over given systems of action. Institutions like Congress, for instance, are not only themselves systems of action but also have special authority to develop controls—or policy ordinarily expressed in the form of law—which others perforce must obey.

Conflict within and between systems of action may be adjusted in a variety of ways, for government (through whatever institutions are used) may be utilized to prescribe particular action which the various systems are to follow: It may adjust conflict between various systems; it may regulate through specific controls; or it may even operate some of the systems itself. In particular, the government is concerned with establishing an internal order which will promote the conditions necessary for survival—public health, shelter, the production of commodities, and the continual adjustment of disputes of whatever magnitude. It is also interested in providing order in the sense of external security, of safety from hostile, competitive systems, and this may encompass the possible use of force. It is additionally interested in making provisions for anticipated future needs, for the protection of human and physical resources, and the continuing needs of society as one generation follows another.

The legislature is, of course, a very special type of institution for establishing order. The fact that it has broad territorial jurisdictions means that a variety of complex activities can be carried on under the aegis of its authority. The fact that controls are specifically stated in the form of law means that there is an element of stability and continuity of policy. The fact that controls pertain to certain select aspects of action means that a large amount of freedom, or of flexibility, is possible. However, legislatures can operate only within the confines of certain types of social organization. They would not be of much value in a static society where there was little or no change and adjustments were made by custom. Nor would they be of much value in a society characterized by chaos or anarchy, or where there was no freedom to make or discuss policy, or where there was a general disregard of legislative decisions. The legislature requires, in short, conditions of some mobility in action and change in social factors; some general acceptance of the basic plan of order by those who are affected by it; and some easy means of communicating ideas within the society.

As a constituent part of a larger governmental system of authority, Congress may be said to perform a natural function in the sense that it is necessary for some institution to be concerned with establishing an ordered relationship between the various internal systems of action. It does not follow that such an institution needs to be Congress or, if it is Congress, that the particular arrangement of authority or the relationship with other institutions is the only one possible. It does mean, however, that if Congress did not exist or was concerned with other matters it would still be necessary for these control functions to be performed. It would be misleading to imply that these activities are the exclusive concern of Congress, a more correct statement being that Congress is concerned in various degrees with providing the conditions and laying down the rules which will enable these essential activities to be carried on. To put it another way, the interest of Congress in these activities is shared in various degrees with other institutions within society, the role of Congress being that of prescribing the rules or creating an ordered pattern of behavior by which members of society can achieve their various purposes.

SECOND REQUIREMENT: SELECTION OF ALTERNATIVE CHOICES

Congress establishes controls and develops policy through a set of generalized rules regulating the actions of other people. The adjective "generalized" is emphasized, for the rules are ordinarily broad enough to cover a variety of contingencies which may arise in the future. The activity involved in adjusting interests, modifying or mollifying expectations, and altering the existing pattern of order lies at the heart of the legislative process.

In the political world, one is constantly dealing with situations of action and change. Within a given system of authority people express their emotions, speak, change their minds, and enter and leave the system, and additionally the external environment and the existence of other groups may affect the nature of the ordered situation. However necessary controls may be, their utility may be limited and their application may be difficult. The harmonious adjustment of interests within and between the various systems of action may be relatively short-lived, with new adjustments being required, or the order may break down completely, retrogressing into a form of chaos, with latent conflict developing into open violence.

The term "equilibrium" is used frequently in this volume as a general term to describe the condition of systems of actions which appear to be operating satisfactorily; that is, they are performing satisfactorily the functions they are expected to perform. Similarly, the term "disequilibrium" is used to describe the condition of systems in disorder, when they no longer appear to perform satisfactorily the functions expected of them. A given system of action may appear to work satisfactorily for a time, but internal or external changes may require a new adjustment. The new adjustment may be easily made and an equilibrium reëstablished, but the reëstablishment of an equilibrium may present difficult problems if the change is of considerable magnitude, such as that resulting, for instance, from a war or civil rebellion. To take an example from the domestic political world during the Second World War: The regulation of wage rates and the conditions of work were developed within a highly unstable political equilibrium, the rules being enforceable only so long as industry, labor, and government maintained their respective memberships in the War Labor Board.

There are some disadvantages and possibilities of misunderstanding in using a term such as "equilibrium," which is borrowed from the physical sciences and is used there to describe conditions which have no precise counterpart in the social realm. However, the term does have the advantage of calling attention to the continual change in the social system. Attempts to control one aspect of a system of action may throw in disarray other systems of action. During the Second World War, for instance, the bakers were permitted to sell unsliced bread as an alternative to raising prices; but housewives then clamored for bread knives, which were unavailable in stores and the manufacturers had no steel to make them. Controls do not always operate specifically or solely on the object to be regulated; rather, change in one area may in turn lead to change in another area. It is part of the job of a wise legislator to anticipate the broad results of any type of imposed controls—not merely to "represent interests."

The forces affecting the various systems of action are continually being upset. With the passage of time, older men are replaced by younger men with different ideas, experiences, and expectations; the physical environment may change; there may be new and different types of adjustment to make. In order to maintain the balance and keep the system operating, in order to maximize the returns for the groups involved, in order to decrease the chances of instability developing, attempts are made continuously, by those affected and competent, to establish controls over significant factors affecting the system. But others may also want to do the same thing for different ends. They also may wish to secure the same franchise, to elect their own man to office, to have a committee consider a bill, to spend public money. Hence, political conflict, political agitation, and political agreement.

In establishing political controls, one is in effect allocating scarce commodities in a situation where the demand for the product outruns the available supply. There is one office but many candidates; X amount of money but Y amount of proposals for spending; few committee chairmen but a large number of claimants. Advocates from disaffected groups, from those groups which are apprehensive about how certain regulations affect them, are continually appealing to Congress for a modification of the prevailing rules. Response to change is not necessarily automatic, and people will interpret differently either the desirability of the change or the specifications for the proposed alteration of the rules.

The functions of Congress in making general rules may be examined by considering the values held by individuals, groups, and members of society as a whole. Many values held by individuals can be fulfilled only within some pattern of order provided by the political system. A value such as that of survival would be jeopardized if society were in a state of anarchy where there were continued threats to life and limb, but an individual might be willing to jeopardize his life if such other values as the safety of his family or even the continuity of the political system were threatened. In other words, some values held by individuals and groups within society can be fulfilled only within a pattern of order provided by the political system. However, not all purposes require such direct assistance, and some individuals may very shortly reach the point where they would prefer no additional political interference with their lives.

Within Congress there may be conflict over the values that should prevail in making decisions. There would be an obvious conflict of values between a gang of kidnapers and the parents of the kidnaped child. Here the decision of which set of values should prevail would be obvious. But the relative merits of the conflicting political claims may be less obvious, and it is the function of the legislature to weigh these relative merits through deliberation before making a final decision. A hypothetical proposal, let us say, to redraft combat veterans of the Korean War for whatever fighting may occur in the future would pose such a conflict. To the veteran, such a proposal might appear to restrict his liberty and to demand unreasonable and inequitable sacrifices on his part; to others, the measure might appear to be necessary to secure the safety of all.

In any complex political decision, the interests of many people and many groups are likely to be involved, whether or not the people affected are conscious of or directly concerned with the decision at the time it is made. One may illustrate this point by referring to the amalgam of individuals and groups who would have an interest in a decision to draft men into the armed services. They would include the individuals to be drafted, their families, schools, and employers. Various government units would also be immediately concerned, including especially the armed forces. We could project the effect of the draft into the future by considering, for instance, its impact on the future supply of scientists and other specialists. All interests are not immediately perceptible and clearly definable, as was shown in the draft case, so that any attempt to think of legislative action solely in terms of interests immediately represented will have serious shortcomings. In establishing policy, the legislature places the conflict in a broader perspective and readjusts the relationships within the whole fabric of society.

Controls are necessary, for without direction and perhaps duress, men will not necessarily behave individually in such a fashion that the present and future interests of society are protected. Men can hate and covet as well as they can love and share, but even under the best of conditions and the most exemplary behavior on the part of all, they will have different needs and different interests which require adjustment. It may be true, of course, that correct training and general acceptance of a common moral code of behavior will lessen tensions and conflicts in society so that individual goals may be achieved with little or no duress. However this may be, some type of authority would still be required to make generalized decisions affecting the totality and to create a pattern of order among the various constituent parts. In our present age, disturbance in the political equilibrium results from conflict between and within various types of internal groups—economic, social, ethnic, religious, and regional—and between the largest of the ordered political groups, the nation-state. Many of these conflicts are adjusted daily in the normal course of affairs; some are adjusted by local political institutions; but some—where many types of interests are affected—are adjusted on a national scale by Congress.

THIRD REQUIREMENT: AN AUTONOMOUS ORGANIZATION

It is, of course, necessary for Congress to develop its own internal organization and procedure for making policy. A legislature takes action in a prescribed fashion within a predetermined organization, which is not the same as individual legislators taking unrelated and independent action on their own. Not only must Congress create procedures and processes for making policy, it must also develop an internal organization for establishing controls over them. The nature of the procedures and the organization is conditioned by constitutional provisions, such as that relating to Congress' having two chambers, and in part by internal rules, such as the committee system. The internal system of authority must have enough stability for Congress to merit the name "institution," but it must also be flexible enough to accommodate the continual inflow of new members and to reflect changing attitudes of the public and the electorate.

The fact that many people participate in making legislative decisions place some limitations on the types of action that can be taken. Congress is not organized to fight a battle or run a department or make a budget or build a ship. But it can decide whether to fight, to create a new agency, spend money, or build ships. In short, it can make policy, and the term "policy" is used to indicate a fixed pattern of action toward any complex, interrelated set of events. It presupposes a continuity of attitudes toward reaching agreed ends, although details of execution may readily be modified. But what kind of policy? On technical subjects? On those requiring secrecy? On those relating to scientific invention? On individual cases?

The range of policy alternatives makes it necessary to reduce this superfluity of choices into manageable limits. Congress needs to be selective in its deliberations, rigidly limiting the type and number of choices available. Controls are placed over such crucial aspects of the legislative process as the subject to be considered, the time allocated for its consideration, and the individuals who will be permitted to utilize this time. Procedures, in turn, require that the various legislators be given functions to perform. Although on a theoretical plane

all legislators have the same legal authority, and in making final decisions the vote of each man counts for one, there is in reality some
differentiation in the nature of authority as well as in the extent of
influence which the legislators possess.

In the process of developing policy, there is a steady narrowing of
the areas in conflict and a broadening of the areas in concord, until
in the end there is firm agreement on the single Act. The difficulty
one might expect Congress to encounter in making decisions on the
wide variety of subjects is met in part by decentralizing the consideration of policy into smaller groups. These smaller groups—committees
—may not only be more adept in securing the required knowledge
but they may also be given considerable control over the content of
policy. In considering tax legislation, for example, the House of
Representatives is frequently limited in its choices to approving or
disapproving the particular bill reported by the Committee on Ways
and Means; in other areas of policy, however, the possibility of offering amendments may widen the scope of choices. Such decentralization may lessen the effectiveness of Congress as a corporate unit; its
part may be confined to legitimating the action of committees, or in
some cases no further legitimation may be required.

In the legislative process, the consent of the members is given
sequentially, by different units, over a period of time, with the final
act of approval or disapproval being precise, orderly, and, hopefully,
meaningful. In its simplest form, the enactment of legislation may be
considered as a process in which policy is approved by a group
somewhat larger than that which originally proposed it. Those who
advocate policy must first persuade others so that, in the end, the
policy will have the support of a large enough part of the totality
to make the decision effective. It is the essence of the process that the
procedures do not give undue advantage to any group, that they
serve to develop a corporate opinion, and that they effectively create
an ordered pattern of behavior for others to follow. In the actual work
of Congress, many types of decisions are made concurrently, with the
component units continually making decisions, major and minor, on
and off the floor, in committees and in the chambers, with many

people talking or listening or thinking in different places about different subjects. An underlying system of procedures gives unity and coherence to what might otherwise appear to be discrete and unrelated actions.

It may be pertinent at this point to distinguish between the methods of making decisions used by individuals and those used by an organizational system in which a number of people participate. In making up his mind, an individual uses his own personal thinking, and the actions he takes are his own responsibility. The thinking which takes place when a corporate body such as Congress makes decisions must still be done by individuals, but with this difference: The corporate decision is concerned with particular categories of individual thought, not with everything that goes on in a member's mind, and Congress uses artificially created procedures to relate and identify the abstracted thought of a large number of people with that of the corporate whole. In its deliberations, Congress follows a prescribed order for considering topics and for making decisions on them. Such procedures make it possible for Congress to make reflective decisions on a wide variety of topics, with the participation at some phase of the process of all its members. If one were to generalize, it would appear that procedures are slower and their significance more emphasized when there is a superfluity of unresolved differences and little solidarity exists within the assembly. Procedures may seem less important and are often followed perfunctorily when a broad consensus already exists.

The existence of political conflict may result in displays of emotion, with partisans expressing themselves in strong terms. Procedures are designed in part to prevent emotions from becoming so high or tempers so hot that it is not possible to make acceptable decisions. It is not in order, for instance, to refer to another member by name or in the second person; to indulge in personalities; to use language personally offensive; to refer to debates, votes, or probable action of the other House, or to cast reflection on the membership, past or present. Emotions may be more restrained than they seem, however, for politicians are skilled at appearing to be angry or outraged or rebuffed without actually losing their tempers, and they may also be able to argue a point forcefully although having little personal concern with the outcome of the conflict. Politicians seem to become inured to opposition, with personal feelings held sufficiently in check to permit sharp opponents on one issue to unite on other issues.

The fact that some of the decisions of Congress have the effect of law points up the close relationship between procedures and legitimacy. The right to make law, given Congress by the Constitution, must be exercised in a prescribed manner, so that in effect the nature of the procedures affects the legitimacy of the action. In making law, it is assumed that certain procedural conditions have been fulfilled, that the legislature is independent, that members have been selected legitimately and are not coerced, that a minimum number is present to carry on deliberations, that proponents have the opportunity to explain and defend and the opponents to question and attack, and that a record is made of the final decision. The procedures must be known and accepted in advance and be above any suspicion of partisan preference; though sometimes tedious, they do perform an important function in the legislative process. After the enactment of a law, the courts may be interested in knowing whether procedural requirements were fulfilled, but an official statement to that effect is ordinarily considered to be sufficient evidence. The courts rarely make an independent inquiry to determine whether a quorum was actually present, whether the vote was tallied correctly, or whether correct procedures were observed. However, if the court enforces the law, it presumes that the law was properly enacted.

One may think of law as a permanent rule, immutable and unchangeable, a standard which is inviolate, rightly governing the behavior of animate and inanimate objects. Legislatures developed historically as institutions which could clarify the meaning of law, but later it was discovered that in so doing they were actually creating new law. The law now made by Congress may be a good deal less stable and perhaps even less wise than the above adjectives imply, for it may be made by a shaky majority, affect a small number of people, and be subject to repeal if there is sufficient discontent with its operation. Nevertheless, the role of law in the legislative process should not be underestimated, for the basic assumption of the total political system is that authority must be acquired legally, that the actions of those in authority must be based on law, and that on the national level the law is made by Congress.

FOURTH REQUIREMENT: EXTERNAL RELATIONSHIPS

Although in making policy Congress must retain a position of autonomy, it nevertheless has continuing relationships with the external world—with the nonofficial but nonetheless political world of voters and constituencies and pressure groups on the one hand, and with the official government bureaucracy on the other hand. Its members are selected from the outside, and these members in turn depend on electoral support to return to office. Its decisions affect other people, and the reactions of other people affect the attitudes, the membership, and even the stability of Congress itself. In short, Congress must continually be aware of public reaction, and, in making policy, attempt to mobilize the support of the public—for particular policies, the continuation in office of its own members, and even the existence of the institution itself. Congress must also be aware of the effect of its action on the government bureaucracy, whose internal organization, legal competence, and fiscal supply are highly sensitized to congressional decisions.

Legislation must be of such a nature that it can actually direct and control action. It must be sufficiently clear to show the sensible intention of the legislators; it must also be acceptable, in the broadest sense, so that it will be obeyed; it must be in such legal form that it will be considered valid by the courts; and it must provide for some continued legislative control. Moreover, legislation must be integrated with other activities, and in approving policy Congress in effect agrees to a particular type of integration. However, subsequent developments may reveal that the integration was less effective or less desirable than was hoped, and a new decision may therefore be required.

Integration must be anticipated in several areas of action—in the government hierarchy, the legislative structure, and in society in gen-

eral, including both the broader public as well as the groups more
immediately affected by the decisions. The fact that policy may be
integrated in one area, however, does not necessarily mean that integration will occur in all areas. The focus of integration within the
government may vary—the presidential office, the Bureau of the
Budget, the National Security Council, the various departments—the
broad legislative requirement being the enactment of policy which
can be integrated structurally within the government. The President
and the bureaucracy will perforce be especially attentive to the manner in which a proposed policy will blend with existing policy and
existing structure; a proposed new agency might duplicate work
already being carried on by an existing agency, or a proposed new
policy might conflict with policy previously authorized under other
legislation. In this area, the President may be able to prevent un-
toward congressional action by the use of his veto.

Integration is also necessary within Congress. It is apparent that
some degree of integration among the various committees is necessary
so that, at the very least, Congress does not enact contradictory laws.
Integration is also needed in terms of goals, anticipations, and expectations; each particular piece of legislation, each separate policy,
requires integration with other policies and must be generally acceptable to the groups most concerned. And Congress must also remain
integrated with the rest of society if it is to make legitimate authoritative rules. In the midst of these larger happenings each individual
member must also carve out for himself a place of influence and a
haven of security.

During deliberations, justifications of the proposed course of action
are made in terms of public satisfactions and necessities, and individual members also attempt to secure support for their action, however unpopular this action may have been with some groups. It is,
of course, a truism to say that political decisions affect people differently and in different degrees. Different groups have different interests, and in making political decisions it may be necessary to make
various compromises and adjustments. Compromise may be needed
to secure the required support; adjustment, to create a harmonious
and workable pattern of action. Issues are ordinarily not so simple as

to present a clear choice between two interests in conflict, with the decision going to the side with the most adherents. Law is a settled rule, but the rule may be a framework for a vastly complex administrative organization which, somehow, will have to blend with the lives of many people.

Although legislative decisions are decisive, have the force of law, and carry sanctions, something more is required in securing integration of policy than the possible threat of force or economic reprisal. Public support is mobilized; individual and group demands and expectations are considered and integrated. The process of securing the integration and the acceptability of policy goes on continuously. The legislators may be able to perform this function more effectively (although they do not act exclusively) than the government specialists because of the formers' acquaintance with the leaders of the community, because of their access to channels of communication, and because of their skills in utilizing the political process effectively. Elections are perhaps the best known method for securing consent and integrating goals, but other methods are also used. The channels of communication between society and Congress are always open, so that many people, many groups, many individuals have access to the legislators.

Inasmuch as integration is not necessarily accomplished with the passage of legislation, the legislature will wish to know how effectively the policy has established a new and more satisfactory equilibrium. It will be especially concerned in areas where governmental control is new and where there are no well-developed anticipations of what will occur. During the Second World War, for instance, various administrators of price control had to spend a considerable share of their time "making their peace" with Congress by arriving at some agreement on what might rightly be anticipated in the development of price control policy. The legislature may make requests for information, or it may rely on public opinion and established procedures for securing the information it requires. In areas of secret operation, of course, it is necessary to construct carefully guarded channels of communication to which few people have access. The legislature, in short, must have an opportunity for examining the effect of its decisions by creating a system of communication which will supply the congressional system with information on how law is being administered. This is the area of controls, of establishing responsibility for policy. Here the actions of Congress may not be definitive, although the information brought into the communications system may reveal enough discontent for Congress to create a new equilibrium by enacting amendatory legislation. Some controls are regularized, and most notably in the budget, where Congress can in theory make an annual review of the whole operation of the government bureaucracy. In other areas of activity—foreign and military policy are noteworthy examples—policy cannot be easily encompassed in the form of law, and not always in the form of monetary allowances, so that legislative controls over such activities may be nebulous and tenuous.

SUMMARY

Congress is chiefly concerned with resolving conflict by establishing a pattern of legal order which those affected are constrained to follow, and it resolves such conflict by establishing generalized rules ordinarily administered by the governmental bureaucracy. In order to operate as a legislature capable of resolving conflict, Congress must develop an internal system of authority and action as well as establish communications with the external world. These requirements are mandatory in the sense that they must be performed if Congress is to be a legislature, but they are not fulfilled regularly with equal thoroughness and emphasis. Their fulfillment represents an equation of relationships and degrees of effectiveness, not a set of either/or alternatives. It may be easier to fulfill some requirements than others, depending on time and circumstances; for example, it may be more difficult to deliberate on policy during an election campaign than at other times, but elections do not occur every day. Although the various functions may be fulfilled with differing degrees of thoroughness, interest, and energy, the performance of no single function can be permitted to lapse completely for any period of time without destroying the legislative system and its involved interrelationships with society and with other government institutions.

CHAPTER 2

Selection of Members

THE LAST CHAPTER DEVELOPED THE POINT THAT Congress must create an internal system of authority in order to make policy and that it must develop channels of communications with the governmental bureaucracy which carries out the laws and with the people who are affected thereby. These functions are conditioned by the system used by Congress in recruiting its members. The selection of the membership, with all the accompanying preparations, precautions, and procedures, brings a world of outside interests within the scope of the legislative process and plants the roots of Congress within the framework of the American social order. An opportunity is opened for relating in some fashion the selection of the membership to the large number of systems of action and interaction which require the exercise of controls on the part of governmental authority. In addition, of course, the selection of the membership determines definitively which specific individuals will be permitted, from a legal point of view, to participate in the legislative process. In the continuous competition to influence political action, a significant step is taken in determining who, specifically, will be placed in positions of authority.

In acting as a conduit of communications, the electoral process must serve the particular needs of the legislature and of the people who are governed, and the two may sometimes be in conflict. It must supply the legislature with the precise number of people—never too many or too few—who, as legislators, are permitted to make authoritative, binding, legal decisions. For constitutional purposes, legality is the thing, inasmuch as legality makes the process authentic and the members legally competent.

The electoral system does not stand as a unit by itself, unassociated with the purposes of the legislature, and its effectiveness requires something more than the selection of legislators. Numbers are not enough. Additionally the system is expected to provide men of talent and character who will be able to perform the numerous roles required in the legislative process. The legislator must, above all, be able to work with the corporate group in making authoritative decisions on the nature of order within society. As Sir William Blackstone once put it, "Every member, though chosen by one particular district, when elected and returned, serves for the whole realm; for the end of his coming thither is not particular, but general; not barely to advantage his constituents, but the *common*wealth." [1]

If Congress is to perform its functions, the legislator—or some of the legislators—must be something more than a pleader for special interests, no matter how vital those interests appear to be to the life of his community and to his own political future. As a legislator, he must be capable of deciding between alternatives, even to the extent of making unpopular decisions, and he must also be concerned with subjects which may be of no immediate or special concern to the vocal groups in his own constituency. The exercise of such authority requires the legislator to have some autonomy—but not too much. He must have enough autonomy to be able to make free choices in the legislative process, but he must not be so independent and free from controls that he can use his special prerogatives for his own gain or to prevent others from competing for his office.

The electoral system serves as a proceduralized method of obtain-

---

[1] *Commentaries on the Laws of England,* Vol. 1, p. 159.

ing consent which in the political ideology of the West is necessary for establishing governmental authority and making its actions legitimate. There is a presumption that consent is necessary if political authority is to be legal and if stability is to be achieved by means other than coercion. An indication of the degree to which the consent of the governed is considered politically necessary is revealed—negatively— in the attempts of such dictators as Mussolini, Hitler, and Stalin to use the façade of elections, however rigged and controlled, in order to achieve a spurious appearance of consent.

The participation of the electorate in the electoral process is also helpful in integrating the conflicting purposes of society. During elections, internal conflicts are debated and alternative policies are offered by political competitors. In determining who will be selected, a partial tentative agreement is also reached on the issues which are considered important and ripe for decision as well as an indication of how they might be decided. Once decisions have been made on who will have authority and, in general, on what policies will be followed, some of the nettling conflicts are resolved and perhaps forgotten, purposes become clearer, and society tends to pull itself together for a fresh start. However, it should be pointed out that there are painful examples where society has failed to become reintegrated after an election, the most tragic case in our own history being the great Civil War which followed the election of 1860.

The legislature and its members must establish continuing relations with the constituent-public in the never-ending process of making public policy. The requirement of maintaining local support and responding to the wishes of different parts of the constituency continues after the election. It is broadly necessary that the government maintain the support of the people and that no section or group become too overtly dissatisfied. It is also necessary for the individual legislator to maintain his own particular support, and, in all, an amazing amount of time is spent by Congressmen in courting their constituents. The office of a Representative or Senator is often a service agency which is called upon to arrange interviews for constituents with government officials, expedite the approval of local projects, inquire about delays, and secure useful information. Insertions are placed in the *Congressional Record* which are reprinted at a nominal cost and then franked to constituents. Congressmen keep their constituents informed through columns prepared for the free use of newspapers and by canned radio programs for the home station. Letters of congratulations are sent on the birth of babies, on graduations, and on marriages. Some Congressmen regularly sample public opinion in their districts in an attempt to know the nature of the prevailing sentiment. Representative William E. McVey (R., Ill.), for instance, who frequently polls his constituents, has written that a legislator "must know what the thinking of that constituency is" if he expects to represent the constituency in a satisfactory manner. It is not always possible for Mr. McVey to follow the views of the constituency, "especially when the general welfare is concerned and where 'the people back home' are not fully informed," but such instances are rare. Representative McVey's own voting in Congress "has conformed pretty closely to the majority opinion of those who filled the questionnaire."

In making policy, various conflicts in society are in effect transferred to the legislative chamber and provide there the raw material with which legislators work. This is, of course, an oversimplification of the process. Interests are not themselves necessarily concrete objects but rather expressions of valued relationships between the individual or group and the object concerning which a political decision may be made. The representative process gives members of society an opportunity to have some access to the legislators and some influence over their selection, and this to the end that the various interests in any system of action will not be overlooked. Of course, other channels are also open for expressing attitudes and applying influence, but this does not vitiate the significance of the electoral process also being used for this function.

It is, of course, not possible to give separate representation to all identifiable interests, for the number would run to infinity. Nor is representation given directly to groups especially concerned with important and productive systems of action. Rather, the system of representation is designed to encompass all of society—all the groups having particular interests and all the systems of action in which they are involved. Here the presumption is that the organized units prevalent in society will utilize the electoral system in a useful beneficial manner. The interests in society are so numerous, the systems of action so diverse and yet so interrelated, that the continuous problem facing any electoral system is that of providing adequate concern for all the interstices of society in terms other than numbers alone. The needs of some groups may not necessarily be expressed in terms of the greatest number, yet their participation in the total system of action is vital. In adjusting conflict, decisions cannot be made in terms of numbers alone, which would be comparable to measuring the significance of the carburetor of a car in terms of its relative weight. The gross numbers representing election totals may be presumed to have some significance other than that one side has a plurality. They also have an internal meaning which is concerned with adjustments and combinations and modifications of interests, attitudes, and preferences. Society is not a single mass with a single interest, although it may be organized under this assumption by mass political parties.

THE NATURE OF THE ELECTORAL SYSTEM

In the electoral conflict, a limited few are chosen to be legislators from a larger number of willing aspirants. For purposes of simplification, we may consider the electoral system initially as an abstract entity, separate from the social context in which it functions, although in operation the system becomes entwined with other aspects of society. Real communities exist where in theory there is only a presumed equality of numbers of people.

There is an element of artificiality about the electoral system, for not only has it been created by law and is thus subject to imposed change, but in addition it is superimposed over other systems of action which have varying types of relationships with the system itself. In order for the system to function at all, it is necessary that controls be established over various facets of the system: These controls determine the general nature of the system, protect it from abuse, and seek in some fashion to equalize the competitive opportunities of the contestants. Without adequate controls imposed by some external source, political competitors may attempt to gain an unfair advantage and bring the whole system into disrepute.

In creating the system, a balance must be maintained between the demands imposed by government and those of society. The system will be threatened if local interests lay too great a claim on the legislature or, alternatively, if the legislature becomes too remote from the interests of the local areas. In some countries the electoral system is required to carry the somewhat heavier burden of selecting a government which commands the support of a majority of legislators and which is capable of carrying out certain prescribed policies. The congressional electoral system is faced with a less onerous burden. However, if it succeeds in electing the required number of legislators and there is no disagreement on who the President is, the government should possess considerable stability and, with the location of authority not in dispute, be capable of making intelligent, binding, legal decisions.

The basic structure of the electoral system is found in an abstract legal framework which determines the size of the membership, the nature of the units represented, the nature of the recruitment process, and the rules of the game. The flexibility and diversity of the system reflect its origin, for the system is the product both of federal and of state legislation. Some latitude exists in the prevailing standards for creating legislative districts, for voting, and for the conduct of elections. Some may be surprised to learn that single-member districts for the House of Representatives are not mandatory, the states being free to provide other methods for selecting their representation if they choose to do so. Congress determines the total number of members to be selected and their apportionment among the states, while the states determine the boundaries of the districts, the qualifications of the voters, and many of the rules for the conduct of elections. Congress may enact legislation to prevent certain types of discrimination or, if it chooses, it may go further by superseding the authority of the state in determining the time and place of elections and the conduct thereof. It may also refuse to seat an otherwise successful candidate if there were election irregularities or if there is some notable blemish in his character.

SIZE

If one attempts to strike a fair balance between a legislature of ideal size and the demands for extensive and extended representation, it will be seen that the legislature and the electorate may have different needs. Other things being equal, a small legislative assembly will probably be more effective and efficient than a large one, but the groups in society which might otherwise feel themselves to be underrepresented might prefer an assembly with more members. However, there are some limits imposed by the function which a legislature is expected to perform, and the size of the body cannot be inflated indefinitely to keep pace with a growing population and an expanding electorate. The maximum size of a legislature which could still maintain its autonomy, deliberate intelligently, and make effective decisions, would probably be considerably less than a thousand. It is difficult to deliberate—as opposed to orating, speechmaking, and haranguing—in an assembly of great size, and it is further possible that a large assembly would lose its autonomy, with internal political controls exercised by outsiders. On the other hand, if the population increases while the legislature remains fairly constant, the larger electoral unit will affect the relationship between the representative and the electorate. It will also affect costs, the need for organization, and access to channels of mass communication, whereas a small constituency having a sense of community may provide a more favorable environment for establishing direct personal relationships.

The Constitution does not give much of a lead for determining the optimum size of the Senate and House of Representatives. The size of the Senate is governed by the number of states in the Union (times two), but Congress sets the size of the House of Representatives, providing only that the ratio of members to population is no less than 1:30,000 and that each state has at least one member. This flexible standard would permit the House to have as few as 48 members and as many as 5000. Congress is also obliged to reflect the shifts in population by reapportioning its membership after each census. In the nineteenth century the membership of the House customarily expanded with the increase in the population of the country, but not at the same rate; there has been no increase in the size of the House since 1912. The congressional districts have grown in size from a mean of about 37,000 in 1792 to a mean of almost 350,000 at present.

We may now raise the important question of who precisely will be permitted to select the membership. It is possible to choose members by a variety of methods—elections, appointment, inheritance, or even coöpting government officials as in newly-established legislatures in colonial areas. Congressional membership, of course, relies on the electoral system of recruitment, although appointments for limited periods are permitted in some cases. Cabinet members are excluded from membership in Congress as a result of a constitutional prohibition that "No person holding any office under the United States shall be a member of either House during his continuance in office." The origin of this clause is found in the British Act of Succession of 1707 which prohibited anyone who held an office of trust under the crown from being a member of the House of Commons, but the provision has been interpreted differently in the two countries. Although it has been no bar to the development of the cabinet system in Great Britain, it has forestalled any development in the United States of a system in which the heads of the departments are themselves members of the legislature.

The various forms of electoral systems may, in fact, affect in some manner the nature of the representation and the pattern of politics within the legislature. This comes about because the various systems require different combinations of voters and candidates, and the commitments and alliances stemming from these elections may influence the action taken in the legislature. The considerable experimentation with electoral systems during the past century has shown that there is no single "general will," readily reduced to representative form, but that different systems of representation may provide different results.

Representation would be somewhat different, one may presume, if Congressmen were elected from the nation at large, for such a plan would alter the present pattern of political influence and, incidentally, require a longer purse to finance the elections.

For representation in Congress, the electoral unit which is exclusively used and which has bested all rivals is based on territorial and population standards. There are no hereditary offices, no *ex officio* members, no members selected to represent state government or city governments or the federal government. There are no free-forming constituencies, whereby a certain number of like-minded voters can secure representation, and no schemes for proportional representation favoring the interests of minority groups. Ordinarily there is but one representative from each electoral district (with two Senators from each state); these legislators are considered to be legally competent to represent all interests, not merely the interests of those who were influential in the elections, and their concern extends to all systems of action with the districts, the states, and the nation.

An electoral system suitable for a federal type of government adds such complicating factors as the representation to be given to the federal units, the location of the legal authority for controlling the system, and the effect of a federal governmental structure on national political parties. The various states of the Union provide the representative base for election to the House of Representatives, the Senate, and the presidency as well. The electorates of the various states are, in effect, combined for the purpose of selecting national officials, but the fact that they have different choices may result in the selection of leaders of more than one party. The Iowa electorate of 1948, to cite one example, voted for President Truman, a Democrat, and for a Democratic Senator, but each of the eight Iowa congressional districts elected a Republican.

In the Senate, as is well known, the doctrine of legal equality permits each state to have two Senators, and the vote of every Senator has identical weight. Even though the ratio of quantities of population per Senators from the largest and smallest state is in the range of 100 to one, there is surprisingly little objection to the prevailing base of senatorial representation. This may be explained in part by the fact that equal representation of populations is not the only factor to be considered in developing a viable electoral system, for there are difficulties in using numbers and quantities to express qualities not readily measurable. The states appear to be willing to support the symbol of state equality, found in their equal representation in the Senate, in return for the reality of state autonomy.

The states have a considerable stake in preserving their autonomous position, and this autonomy is fostered by the doctrine that, in legal terms, all states are on an equal footing. Moreover, the states (or the population thereof) do not necessarily *feel* underrepresented (or overrepresented) on any grounds directly associated with the size of the population. The small states appear to have few (or no) singularly identifiable interests which are promoted exclusively at the expense of populous neighbors. Moreover, in the whole vortex of establishing relations with Senators, the proponents of specific types of policy (for example: tariff, taxes, foreign aid, price support, labor laws, housing, immigration) may find that Senators from small states are as subject to blandishments and as responsive to their requests as Senators from large states. Ideological reasons apart, there seems to be no pressing reason to find fault with or to change a pattern of political representation which is otherwise satisfactory.

Given the nature of the federal system and the historical debates over the legal rights of the states, there is perhaps less direct relationship between Congress and the states than one might initially suppose. The state governments are not themselves directly represented in Congress, as they were under the Articles of Confederation, and there is no specific governmental procedure through which the states may advocate or oppose legislation, although state consent is required for amending the Constitution. It is, of course, true that Congress and the states are frequently interested in the same topic, such as the sources of taxation or programs extending grants-in-aid, but there is no institutionalized procedure for carrying on direct negotiations between Congress and the states. In other words, although the states may be said to be represented in Congress, they are not represented directly as organized, policy-making entities.

APPORTIONMENT

Once Congress has determined the size of the House, the apportionment of the seats among the states involves a problem in mathematics; but it involves something more, also, and with many vocal, competitive claimants anxious to retain or increase their representation even mathematical solutions may develop a thick political overcast. The directions in the Constitution say simply that "Representatives shall be apportioned among the several states according to their respective numbers, counting the whole number of persons in each state, excluding Indians not taxed." This simple and apparently straightforward declaration has many possible mathematical solutions, so many that a sizable bibliography on the mathematics of congressional apportionment has developed over the years. Rudyard Kipling's line that there are "nine and twenty ways of making tribal lays, and every single one of them is right" is also applicable to the business of apportioning congressional seats among the states. The mystifying nature of the problem can perhaps be suggested by recalling the so-called Alabama paradox, which developed after the census enumeration of 1880. Appropriate tables were prepared for Congress showing how many seats each state would receive with each unit increase in the size of the House. Surprisingly, the tables showed that if the size of the House were increased from 299 to 300, Texas and Illinois would each gain a seat and Alabama would lose a seat. This was a paradox indeed.

Inasmuch as the loss or gain of a seat may affect the fortunes of political parties, mathematicians have discovered to their chagrin that impartial proposals could be turned into partisan issues, with politicians clustering around the mathematicians who supplied what they considered to be the most attractive formula for advancing their own interests. The core of the apportionment controversy relates to the allocation of seats for fractions of population less than the required quota. In recent years Congress has replaced the method of major fractions (which awards the extra seat to the state with the largest fraction of unallocated surplus population) with the method of equal proportions (which awards the extra seat to the state with districts having the highest average population). Although sound mathematical arguments can be advanced for the change, the motivation can perhaps more correctly be credited to the desire for partisan advantage.

Following the 1940 census enumeration, the two methods apportioned seats somewhat differently: The method of major fractions awarded an extra seat to Michigan and took one away from Arkansas, and the method of equal proportions preserved the existing allocation (for those two states). The prospect of losing a seat in Arkansas distressed the Democratic majority to the extent that they amended the Apportionment Act by substituting the method of equal proportions. The partisan nature of the amendment is indicated by the vote in the House of Representatives, where 96 percent of the Democrats favored the change (all the Democrats except those from Michigan) and 99 percent of the Republicans opposed it. Following the 1950 census—as a belated fulfillment of justice—the method of equal proportions then in use took one seat away from Arkansas and gave one to Michigan.

THE COMPOSITION OF THE UNITS

Although the electoral system assumes that population aggregates of a certain size acquire an amorphous type of legal equality, politicians are interested in something more than the size of the units. They know that the manner in which the population is distributed among the electoral units determines the composition of the districts and may also determine which party and which individual politicians will be placed in positions of authority. Many questions are pressed forward for consideration in the creation of single-member districts. Is it desirable to have homogeneous constituencies? Should districts be created to augment or retard the chances of party competition? What considerations should be given to natural geographic boundaries? To networks of communications, such as common press or radio coverage? To markets and other economic areas? In creating districts, the existence of political boundaries of states and counties are regularly recognized, but this is not true of precincts and wards, and no basic principles have been developed regarding the preservation of other political, economic, and social units.

From time to time between 1842 and 1911, Congress laid down various standards for creating congressional districts, including the prescription that single-member districts should be contiguous, compact, and equal in size. The present apportionment law includes no such standards, however, the states having full latitude to determine the nature of the districts. The reluctance of Congress to lay down standards stems partly from the desire to preserve the right of the states in this sensitive political area, but it is also due to the thankless job facing Congress if it were to demand compliance or itself had to create the legislative districts. There is general agreement in principle, however, that single-member districts, based on territory and population, should be used for the electoral base, and that so far as possible the districts should be compact, contiguous, and equal to size.

Although it is now presumed that states will permit members to be elected from single-member districts, an alternative plan of electing all members on a state-wide basis, with the winning party taking all seats, has also been tried. This centralizing tendency has gone full cycle in selecting presidential electors for the electoral college; whereas once the electors were selected from districts, they are now chosen from the state at large, with the entire slate of electors going to one party. So, too, with Congress. The states of Alabama, Georgia, Mississippi, Missouri, New Hampshire, and Rhode Island once adopted a centralized, state-wide ticket for congressional elections, doing away entirely with single-member districts. Opposition developed to this centralizing trend, and in 1842 Congress put its foot down by providing that representatives were to be "elected by districts composed of contiguous territory . . . no one district electing more than one Representative." [2]

Some four states defied the law and continued to elect their Repre-

[2] 5 Stat. 491, 1842.

sentatives by a general ticket. When the issue of seating these Representatives was debated, the Committee on Elections argued that while Congress had authority to enact laws superseding those of the states, it had no authority to compel states to make or change their laws. Congress having failed to determine the boundaries of the legislative districts, the proposal that the members from the four states be considered "duly elected" was carried by a vote of 126–57.[3] Over a period of time, the recalcitrant states turned again to single-member districts as the representative base.

The most frequent use of the general slate now occurs when a state fails to create new districts after a gain or loss in representation. Many members shudder at the thought of facing election from the state at large and prefer to stake their political survival within a district where they are known. With two exceptions (New Mexico and North Dakota, for obscure reasons, elect their two Representatives at large), every state with more than one Representative now uses single-member districts. In addition, Connecticut elects at large one of its six Representatives; Ohio, one of its 23; and Texas, one of its 22.

The standards of contiguity, compactness, and equality of size of electoral districts are believed desirable to prevent obvious distortions and favoritism, although in themselves these standards do not guarantee adequate representation. Those who are interested in electoral results will want to know the composition and voting propensities of these districts, the effect of electoral standards on the political fortunes of individuals and parties, and the influence of particular groups within the areas concerned. They will be concerned with the political preferences of the population, whether the area is rural, urban, or suburban, and whether specific political leaders live in the district. Whatever abstract standards are followed, certain concrete political interests will be affected favorably or unfavorably.

Gerrymandering is the term applied in creating districts for some immediate political advantage, often at the expense of other standards. The irregular and often arresting geometric design is the embarrassing evidence that politicians have had no little trouble in finding the

[3] H. Rept. 60, 1844; from 1 Hinds sec. 310, pp. 171–173.

proper concentration of voters. The partisan rule of thumb for gerrymandering is to concentrate the opposition votes in the fewest number of districts which conscience permits and to disperse the voters of one's own party in such a fashion as to create majorities in the maximum number of districts. Population movements, however, may very readily undermine the work of the gerrymanderers.

Although the states ordinarily attempt to keep the districts relatively equal in terms of population, no law of Congress now compels this to be done, and there are some exceptional cases where the range of population is considerable. In Texas, the range between the smallest and largest district is 580,000; in Georgia, 372,000; in Michigan, 347,000; in South Dakota, 334,000; in Ohio, 319,000; in Florida, 315,000; and in Alabama, 308,000.

If legislative districts are notoriously unequal in size, no effective appeal can be made to the courts according to the decision in the case of *Colegrove v. Green* (1946) (328 US 549). This case grew out of an attempt on the part of certain private citizens to compel authorities of the State of Illinois to create new congressional districts. The Illinois districts varied greatly in size, the largest one having a population of 914,000 and the smallest of 112,000. The plaintiff in the case, Professor Kenneth Colegrove (who lived in a district containing a population of 625,000) argued that the residents of the large districts were being denied the equal protection of laws because their vote was theoretically less influential than the vote of those living in small districts. The court refused to consider the problem, however, saying that the issue of redistricting was of "a peculiarly political nature" whose remedy lay with Congress or the state legislatures. The courts were admonished "not to enter this political thicket."

In dissenting, Mr. Justice Black agreed that the petitioners were in fact being denied the equal protection of laws, and it was his opinion that the electoral system, whatever its nature, "should be designed to give approximately equal weight to each vote cast." The Black prescription as stated might also lead into political thickets of other varieties. Each vote would have approximately equal weight only in the event that there were approximately the same number of votes cast in each district, and then under conditions compelling the equality of candidate rivalry. Happily for the petitioners, the issue was resolved when the state legislature of Illinois, without legal compunction, decided on its own to create new congressional districts.

THE ORGANIZATION OF THE ELECTORATE

For purposes of political quantification, there is a precise number of legislative districts, each having a kind of legal equality. However, if we wish to know the nature of the political conflict and how this conflict is resolved, it is necessary to look beyond the abstract qualifications of electoral districts and consider how the electorate within these districts is organized by political parties and other interested groups. Here, the temporal and occasional nature of the electoral process is significant, for the elections themselves occur infrequently. Although a channel of communications between the legislator and constituent is kept open during the interim period, the electoral system with all its ramified relationships has to be recreated every two years. The partisans must be reinspired, new followers must be recruited, new appeals made, new issues developed. The concerted effort of many people is required to mobilize the support necessary for electoral victory. Contestants who hold no office may have an especially heavy burden in recruiting workers, raising money, and appealing for support. The political parties, of course, perform an important function in carrying on all this mobilizing activity, and they have within their membership many specialists in the complex task of persuading citizens to become partisans, and partisans to vote right. While the more prosaic members of the citizenry wait placidly until election day to cast their ballots, the parties anticipate the electoral requirements by putting into operation the procedures necessary for selecting candidates, choosing issues, and mobilizing public support.

The congressional system of elections does not stand apart but is closely associated with other electoral systems created for selecting other types of officials. On the national scale, no election is devoted solely to choosing members of Congress; rather, the election of members of Congress is identified with other elections and may not be considered to be the most significant of the choices which the voters make. The pattern of congressional relationships and associations varies considerably in the different states; it may be associated with big-city party organization, or with a presidential election, or with the success of a state-wide ticket, or even with some independent candidacy. In developing strategy for getting into office, or for staying in office, prospective candidates must take into account the nature of the political groups which may already have organized the electorate.

Within any given electoral district, it is necessary for the successful candidate to attract various clusters of support. He will identify himself with the purposes of groups and movements, and, as a resident of the area, he will presumably be in sympathy with its particular economic problems. Hear the local appeal of Representative E. A. Hall, a Republican from Binghamton, N.Y., as he asked for the support of his constituents. "I am your hometown boy," he said, "and have been elected by you people again and again in spite of their (the enemy's) herculean antics to try to dump me. What will a stranger ever do for you?" Or listen to the local appeal of Representative Lindley Beckworth of Gladewater, Texas, as he listed in the *Congressional Directory* the territorial connections of himself and his relatives. Beckworth represented the Third District, containing the eight counties of Camp, Gregg, Panola, Rush, Smith, Upshur, Van Zandt, and Wood. His father, he said, came to Smith County from Georgia and had taught in Upshur, Camp, Erath, and Palo Pinto Counties; his mother came from Van Zandt County; his grandfather was a 90-year-old Primitive Baptist preacher who was born in Anderson County; his uncle had taught in Smith, Gregg, Trinity, Palo Pinto, Karnes, and San Patricio Counties; his twin sister, Linnie, had attended two colleges and taught in Upshur, Gregg, and Rusk Counties; his father had recently married a lady from Camanche County who was then teaching in Upshur County; Beckworth himself had attended schools in Upshur and Camp Counties and some five college and universities; he had married the daughter of a family who had lived in Mills, Brown, Stephens, Taylor, Nolan, and Eastland Counties.

The interests of the voter may transcend the artificial boundaries of the district and extend to other areas, and it follows that in some districts some interests are better organized and more articulated than in other districts. A minor interest in one area may be a major interest in another area, and the individual associated with this minor interest may feel that he is more effectively represented by members from districts other than his own. In order to see the extent and appeal of organized interests and how they are represented, it is necessary to look at the electoral process as a whole, as well as the subsequent political process; it is unsafe to assume that people are not represented at all if they are not represented directly.

The electoral process is encompassed by a multiplicity of federal and state laws which are variously enforced. One set of prohibitions attempts to achieve honest elections by preventing the stealing or purchasing of votes, the federal law specifically prohibiting the giving of money to any person for voting or withholding his vote, as well as prohibiting a candidate from promising favors to secure support.

Another set of prohibitions attempts to regulate the extent to which particular groups and individuals can influence elections. In particular, corporations and labor unions are prohibited from contributing to presidential or congressional elections, and campaign contributions of whatever nature must be public. Some five times during an election year, reports are filed with the Clerk of the House of Representatives containing the names of all who have contributed one hundred dollars or more to campaigns and of all to whom expenditures of ten dollars or more have been made.

A third set of prohibitions attempts to control certain phases of political competition; a limit is placed on the total campaign outlay, and radio and television facilities are to be made available to the contestants on even terms. The federal law provides that candidates for the Senate may spend up to $25,000 and candidates for the House of Representatives up to $5000. Generous exemptions are made for personal expenses, including travel, for printing and distributing campaign literature, and for telephone and telegraph charges. The above restrictions apply specifically to the candidates. Additional funds raised by "political committees" must also be accounted for, but inasmuch as there is no limitation on the number of committees which can be created, there is no effective limitation on the total amount of money which may legally be spent in a campaign.

A degree of supervision over elections is provided by special election committees, appointed biennially by each of the two Houses of Congress, whose business it is to see to it that campaigns are conducted fairly. The committees can be asked during or after campaigns to investigate charges of improper electoral behavior, and Congress is later given a report of the complaints received and adjudicated. The level of the competence of these committees varies considerably. There is no necessary continuity of membership or of staff, and the committees can determine for themselves the scope of their work.

The two major political parties attempt to organize the various electorates and provide them with common goals. These parties have permeated the electoral system fairly thoroughly, with the Democrats offering candidates in almost every district in the country and the Republicans in almost every district other than the South. Only rarely is a candidate able to win an election without identifying himself with one of the major national parties. The desire of candidates to identify themselves with a political party stems in part from the fact that Congress, being organized along party lines, reserves its positions of greatest authority for the pronounced partisans. Party membership is ordinarily a valuable asset for any member of Congress, and it is required if the member has ambitions of spending some time in a position of authority.

The election of the President also affects the partisan identification of those who seek election to Congress. Only one man is chosen President, not a council, with the result that presidential elections tend to polarize the electorate into two groups. This polarization is reflected in contests for most elected offices, even those of a local nature, and candidates may find it easier to join a party and harness the partisan spirit to their own advantage than to strike out on their own.

Although congressional candidates tend to identify themselves as partisans, it does not follow that the national parties select the candidates, manage the campaigns, or even define the issues. The reciprocal obligations of candidate to party and party to candidate vary widely. In 1952 some Democratic members of Congress from the South (who had no opposition in the general election) supported the presidential candidate of the Republicans, but party independence, or defection if you please, rarely goes this far. Candidates for seats which are closely contested are forced to share the fortunes of their own party. On the whole, however, candidates for Congress wish to preserve some independence from party demands. They may take exception to statements in the platforms or the position of the presidential candidate and will amend or modify the national program to the requirements of the state or district. The modification may go rather far at times. However, one need not begin with the premise that the so-called national program is necessarily right or popular, for it is often the result of happenstance creation. The decentralized nature of the electoral system makes it necessary for candidates to have and to express some independent ideas of their own, and candidates may be able to develop sufficient electoral support to survive even when their party is defeated nationally. It can also be argued that if there were total agreement within a party and all issues were resolved by the election, the function of Congress as a maker of policy might be reduced to that of ratifying the decrees proposed by party bosses.

The national party may at times induce candidates to offer themselves as candidates, but there are no regularized procedures by which the national party officials share in the choice of candidates using the party's name. The fact that nominations are made through primary election of nominal partisans adds a complicating factor, for the national organization may be understandably reluctant to indicate preference in a contest within the party. Covert influence may be exerted in support of a particular candidate, but it does not happen regularly, and there is no special electoral device for accomplishing it. Many local political leaders would resent the "outside interference" of a presidential nominee or the national party chairman stating his preference of candidates.

One should not conclude too quickly, however, that candidates for Congress do not want the support of the national party. This support is ordinarily welcomed, providing it is not accompanied by the price tag of excessive commitments on voting, leadership preference, patronage matters, and other factors undermining the autonomy of the legislator. If the presidential candidate is more popular politically than the candidate, the latter may go to embarrassing lengths to secure some public endorsement, or at least an opportunity to be seen in association with the Magic Name.

Both parties in both Houses have party committees and committee staffs whose job it is to raise funds, supply speakers, and prepare election material for candidates. The participation of "outside" speakers is often a coveted testimony to the fact that the candidate's talents are appreciated more widely than in his own district alone. Comparatively speaking, the national organization extends little monetary assistance to a candidate for the House, although somewhat more may be given to a candidate for the Senate. There is a complex process of raising funds and directing them into the state or district, for funds may be spent by the national committee or the senatorial or congressional committees (Democratic or Republican) or donors may be asked to give funds directly to the particular local political organization where the need is the greatest. Generally speaking, however, the congressional candidate must rely on his own efforts, those of the volunteers whom he inspires, and perhaps also of the local political organization with which he is identified. If the candidate comes from an area with a well-developed political organization, such as exists in some of the states and many urban areas, the party workers will attempt to elect him along with the rest of the ticket. In cities or states which are less well organized, the candidate may have more responsibility for running his own campaign.

The general, reliance on single-member districts has influenced the nature of partisan representation by creating the conditions favorable to the two-party system. In any one district, a third party must gain more votes than either of its rivals. No advantage accrues in almost winning an election, for minority votes are not pooled. The organization of Congress creates additional handicaps for third parties inasmuch as the control of committees and of major offices requires the support of a majority of members. In the decade between 1940 and 1950, the average minority party representation was two members per session. The number was somewhat greater in the 1920's and 1930's, when the Progressives of Wisconsin and the Farmer-Laborites of Minnesota, who competed for political control of their respective states, sent members to Congress also. The high-water mark of minor party representation during the present century was reached in 1912, when there was a split in the Republican party. In that year, nine Progressives, seven Progressive Republicans, and one Independent were elected to the House of Representatives.

The single-member district tends to create pockets of residual strength for the major parties. If districts express a pronounced preference, the favored party has an anchor of support when voters in other areas are unresponsive. A party may lose national and state elections, but it will retain a voice in national affairs by carrying safe congressional districts. In New York State, for instance, the shift in party control is less pronounced in congressional elections than in presidential and gubernatorial elections, neither party customarily gaining or losing on the average more than three or four of the state's 45 Representatives. In general, the tenure of office of members from relatively safe districts is greater than that of members from contested districts, so that this fact, combined with the seniority system, results in positions of authority in Congress being achieved most regularly by those with relatively safe seats.

Single-member districts are sometimes charged with encouraging political parochialism inasmuch as members may attempt to establish their careers on the basis of services performed for their constituents. This parochialism may be enhanced by the unwritten rule requiring a candidate to be a resident of his district. Moreover, the fact that political parties have no central control over party nominees may force members to provide their own support by catering to constituents. However, parochialism in moderation may be defended, for there is much to be said for members of Congress having an intimate and broad contact with the districts and states they represent. In developing legislation, it is necessary to make certain that national policy is cogently related to local needs.

It is necessary that the winners of the elections qualify as men whose character can be trusted, the ultimate enforcement of this standard being left to the judgment of each branch of Congress. The Constitution provides that each House shall be judge of the "qualifications" of its members, which implies that there are standards of behavior one may expect which go beyond the legal requirements of age, citizenship, residence, and electoral victory. Congress has used this authority with considerable restraint, accepting the presumption that the electorate knew what it was about in making its choice.

One recent case where the Senate was asked to deny a seat to a Senator otherwise competent and legally elected concerned charges of moral turpitude raised against Senator Bilbo, of Mississippi. The charges arose during the reëlection of Bilbo to the Senate in 1946 when it was said he told the Mississippi electorate "to resort to any means" to prevent Negroes from voting in the Democratic primary. (Additional charges were made regarding improper government contracts.) When Bilbo appeared to take the oath of office in January, 1947, he agreed to step aside until his case could be heard. His physical condition did not permit him to press his case, and he died in August of that year, with the Senate having taken no further action on the charges.

SUMMARY

The electoral system must fulfill two essential requirements: For Congress it must supply the essential number of legislators who will be able to develop public policy, and for society it must provide a method by which the people can influence the choice of issues and themselves select their legislative representatives. In its technical aspects, the electoral system operates regularly in supplying Congress with the precise number of members necessary for operating the législature. The process of permitting free access to the system and of eliminating peacefully and procedurally all contenders except the successful 531 Senators and Representatives is performed successfully and continuously. This is saying a good deal.

The electoral system also operates so as to give the people continued access to the legislators, or to give significance to the political reaction of the public, and indeed a high premium is placed on the ability of legislators to win public support. The proposition can be advanced that the electoral system promotes stability by establishing close relations between the governing authority and the systems of action which are affected thereby. The necessary and continuous process of adjustment is facilitated by the electoral process and the subsequent activities of the elected members. Moreover, the adjustment has some substance to it and is not accomplished solely by the manipulation of mass symbols or the use of force.

The respective requirements for Congress and for society may at times be in conflict, as when constituent demands prevent legislators from performing their legislative functions. The extraordinarily close relationship between the lawmakers and the constituents may in fact encourage aggressive and perhaps selfish groups to take special advantage of this ease of access to those in authority by making excessive demands as the price for their support. The legislator has a sensitive position where, continually, he must listen to the complaints of the aggrieved and the demands of the ambitious. He may need more protection from pressures, more time to deliberate on alternative courses of action, more autonomy in making up his mind than is actually offered him.

The two-year terms for the House of Representatives may also have a disruptive effect on the legislative process by making the members continually conscious of the pending elections. A case can perhaps be made for extending the term of the House of Representatives to four years, with all members elected at the same time. If elections were not always just around the corner, the members might be able to be more selective in their judgment—and to have more time and be under less pressure to make a judgment. The open communications which otherwise exist would still permit legislators to be aware of actual needs and desires in integrating policy.

The electoral system has adopted itself to the various requirements of a federal governmental structure, of controls imposed by both the national government and the state governments, and of an essentially decentralized political organization. The single-member district has emerged as the electoral unit most widely adopted, but there are no national legal requirements that the single-member unit be specifically used, and Congress has been reluctant to demand standards requiring the population of the districts to be equal and compact and the territory to be contiguous.

The political composition of the various electoral units (for the Senate and the House) varies considerably, and so too does the degree of political affinity of the electoral units with the local and national political organizations. The various political affinities of members of Congress will be demonstrated more clearly in a later discussion on voting propensities. The system of elections, calling for a myriad number of adjustments to constituent opinion but not in fact controlled by any one type of opinion, does in fact provide for large areas of freedom on the part of legislators in which choice may be made. Despite their dependence on party affinity for securing nomination and election, members of Congress are not also compelled to turn over to the parties their minds and their consciences.

There are some who claim that Congress could achieve relief from pressures and the unequal application of influence through disciplined parties. But this may create problems of another nature, for the "disciplining" of parties would call for the transfer to some unspecified location of the forum for reaching concord and would not itself resolve discord. In addition to all of this, pressures—strong, active, even brutal pressures—may insist on dominating "disciplined" parties, as an examination of the party structure in other countries will reveal. The key to political concord is not necessarily found in accepting the solution proposed by Party *A* or by Party *B*. The function of government in establishing controls and creating ordered patterns of behavior is too complex for such essentially simple solutions. The governmental process requires continuous, persistent adjustment, based on reflection, research, discussion, and access to reliable information. Here a case can be made for a free legislator who uses his brain to think, not his voice to say what he is told to say (or to keep quiet and say nothing at all). There is still a need for putting in authority individuals whom one can trust and who are competent to make decisions in which people will have confidence.

It is possible that further controls should be developed to make certain that the electoral system does, in fact, operate fairly, and on this point there is need for increased understanding of how the system operates in all its manifold ramifications. The electoral system is fragile, with many opportunities for abuse, because of the artificial nature of its creation. The stakes of the success of the system are so high, however, that strenuous effort should be made to make the system continuously reliable, honest, and effective.

CHAPTER 3

The Internal System of Authority

IN THE PRECEDING TWO CHAPTERS WE HAVE CON-
sidered the general nature of politics and the function of the electoral
system in supplying Congress with the precise number of legislators
required. In the process of selecting the members of Congress, the
political conflict becomes channeled into specific and acceptable procedures; it becomes more defined and less amorphous, with specific
solutions being proposed, but many steps remain to be taken before
a legal pattern has been created for resolving conflict. One of the
steps concerns the organization of the activities of the members of
Congress in such a fashion that the end product is some form of
public policy. This requires a process for selecting a few significant
issues from the manifold proposals which compete for attention; for
mobilizing information and opinion; and for making a final, binding
decision. Although the legislative process is encompassed by various
types of rules, it does not operate automatically. Controls are established at crucial aspects of the process, and competition for effective
political influence occurs at these various control points.

In the exercise of legislative authority, a limited number of individuals have authority to make decisions on spending other people's

money, settling other people's quarrels, taking other people's wealth, and regulating other people's business. They may be in a position to influence the action of government agencies or intercede for particular persons. The strategically influential position of legislators raises at once several important questions relating to the exercise of political authority. What individuals are to be entrusted with the exercise of this authority? How are they to be selected? What standards of competence are required? What internal controls are needed to secure proper performance of duty? How can society prevent ambitious men from securing office by corruption or from using public office for the benefit of themselves and their friends?

Some answers to these questions are found in the principles governing the internal organization of Congress, as well as in the electoral system of recruitment. Under the theory of constitutional government, the exercise of authority is based on law and is limited in time and scope, with periodic elections required to legitimate the authority exercised by the legislators. In all of the political process, there is an implicit assumption that those exercising authority must be able to explain, defend, and justify their actions before some group which they do not control. However, as will be seen, it is no easy thing to organize a legislature in such a fashion that no special or unfair advantage is given to or taken by those who are in an especially advantageous position for exercising influence.

In examining the internal system of authority within Congress, we may begin with the assumption that the electoral system will produce regularly the precise number of legislators required for making policy decisions. There are some conditions, of course, where this assumption would not hold, such as during periods of civil strife, but, in this volume, electoral stability and efficiency are assumed. The electoral system may have an impact on Congress by influencing the nature of partisan control, the allocation of committee membership, the voting behavior of members, and even the competence of members as legislators. But the electoral system itself does not provide all the conditions necessary for the successful operation of a legislature. The electoral assumption of the legal equality of all members—that each member can participate on even terms, with his vote having the same numerical value as that of every other member—must be supplemented by some scheme for inducing specialization and controlling procedures. Congress is not simply an association of 531 autonomous individuals gathered under the great Capitol dome in Washington; it is fundamentally an organization which can make policy decisions, and, as such, requires an internal system of authority in which various types of controls are placed over individuals and processes.

In developing this internal system of authority, it is necessary to transform, as it were, the successful candidates, fresh from electoral victory, into knowledgeable, hard-working legislators who can tackle political issues of complexity and significance. Inasmuch as the skills required for winning elections may not be the same as those required for an effective legislator, the electoral system itself may not supply ready-made legislators. Service in Congress may provide new members with additional training in proper legislative behavior, and this training is often rigorous and thorough. The new members must learn the required canons of ethical behavior as well as the useful parliamentary skills. In short, the electoral recruit must be trained to fill the various roles required in the legislative process.

It is also necessary that strategic controls be applied so that the legislative process becomes something more than a free-for-all, where issues are thrown up for a chance decision. What is required, essentially, is a kind of structure which will permit Congress to make decisions in its corporate capacity after due deliberation. The requirements that definitive action be taken on some issues distinguish Congress from a mere debating society or advisory council, and the organization is directed toward the end that the corporate entity of Congress can take affirmative action. However, Congress must make decisions in a prescribed fashion with "adequate" time permitted for the exchange of views and the development of consensus. At each significant phase of the process—raising the issue, considering the subject, and making the decision—competitive partisans may seek to influence the action favorably toward their own interests.

In organizing Congress, it is necessary to make some distinction in the duties required of the various members. They are given assignments having varying degrees of influence, and, in some assignments, a few members may have considerable control over their colleagues. The organization of Congress is formalized in the sense that specific officials or concrete units have certain functions to perform, but in many cases the extent of influence exerted by the various members may not correspond with the formal structure. However, one should not overlook the formal organization in the search for effective influence in making decisions, for it is in terms of the control of the formal structure that influence is actually exercised.

Congress is restricted in its choices in developing an internal organization. It cannot go beyond its own membership by coöpting new members nor can it pass over members whose talents do not quite fit; somehow, everyone must be given a part to play. The task, then, is to devise a scheme which will satisfy personal ambitions, give everyone something to do, and still perform the work required of Congress. The adjustment of rival claims must precede the adjustment of major conflicts without being permitted to divert attention for long from the larger task at hand. Some harmony within the legislature—including agreement on the location of internal authority —must exist before the legislature can itself promote harmony between conflicting groups.

The allocation of authority within Congress is related to the question of the degree to which its internal organization should reflect changes in public attitudes. Membership is continually changing through election and retirements, but to perform its function properly Congress requires some continuity and stability of membership. A balance must be struck so that the internal organization is neither immobilized by every electoral breeze nor yet unaffected by elections. The average electoral turnover of 20 percent is not large enough to affect the general stability of Congress, and the seniority system largely determines in advance which particular party members will be given positions of authority. In other words, the contested areas determine which party will control Congress but the safe areas supply the party leadership. This is one of the results of the uneven territorial distribution of partisan voters. During great electoral upheavals, however, even party leaders with considerable tenure may fall, as during the Democratic victories in the 1930's when the Senate Republicans lost almost all their leaders. In general, the internal organization of Congress provides considerable stability, although this is less true of the chairmen and members of some of the minor committees. There is much to be said for stable political leadership, but one of the drawbacks of the present system is the difficulty in rectifying an error once an incompetent person is put in a position of authority. But other institutions (including academic) suffer from the same defect.

In formulating policy, Congress carries out its work through various types of units and alliances. Some of these units and alliances are recognized in the official rules; others are free-forming, as it were, operating within the legislative structure while not being a constituent part of the legal framework. Individual members acquire authority in so far as they belong to some larger group, and no one would suggest, say, that an unorganized member, or the chairman of a committee, or even the Speaker of the House could make law by proceeding on his own initiative. A legislative body makes decisions as a corporate body, and the requirement of corporate action becomes the base line toward which political action is directed.

Congress, considered as a corporate whole, is a procedural abstraction, for it is not organized and does not act as a single unit; the two chambers may meet jointly for limited purposes—to hear the President or a visiting dignitary or to witness the counting of the votes of the electoral college—but there is no unitary assembly as such. Not only is Congress divided into chambers but the chambers are further divided into committees and subcommittees, and the latter have considerable influence in shaping laws and even in controlling the actions of departments. Influence may be exercised by committees acting in the name of Congress, although other members of Congress may not know that the action has taken place, much less have an opportunity to consider it or approve it. In locating authority within Congress, it is often perplexing to find such a large number of diversified groups and individuals who speak in the name of Congress and identify their own acts with that of the whole body. In all there seems to be a growing propensity for certain types of influence to be exerted, for certain types of decisions to be made, which are beyond the control of Congress as a whole. The diminution of corporativeness is displayed, say, when a subcommittee presumably speaks in the name of and for all members of Congress or is permitted to review and to veto administrative acts. It is also displayed in the continuing controversy over congressional investigations, where the committees lack an effective theory for guiding their conduct in exercising authority over private individuals.

THE MEMBER AND HIS OFFICE

The new member of Congress does not pick up the business of legislating as if nothing of consequence had ever happened prior to his election. He will find, instead, that many decisions governing his conduct have been made prior to his arrival and which are practically irrevocable. He will be expected to work through given units within Congress, to assume certain habits of thought, and to exercise his influence in a prescribed fashion. He will also find a fairly well stylized type of behavior to which he, as a legislator, will be expected to conform, and he will be granted special privileges not extended to the ordinary citizen.

Political authority is necessary for the survival of all, but its use must be controlled. The legislator with his special prerogatives is for some purposes above the law, but inasmuch as he may otherwise use his authority for private or ignoble ends—affecting his own fortunes and those of his friends and opponents—he is expected to conform to well-developed standards of personal rectitude. These standards are in part determined by explicit requirements, some of which are found in the law, in political mores, and in the procedural requirements of the legislature. Laws and customs do not themselves make a legislator, but they do supply some of the conditions favorable to legislative action.

The first rule of political morality is based on the assumption that self-interest is less likely to be advanced if the legislator himself has no financial stake in the outcome of the decision. Laws prohibiting bribery and other forms of corruption attempt to prevent a type of influence which rewards an official financially for surrendering his power to make independent decisions. The possible conflict of interest—they are not all financial—cannot be entirely avoided but it can be lessened by a frank admission that a conflict of interest exists. Further evaluation needs to be made of those situations where members receive remuneration from law firms having clients specifically interested in legislation before Congress. It would seem, however, that the honorable course would be for members to declare their personal interest in controversial legislation, especially if they stand to profit financially.

Legislators may also be expected to follow the standard of behavior demanded by society. Loyalty is demanded, as well as honesty, and especially loyalty to the ideas and ideals of the predominant forces in the electorate. The voter may be more willing to trust the legislator to decide various political issues because both share the same set of moral values, and it follows that in representing a constituency the legislator may be expected to share the moral values prevalent in the community. In addition to these enumerated restraints, the legislative process depends for its effectiveness on the personal integrity of the individual, on men who are self-reliant and dependent, who understand or seek to understand the issues, who rely on their conscience to guide them as well as on their party and on public opinion, and who are resolutely determined to be heard. Responsibility is also the concern of the individual.

The member is given certain immunities and rewards which are designed to assist him in performing his job adequately. Here there is the necessity for a judicious balance of generosity and restraint, for the equilibrium of the political struggle might be upset if the immunities and rewards are either too limited or too generous. The job must be stable enough for the legislator to perform his functions but not so stable that there is no competition or so rewarding that the stakes of office are too high.

To provide the conditions necessary for making law, the Constitution grants members of Congress freedom from arrest, except for cases of treason, felony, and breach of the peace while engaged in legislative business, and freedom from libel suits for words uttered in debate. Although these immunities may be abused, they would seem to be essential for establishing the autonomous position of the legislator. If abused, the two Houses of Congress have some authority to discipline offending members; either House may exercise internal discipline in the form of a reprimand, a resolution condemning certain action, or the deletion of offensive remarks.

It is necessary, of course, to provide Congressmen with "adequate" compensation, but the question of what constitutes adequacy has no obvious answer. There is no constant, well-established relationship between the extent of fiscal rewards received (or the lack thereof) and the type of behavior believed desirable. It can be argued that the compensation need not be great in that the job of legislator should attract only those who are interested in the position for purposes other than personal financial gain. The argument, used frequently in the case of elected local offices such as the city council, assumes that the official's income has been provided for otherwise. Despite the morals of the nineteenth century novels, poverty and virtue are not always joined, and an impecunious legislator might conceivably be subject to temptations which would not affect his more affluent colleagues.

The argument for little or no remuneration is less compelling, now that modern legislation requires full-time attention, living costs are high, and legislators with no independent income require some support. And who should provide this support—the government? the party? the corporation? the labor union? Some would argue that the government should pay legislators good salaries, comparable, say, to those received by executives of large business corporations. Here is the other side of the coin, where the job becomes extraordinarily attractive because of the compensation attached thereto. High legislative salaries might have the effect of making members less independent, less courageous, and willing to support whatever opportunistic measures would lead to reëlection. The job would be too

attractive to give up readily. In developing a standard for remuneration, one can say little more than that it should provide sufficient
resources for the member to be independent in debates and votes
but should not provide such a sufficiency that a member would wish
to hold on to his job for the sake of the salary alone.

Members are also given additional assistance which is helpful in
establishing a channel of communication with the constituents; the
member's office becomes, in fact, an important link between the
government and the governed. This assistance includes free office
space and secretarial help; free mailing privileges and a certain
amount of free telephone and telegraph service; the opportunity to
purchase reprints of speeches from the *Congressional Record* at a
nominal fee; facilities for making television and radio broadcasts
for home consumption; and a generous allocation of government
documents. This type of assistance may indeed give the sitting member some competitive advantage in seeking election. Perhaps one can
argue for stability by claiming that a member who has made himself
vulnerable to political attack by voting on contentious issues *should*
have some competitive advantage over the uncommitted contestant.
In any event, the relatively high degree of turnover in the House and
Senate would seem to indicate that the prerogatives of office are by
no means decisive factors in enabling members to stay in office.

The office of a member is also used in integrating policy with the
patterns of order with which the legislator is especially concerned, and
the attention of the bureaucracy can be directed to complaints of
unsatisfactory administration. Although many such complaints are
cleared up through the routine exchange of correspondence, it is
easily possible for an incident to be given additional attention in a
committee hearing or perhaps even to be the subject for debate. In
some situations a member may use his position in the power structure
of Congress to bully the bureaucracy into taking action which might
not otherwise have been favored on its merits. The situation may
develop where a member will request or demand special favors, such
as granting contracts, issuing licenses (as for a radio or television
broadcasting station), establish flood control or other public works

projects, and on and on. The defenseless bureaucrat often needs more protection from this kind of external pressure than the present system provides.

Although it is not necessary that all members be masters of parliamentary skills, the members must hold in common certain basic assumptions about the nature of the legislative process and their relation to it. These include the following:

1. The members must believe in the necessity for making decisions through a given process, with the participation of more than a few people and the contribution of many minds. It follows that the opposition must be given a hearing, that the decisions (made procedurally) are considered binding, and that if the process is to work members may have to modify positions taken previously.
2. It is assumed that members are willing to participate in considering types of policy in which they may have no personal overriding interest —in which, perhaps initially, they have no knowledge whatever—and that the legislator will develop some concern for subjects of general interest.
3. It is assumed that the sole authority of the legislator is acquired by membership in, and is exercised through, the legislative system.
4. It is assumed that all actions of a legislator must be defendable. Although accountable to his constituents, he is not accountable solely to them; while respecting their wishes, he is not bound to follow them. He is free to attempt to persuade his constituents that he is right; they are free to elect someone else. So far as decisions are concerned, the member is autonomous, and he cannot be compelled to change his mind by any outside force.

In addition to these basic requirements, it is necessary that at least some members acquire the parliamentary skills of debate, of negotiation and adjustment, of adroitness in the use of rules, and the ability to acquire new information quickly and to translate technical terms into language that is politically compelling. New members continually identify themselves in a remarkably short time with what might be called the congressional point of view, but the period of full maturation, when the politician becomes also a seasoned legislator trusted fully by his colleagues, may require several years. Until relatively recently, the Senate expected a new member to remain sedately quiet for most of his first term in office, but with the greater number of Senators who serve for a single term, this practice is no longer followed. In both Houses, new members are tested and trained before they are given major responsibilities and before their words carry weight.

THE TWO HOUSES

There is a close relationship between the physical facilities and the functioning of a legislative chamber, but the design of the buildings of Congress is more the product of architectural tradition than of any attempt to facilitate the work of the legislative process through specially-designed architecture. The comments made by Prime Minister Churchill relating to rebuilding Parliament after its partial destruction by bombing are pertinent here. Mr. Churchill said that he favored an oblong chamber rather than a semicircular chamber which "appeals to political theorists and enables every group to move around to the center, adopting various shades of pink as the weather changes." The party system "is much favored by an oblong chamber. It is easy enough to move through those insensible graduations from left to right, but the act of crossing the floor is one which requires serious consideration. . . . Logic, which created in so many countries the semicircular assemblies which give every member not only a seat but often a desk with a lid to bang, has proved fatal to parliamentary government." Nor should the Commons be large enough to hold all the members at once without overcrowding, for its hold on the electorate depends to "no small extent upon its episodes, even its scenes and rows, which everyone will agree are better conducted in close quarters. . . . One of our war aims is a parliament which will be a strong, flexible instrument free for debate. For this purpose a sense of intimacy is indispensable. Harangues from the rostrum would be a bad substitute for our conversational style." [1]

The spatial arrangement of congressional seats is more like the

[1] New York *Herald Tribune,* October 29, 1943.

French than the British method, but it does not here produce "those insensible graduations from left to right" about which Sir Winston complained. In the Senate chamber, desks are individually assigned and arranged in a semicircle, with an aisle dividing the two parties. In the House chamber, the members sit on unassigned benches arranged in a less pronounced semicircle, but with partisans clustered together on either side of the main dividing aisle. Some feeling of party identity may be engendered by such physical propinquity, but it is not overriding. When party members of either House vote with the opposition, they do not at the same time change their seats, although occasionally, as in the case of Senator Wayne Morse of Oregon, a member crosses the line and sits with his new-found allies upon changing his party membership. In colloquy, a Senator speaks from the floor by his desk, a practice better designed for debate than the House practice of speaking from the well of the House, as if delivering a lecture. The suites for committee rooms and member offices are for the most part located in buildings separate from the capitol building itself. The commodious arrangements and the magnificence of the general physical surroundings perhaps impress Washington tourists and make them feel they are getting value received for their tax dollar. Nevertheless, the dispersal of congressional facilities over vast acres of grass and marble detracts from a sense of congressional unity. An improvement in convenience and effectiveness might be achieved by housing all facets of Congress—the chambers, offices of members, committee rooms, and a research library—in one building.

The bicameral structure divides Congress into the two assemblies of the House of Representatives and the Senate, each of which possesses an intricate system of partisan and committee organization. The two chambers have approximately the same legal authority, with similar proceedings, so that Congress continually makes duplicate sets of decisions on the same subject. The difference between the two assemblies, while not considerable, is nevertheless significant in some cases and may be summarized as follows: The strict House rules give the leaders firmer control over the agenda, the debate, and the decision; the more viable Senate rules permit extensive deliberation, with many types of decisions being made by unanimous consent. On the whole, Senate debates are more extensively reported in the press, with the result that the public may possibly be more familiar with the views of Senators and perhaps considers the actions of the Senate to be more important than those of the House. The party organization is stronger in the House, and there is a greater tendency for the voting to be along party lines. The considerable influence which individual Senators may exercise over legislation is due in part to the persuasiveness inherent in unlimited debate, which may lead to filibustering (and concessions to stop the filibuster). The organization of each assembly provides for a moderator to preside over the debates, for a parliamentarian to furnish precedents, for doorkeepers and sergeants at arms to prevent intrusion from without and disorder from within, and for clerks to keep the records. The Senate has special authority over treaties and personnel appointments. Despite some differences, the Senate and the House have basically similar types of constituencies, so that no one assembly represents exclusively, say, the farmers, or the cities, or labor organizations, or manufacturers, or even states. Although there is intermittent disagreement between the two assemblies on matters of policy, the differences rarely become so ossified that no reconciliation of views is possible.

PARTIES AND OTHER ASSOCIATIONS

The members of Congress must perforce combine their efforts through association either to carry on the business of Congress or to advance their own more particular interests. Concerted action is required to advance through the three crucial phases of the legislative process: the determination of the agenda, the deliberation, and the final decision. Members combine with other members in order to achieve certain specific ends—farm relief, veterans' pensions, navy expansion, tax cuts, and all the rest. Their associations in Congress may be important in establishing public support for the member, the party, and the government itself—all having particular pertinence to the upcoming election. They combine also in order to create the organization which controls congressional procedures, and it is through association of this type that members develop careers in Congress which carry prestige and influence and honors and satisfaction.

Associations within Congress command various degrees of allegiance, and it is often through these associations, particularly of parties and committees, that Congressmen participate in the legislative process. Associations may be formed of political parties, of legislative committees, of regional representatives, state or urban delegations, and groups interested in particular types of policy, such as oil or flood control or utility regulation or civil rights. Friendship may count a good deal on some matters—especially in the Senate—and action which does not conform to action otherwise anticipated may be taken out of deference to personalities. Some associations are permanent and well organized (such as parties and committees); others are temporary and transient, formed briefly to secure some temporary goal and then disbanded. Some are punctilious about their membership, being circumspect in recruiting, and demanding on time and allegiance; others appeal for adherents *en masse,* making few requests other than appeals for support of the immediate issue. Within the organization of Congress, some groups attempt to control the selection of personnel for positions of authority, or the policy to be followed, or the strategy to be adopted.

The parties and the committees are the two major political associations within Congress, and members build their legislative careers and find a scope for their talents under the discipline of these systems. A member may have other associations which he prizes highly, or he may be the cat that walks alone, but if he hopes to be influential in the legislative process he must work within the orbit of the party system and the committee system. New members are caught up in the vortex of this twin system of authority; given time, patience, reëlection, and perhaps some luck in securing favorable assignments, they will be able to work their way upward in the hierarchy of congressional authority and, at some future date, achieve a position where they can exert a commanding influence in certain areas of policy or certain phases of the legislative process. With an occasional exception, political candidates find that identification with a political party is essential not only for election but also for securing committee assignments, advancing within the hierarchy of congressional influence, securing time for debate, and achieving various other ends in which Congressmen may be interested. Although voters may wish to retain their independence in voting for the best man and not for the best partisan, the candidate himself can rarely be so independent as to disavow completely all partisan affiliations.

The political parties perform several functions that may be considered essential, or at least helpful, in making it possible for Congress to act as a legislative body. Primarily, the parties assume the responsibility for "organizing" Congress, which means the selection of personnel to control the three phases of the legislative process. In the selection process, the long list of possible claimants for positions of authority is reduced to a precise number of known individuals; these individuals, in turn, are assigned certain tasks and are expected to meet an acceptable standard of performance. This process of selecting the personnel for the key legislative positions is another step in the series of events set in motion even before the elections. At long last, after many contests, tests of strength, and partisan rivalry extending over the entire nation, the precise number of individuals is finally chosen for positions essential to the operation of the legislature.

In organizing Congress, the parties naturally receive the support of their own members, for one of the attractions of membership is the ability of the party to place its members in positions where they can participate in the crucial phases of the legislative process. The parties make certain that their members are represented in some fashion at all points where crucial decisions are made. This does not necessarily mean that the parties will dictate what decisions are to be made. It does mean, however, that the parties have established firm control over the selection of personnel and that members who hope to influence policy or achieve a position of stature in the legislative hierarchy will find it expeditious to belong to a political party. The legislative parties may also be able to assist members in their relations with their constituents, especially in elections, although some may feel that they can command more support than the party.

The parties play a useful function in the legislative process because of their exceptional talent for resolving conflict. The conflict which exists in real life is transformed into the sham battle of perpetual party conflict, played according to well-defined rules which permit some exaggeration in forensics while demanding punctilious regard for procedures. Major issues between social groups may be reduced to contests over legislative tactics. Issues are looked over and examined by partisans and tested for possible exploitation before a broader audience. Few of the issues before Congress develop into national issues that command the attention of the public, but the partisans are constantly feeling their way, as it were, in examining issues closely to determine whether they might be advantageously exploited. Unless a measure is relatively innocuous and politically inert or is so widely popular that overt opposition would be imprudent, it can hardly pass through the various stages of the legislative process without some partisan clash taking place. The possibilities of partisan exploitation are so considerable and the number of partisans so great that it is rare for a measure to remain free from partisan bickerings at all stages of the process. Whatever the case, skilled leadership is required to secure the passage.

The party machinery of Congress is a sprawling, loose-knit sort of organization which has few general principles to guide its conduct and is perhaps not completely satisfactory from anyone's point of view. It is not the product of any attempt to define closely the nature and expectations of legislative party organization, but it reflects, rather, the diverse and sometimes contradictory approaches that have been made to resolve the demands and strains at some past crisis. Within each major party some trends have favored centralized control while others have favored decentralization, and claims additionally made on behalf of regional interests, the special position of particular political personalities, or the voting propensities of certain groups have been reflected in the organization.

Centralized control presumably enables the legislature to act more effectively and expeditiously than otherwise, to plan a session so that Congress can consider the various items on a crowded agenda, to integrate the activities of the various parts, and to locate specifically those responsible for taking action (or not taking action). The strong party caucus, used frequently in the nineteenth century, provided a forum for resolving internal conflict and developing a program which members were constrained to follow. In the House, the use of the caucus as an instrument of control tended to be augmented by a Speaker whose considerable prerogatives made him a man of commanding influence. He was a strong factor in selecting the agenda by virtue of his membership on the Rules Committee and his ability to appoint and remove members of legislative committees. He had considerable control over the deliberations in the House, in part because he did not hesitate to use his authority as presiding officer for advancing partisan ends. Finally, his control over appointments and other spoils of office added to his ability to mobilize his party in support of a measure.

Whatever advantages such a system may have had for establishing centralized control over proceedings, many Representatives found it galling to be controlled so strictly by a party leader. A reaction to the Speaker set in, and in 1910 the prerogatives of the Speaker were considerably curtailed. In the new order of things, the base of authority was broadened, enabling more members to participate in controlling the proceedings, and a number of lesser authorities were established over specific areas of policy or facets of the process. The authority formerly centralized in the Speaker was dispersed widely among committee chairmen, party organizations, political leaders, and the members as a whole, with no formal provisions made for coördinating these diverse strands.

In theory the Senate also distributes authority widely, although sometimes a strong figure, such as a Senator Aldrich or a Senator Taft, is able to exert considerable influence over the proceedings. The general rule in both chambers is for authority to be dispersed, formally and informally, among a large number of committees and subcommittees, individuals, partisan organization, and other groupings. The smaller units within the greater have varying degrees of influence. No one speaks for Congress on all things, but those who speak for Congress on some things have been in office a long time.

A description of the formal machinery for making party decisions may give a false impression of its significance. In locating the area where decisions are formulated, one might have to go considerably beyond the party structure, but the latter is important in so far as decisions are made under the symbols of its authority. The basic unit of the caucus (or conference) gives technical approval to party officials and party nominations and, occasionally, to policy proposals. The caucus may be considered to be the constituent body of the party in each chamber—there are no joint caucuses—with which all party members affiliate. Once it has met, selected its leaders, and ratified committee assignments, party action is henceforth taken under its authority, but the caucus seldom acts further in its capacity as a corporate group.

Ordinarily, membership in the caucus is axiomatic, but a question of loyalty may arise in connection with the attitude of a member during the election, and especially whether the member supported the presidential candidate of his party. Parties have adopted varying attitudes toward their more inconstant members. After Senator Robert M. La Follette, a nominal Republican, ran for President as a Progressive in 1924, he was removed from the Finance Committee and placed last in rank on the Committee on Manufacturers, thereby losing his position as chairman. On the other hand, two Senate Democrats who ran for Vice-President on third-party tickets suffered no such reprisals. Both Senator Burton K. Wheeler of Montana, who joined the La Follette movement in 1924, and Senator Glen H. Taylor of Idaho, who joined the Wallace movement in 1948, retained their committee assignments. "Taylor commented afterward that he was never subjected to punishment via patronage, but that he had been studiously left out of all consultations. 'A kind of negative hazing,' he labeled it." [2]

[2] Bailey and Samuels, *Congress at Work*, p. 75.

The party caucus has gone into disrepute as a formulator of policy, partly because of the issue of compulsion. Objections have been made that the party caucus limits one's freedom of action, and the rule of the majority no longer prevails. The House Democrats now require a two-thirds vote to bind members, but the member must have participated in the decision, and he can be otherwise excused if he has committed himself differently to his constituents or if he believes the proposal to be unconstitutional. The Republicans no longer attempt to commit their members. The formation of policy becomes less the concern of the formal party organization and more the concern of groups and individuals who speak in its name—the steering committees, policy committees, legislative committees, and party leaders.

The main function of the party caucus (or conference) is less to make policy than to assign personnel to the various positions essential to the legislative process. First in importance comes the committees. It has been mentioned that party membership is requisite for securing the best committee assignments and advancing in the hierarchy of committee authority. Party identity, yes, but not party regularity, which is not an essential requirement for appointment, or advancement, or even for securing the chairmanship. The party places its members on committees but does not instruct them how to vote; once appointed, a committee tends to have autonomous authority, fully subject to party influence but not to party discipline. A more extensive discussion of the requirements of committee organization will be contained in the subsequent section; here the discussion will be restricted to the more formal aspects of the party's role in selecting the membership.

It may be misleading to describe the selection process in too great detail, for negotiations, past commitments, regional representation, and personalities play a part, and influence may change rapidly in the fluid orbit of congressional politics. Assignments are formally made by the party caucus (or conference) which presents for approval to each chamber a slate of names prepared by a committee on committees. Speaking legally, the committees are appointed by each chamber, but the names presented are those proposed by the party organization. In tracing the origins of the committee assignments, we can wind our way back to the party caucus, which in turn approves the assignments proposed by the committee on committees. A member of such a committee in the House has written that so far as he knows, "there are never any appeals from the committee to the caucus." Going further back, we can ask what criteria are used in selecting the committee on committees and what *their* criteria are in selecting the members of the committees.

The pattern of selection is varied, with the formal party structure being used in many cases to approve action or confirm agreements made elsewhere—perhaps by other people. Each of the four major party organizations in Congress follows a somewhat different formula in selecting its committee on committees, although the common problem is to find a formula by which the various diverse party interests can be represented. In the House, the committee on committees of the Democrats is composed of the Democratic members of the Committee on Ways and Means, and these members, in turn, are elected by the party caucus—often after a competitive struggle. The committee on committees is divided into zones, each zone having a member, and each zone member nominates candidates from his zone for various committee places. The full committee then votes on these nominations by secret ballot. The committee on committees of the House Republicans is composed of one member from each state having Republican representation. In this fashion, all areas electing Republicans are represented, although not necessarily in proportion to the extent of their partisanship. In the Senate, committee assignments are determined by the steering committees, Democratic and Republican, although in both cases negotiations and discussions may take place elsewhere.

The parties must also determine who will be permitted to speak on party matters, and over what measures and in what spheres of activity party leaders or party committees are to have authority. So-called steering committees appear to have considerable control over policy and strategy from their position in any box-and-string diagram of party organization, but they are not customarily a vital factor in formulating policy. In 1946, the Senate created majority and minority policy committees, and the Republicans, especially, have made effective use of their committee as an agency for legislative research, legislative planning, and legislative conference. To add to the confusion of organization, the legislative program in the House is largely determined by the Rules Committee, a standing committee having bipartisan membership. Although the majority party maintains a majority of eight members to four, the committee may in fact act independently of party wishes.

The party leaders have little legal authority but they may nevertheless have considerable influence over the legislative process as a result of their talents of persuasion or abilities as negotiators. The Speaker of the House, selected by the majority party, has an anomalous position for he is simultaneously the presiding officer and leader of his party. As presiding officer he is neutral, his function being to see that the consideration of legislation is procedurally correct, and in this he has the assistance of a parliamentarian—a permanent employee of the House—who prepares precedents and otherwise advises the Speaker. As party leader, the Speaker takes little part in debate, but he will occasionally speak out, either in admonition or in rallying the party to a cause, and he has the assistance of the Majority Leader and his floor organization.

In the Senate two officers perform functions similar to those of the Speaker of the House. The presiding officer is, of course, the Vice-President of the United States who has been thrust upon the Senate, as it were, and is considered to be somewhat of an outsider. The Senate has never thought it necessary to expand the meager functions of the Vice-President listed in the Constitution, and he does not even exercise the customary senatorial prerogatives of debating or voting (except in a tie). His supposed right to appoint conferees and other committees is determined by custom, restrained by party leaders, and subject to revision by a Senate majority. However, if consulted by party leaders he may play an influential role in developing legislative strategy. The Senate also utilizes a president pro-tempore, who performs routine functions in the absence of the President of the Senate. The position carries with it such attractive prerequisites as the use of a limousine and on the whole is more honorary than onerous.

The real work horses of the party are the respective leaders, the majority and minority leaders of the House and Senate, who are selected by their party organizations, often after a spirited contest, for seniority is not a requirement. A contest of heroic proportions developed in 1937, when the Democrats chose a replacement for Senator Joseph T. Robinson of Arkansas, who had died during the heat of the controversy over the bill to enlarge ("pack") the Supreme Court. Senator Alben W. Barkley of Kentucky had the advantage of being acting leader at the time, and he also had the support of President Roosevelt, who had written a letter with the memorable salutation, "Dear Alben," which expressed the hope that Barkley would assume the leadership of the party. The letter stung, for Presidents, if you please, are supposed to keep out of Senate politics. Opposing Barkley was Senator Pat Harrison of Mississippi, who not only had friends of his own but was also supported by those annoyed by the President's indiscreet letter. The party caucus chose Barkley by a margin of one vote, 38–37, which included a vote from Harrison's Mississippi colleague, Senator Theodore G. Bilbo. Not until the spring of 1944, when Senator Barkley attacked President Roosevelt's veto of a tax bill, did some Senators believe that Senator Barkley was actually the leader of the majority and not merely the President's man.

The party develops majorities in voting not only as a result of commonly shared attitudes but also through the work of the party mobilizers who see to it that all members are present and voting at the strategic time. Here the so-called whip organization is called into action. Its devolved responsibility resembles an army unit, where the major tells the captain and so down the chain of command until shortly the corporal arrives with his squad. If the whip organization is active, alert, and disciplined, a party may win votes by quickly mobilizing its strength even though it has only a nominal minority.

Although permitting a wide tolerance of opinions on the part of their members, parties nevertheless provide a measure of cohesiveness by inculcating attitudes of loyalty, trust, and mutual reliance. These are conditions under which authority can be widely dispersed and which assist in mobilizing majorities on controversial issues. It may appear to some people that partisanship is an undesirable adjunct of the political system in that it substitutes prejudice for open-minded deliberation and gives preferment to partisan cronies regardless of ability. Such complaints may have merit, but that is not the whole story. Partisan alignment also performs a useful function in mobilizing opinion and creating attitudes of mutual trust necessary for a large group to make decisions. It also enables the individual member, chosen by this particular electorate, to be a meaningful part in the collectivity of the total assembly. Some sort of organization, some sort of mutual reliance, is necessary if the legislature is to be a corporate body, capable of making decisions. The political party is the vehicle, in other words, for creating a common bond in a common purpose between legislators.

In addition to the function of developing majorities, partisanship also "sets the tone" for legislative deliberation, which characteristically includes trust of one's colleagues (if not suspicion of one's opponents), and this, in turn, may add to the facility with which conflict is resolved. To place partisanship in the most favorable light, it can be said that it develops in members a willingness to trust the decisions of others, especially in those areas where they are not informed, and to place political loyalty above many other loyalties. In the words of Speaker Cannon, "it's a damned good thing to remember in politics to stick to your party and never attempt to buy the favor of your enemies at the expense of your friends." [3]

Partisanship does not necessarily mean that all partisans share common beliefs, but it may mean that, in certain areas and on specific occasions, they will trust the decisions of other partisans, and above all, remain loyal in a crisis. "Each of us has more than one duty to perform in the United States Senate," Senator Elbert D. Thomas (D., Utah) once said in explaining why he was now supporting a

[3] Busbey, *Uncle Joe Cannon*, p. 269.

measure which he had hitherto opposed. "Sometimes we find ourselves to be advocates for our committees, sometimes advocates for
the administration, and sometimes for our party." Now, during the
war crisis, "when it was decided in this instance unity was necessary
because of the uncertainty incident to the great military campaigns
that are now under way, we all gave way, and accepted the theory
of our leaders." [4]

The feeling of trust and mutual obligation developed by partisanship creates the conditions under which members are trusted in some
areas simply because they are fellow partisans. You don't let the
side down. On some issues it is *de rigueur* for all partisans to be
united and agreed. If some members are given special authority to
make decisions in some areas, they need to have the confidence of
their colleagues. Senator *A* supports a bill reported by Committee *B*
not because he is himself convinced of the merits of the bill but
because he trusts his fellow partisans on the committee who are so
convinced.

The partisan attitude toward the opposition is one of ceaseless
querulous questioning. The introspection and self-analysis which partisans may lack in themselves is supplied in full measure by the
opposition. However, the raising of questions by one set of partisans
means also that these partisans must be prepared to answer questions,
and this involves a type of internal therapy. These partisan contests
go on incessantly: some are petty, some prodding, some important.
Whatever the nature of interpartisan relations, the opposition is not
only tolerated but continually represented in making legislative decisions, for the loyalty of legislators to one another and to the
legislative process is greater than that of partisan to partisan.

Although all legislators are partisans, the nature and scope of their
partisanship varies considerably. Some are content to remain at the
elementary level of political quibbling, which often characterizes
House debate. Some are partisan in the sense of trusting fellow
partisans to make important decisions. Still others are partisan in
the sense of supplying leadership; they define and clarify the basic

[4] *Congressional Record,* February 26, 1945, p. 1419.

issues, take a positive stand, and attempt to persuade others to follow them. The following traits are common denominators of congressional partisans: (1) A partisan identifies himself in the *Congressional Directory* as a member of a party; (2) he is a member of his party caucus or conference (a few may not attend); (3) he votes with his own party in choosing the Speaker of the House or the president pro tempore of the Senate, and he supports the list of committee assignments offered by his party; (4) he will almost inevitably support the presidential nominee of his party; (5) he will ordinarily support the partisan appointments of his own party; (6) he will ordinarily vote with the party on issues where partisanship itself develops into a significant issue—such as creating an investigating committee which potentially might embarrass the opposition party; (7) if his party is out of office, a member will attack the Administration in broad terms, or conversely will defend the Administration for general electoral purposes.

THE COMMITTEE SYSTEM

The system of standing legislative committees developed early in the nineteenth century and now plays such an important part in the proceedings of Congress and the careers of members that questions are seldom raised about the general utility of the system. The committee system provides legislative careers for members of Congress, giving them unusual opportunities for influencing political decisions. Relatively few members become the heads of government departments, which in any event would require them to give up their seats in Congress. It also provides policy specialists for the parent chamber, for the committees are influential in determining what legislation is to be considered, in examining the content of the legislation, and in the deliberations. Committees also provide an instrumentality through which Congress can exercise control over the administration of policy by the governmental bureaucracy.

The somewhat formalized method of allocating authority among the various legislative committees is based on the principles of limited and exclusive membership, relative partisan strength, seniority, and major policy areas. Limited and exclusive membership means that the components of committees are fixed. A member cannot join whatever committee he pleases merely because of his interest in the subject matter, and he can belong to but one or two major committees. The committees have a set membership component, divided according to partisan affiliation and ranked by length of tenure of assignment, with opportunities for new appointments developing only when vacancies occur. Membership on a committee is expected—and it is required if a member expects to have influence in Congress—but initially the new member can consider himself lucky if he gets the assignment he covets most.

The fact that all committee assignments are not equally attractive, although all must be filled, requires the development of a system of assignment priorities. In all, counting both Houses, 700 or more committee assignments must be made, some of which carry considerable prestige and influence and all of which have authority over policy important to some people. Although the priority system does not always give the available assignment to the most competent member, it has other features to recommend it. Its greatest strength perhaps lies in the fact that it fills all committee assignments regularly, thus ensuring the consideration by some legislative group of all subjects coming within the orbit of congressional interest. Not everyone can be a chief; some have to be Indians. The conflict between talent and the availability of committee assignments can be illustrated by the experience of Mr. John Foster Dulles when he was appointed to the Senate in 1949. Although Mr. Dulles later became Secretary of State, he did not receive an obvious assignment to the Committee on Foreign Relations, where there was no vacancy, and he was named instead to the Committee on Post Offices and Post Roads. One might conclude that this was a case of misappointment in which the Senate failed to make the best use of the talent of its members. However, Congress has functions which must be performed and assignments which must be filled; if someone must serve for a while on a less attractive committee, why should it not be a newcomer? ·

New legislators ordinarily have more knowledge of the problems of their constituencies than of the nation and will tend to gravitate toward committees with jurisdiction over interests in which they are especially concerned—farm, labor, maritime, petroleum. This preponderance of local interest raises for Congress the problem of how to develop in its members a broader conception of the interests of the whole nation. The committee organization assists in this broadening process by forcing the members to become familiar with political issues which are not closely associated with their constituencies and about which they may know little on arriving in Congress.

Another result of limited and exclusive membership is the development of a hierarchy of committees in which some assignments are more coveted than others. New members must ordinarily wait their turn to secure the most coveted assignments, and in the meantime their colleagues will be sizing them up and testing them out. A member may serve on several different committees before he is satisfied, but once satisfied he will want to stay on the committee and build up seniority.

The principle of relative partisan strength awards committee assignments in proportion to the magnitude of the party's electoral victory. Thus, if a party wins 70 percent of the seats in the House or Senate it will be entitled, roughly, to slightly more than 70 percent of the committee assignments. The rules governing the allocation are somewhat complex, but the net result is that a party with a narrow margin of victory has little flexibility in making assignments and a small margin of strength in each committee. The majority party is in effect awarded a small bonus of seats which can be used differentially to bolster its strength on committees where its control might otherwise be tenuous.

The advantage of party alignment in securing favorable committee assignments is illustrated by the case of Senator Wayne L. Morse of Oregon, a nominal Republican who became an Independent during the 1952 presidential campaign and supported the Democratic candidate, Governor Adlai Stevenson. Senator Morse subsequently lost his seat on the Armed Service Committee. The public may have gathered that Senator Morse was being disciplined for his insurgency, and this may have been so; it should also be said that the Republicans did not have a margin of political strength great enough for them to be charitable to Morse without, at the same time, jeopardizing their control of several committees. Republicans as well as Democrats wish to award their quota to their own members. The Republicans held most committees by the margin of a single vote and would have jeopardized this control by any committee composed of six Republicans, six Democrats, and one Independent. The Republicans could have continued control by a committee membership of seven, five, and one, but this solution would have required the Republicans to give up one of their few bonus seats and would have reduced the number of Democrats on the committee. Short of enlarging the committee membership by changing the rules, any seat given to Senator Morse on an important committee would have affected party control. So Senator Morse lost his seat on the Armed Services Committee.

Another organizational principle followed is that of seniority. This standard controls the advancement within the committee hierarchy, the member first in rank becoming chairman if his party succeeds in organizing the parent chamber. Continuous membership on the committee is necessary to advance in rank, inasmuch as accumulated seniority is forfeited if there is an interruption in service for a session or longer. A member who is reëlected after being out of Congress for a term has no overriding claim to regain his old committee assignments, and if he is reappointed he is last in rank. Senator Alben Barkley, for instance, was reappointed to the Finance Committee in 1955 after serving four years as Vice-President of the United States, but he forfeited his seniority in resigning; when again assigned to the Finance Committee he was last in rank.

A member advances in the hierarchy of the committee at an unpredictable rate. Two members, A and B, may be elected at the same time and assigned to different committees: A may have the good fortune to become chairman within a relatively few years; B may never become chairman. The rate of committee attrition is uneven, with vacancies developing more rapidly on some committees than on others. Other things being equal, progress is slower on committees which are popular and sought after than on committees which do not retain their membership. Some constituencies and some states tend to reëlect their membership, so that a committee member who is outranked by one from such an area must be prepared to wait and wait and wait.

The career of Representative Adolph J. Sabath (D., Ill.), the former chairman of the House Committee on Rules, illustrates how one may eventually become chairman if he holds his seat with uncommon tenacity. Mr. Sabath was elected to the House in 1906 at the age of 40; some 22 years later he was named to the Rules Committee, the last ranking Democrat. The Democrats organized the House in 1931, making Representative Sabath a member of the majority, and one by one those members who outranked Sabath on the committee dropped out. Sabath became chairman of the committee in 1939, after 32 years in the House, and he remained the ranking Democrat on the committee until his death in 1952 at the age of 86.

The varying results of the seniority system prevent one from being too dogmatic about its results or from being too sanguine in offering alternatives. Its merits are that the choice of chairman is certain, that it is known in advance, and that it avoids controversy between personalities, and all this in addition to the fact that the member with the greatest experience may indeed be the logical choice. On the other hand, seniority may put in authority one who is somewhat of a misfit, and this in turn may cause difficulties and embarrassments, the saddest cases being of those who are too old to assume the responsibilities of the office. The protective handling of such committee patriarchs may strain the political acumen of the party leaders, the committee members, and the family advisers. Each party has its venerable ancients, and while some are very good legislators, the time may nevertheless come when their usefulness decreases. One case concerns Senator Arthur Capper (R., Kan.) who after a long political career became chairman of the Committee on Agriculture and Forestry at the age of 81, and it was said of him at the time that he could hear no one and no one could hear him.

However, there are ways to modify the seniority system, such as occurred with the shifting of chairmanships which took place when the Republicans organized the Senate in 1947. Senator Robert A. Taft (R., Ohio) decided to accept the chairmanship of the Committee on Education and Labor, although he was also eligible to become chairman of the Committee on Finance. Taft's sacrificial choice gave Senator Hugh Butler (R., Neb.) the choice of being chairman of Finance or of Public Lands. When he chose the latter committee, he was given the honorary title of "Dean of the West," and Senator Milliken, a former banker, became chairman of the Finance Committee. In this arrangement the principle of seniority was maintained, but the arrangement also permitted competence and interest to be considered. In the long run, the problems raised by the seniority method of selecting chairmen may perhaps best be met by modifying the functions of the chairman, making him simply the presiding officer of a collegiate body and not an official having independent authority by virtue of his title.

The legislative committees of Congress are organized around major policy areas, such as taxation, foreign policy, or labor relations, so that the committee structure does not correspond with any exactitude to the structure of government agencies. The reasons for this type of organization are in part accidental, but the structure can be and has been rationalized. The number of government agencies and congressional committees has been expanded and contracted independently, with no necessary correlation between the one and the other. Thus, the organization, or reorganization, of each branch of government does not directly or immediately concern the other. Moreover, the argument is advanced that a committee interested in a policy area may be able to take a broader point of view than a department and be in a better position to review and to integrate total policy. For instance, the Committee on Banking and Currency would be able to examine the fiscal policies of the Treasury Department as well as the Federal Reserve System and it might have a broader and more comprehensive view than either of the two agencies. In practice, however, there is a close relationship between departments and committees which may belie the organization based on policy areas. The effect of organizing committees around policy areas may mean only that one committee considers legislation for parts of several departments, that one department may have relations with several committees, and that no one committee examines the total operation of any one department.

Even such a convenient rubric as foreign affairs may not catch all aspects of foreign policy in its net. The authority of the Senate Committee on Foreign Relations or the House Committee on Foreign Affairs is not exclusive and other committees may also claim jurisdiction over some aspect of foreign policy. The requirement that funds must be authorized before they are appropriated means of course that both legislative and appropriation committees are involved in foreign policy debates and that, in some cases, it is necessary to make a series of duplicate decisions. In the consideration of the European Recovery Program, to take one example, Congress was continually asked to make policy in the form of law, following which it would make policy in the form of appropriation. The Appropriations Committees must be included, then, in any description of the sources of congressional authority in foreign policy. The Armed Services Committee also has a share, a fact which was emphasized when the hearings on the removal of General MacArthur were held jointly by the Armed Services Committee and the Foreign Relations Committee of the Senate. The agriculture committees may also have a share, as when they have custody over legislation distributing food stockpiles to "needy governments and peoples." On economic questions, the banking and currency committees must be included, and for good measure one should add the judiciary committees, which have jurisdiction over such constitutional amendments as the Bricker proposal for modifying the procedures for making treaties.

There are several types of committees other than the legislative committees organized on a basis of major policy areas. The two appropriations committees have jurisdiction over money bills, although legislation authorizing the appropriations is handled by the standing committees. There are also so-called watchdog committees, the best example being the Joint Committee on Atomic Energy, whose distinguishing features are that its members are drawn from both Houses and that it was created particularly to supervise the operations of a single agency. The special investigating committees represent still another type; such committees may be created for a particular purpose for a limited time and ordinarily are not authorized to consider and report legislation. There are also service committees which supervise the operation of the Government Printing Office and the Library of Congress. Finally, there are commissions and boards of visitors.

The jurisdiction of committees is defined fairly precisely by the rules of each chamber, and most bills are referred as a matter of routine. However, the presiding officer has some choice of referral, but he may be overruled by a vote of the membership. Alteration in committee jurisdiction may occur if a committee becomes interested in a particular topic, so that in the process of time the jurisdiction of some committees may be expanded and that of others contracted. For many years the Senate Committee on Manufacturers was overshadowed by the Senate Committee on Interstate Commerce; it was starved of legislation and was eventually abolished by the Reorganization Act of 1946. During World War II, strike legislation was referred to the Military Affairs Committee or the Judiciary Committee, rather than to the respective committees on labor. The technical justification was that the proposed legislation amended the Selective Service and Training Act or the Criminal Code, subjects which had been considered earlier by the two named committees. The more obvious political reason was the unlikelihood that the labor committees would report out the kind of legislation its sponsors wished.

Whatever the committee structure, proposals will be made for creating new legislative committees, or establishing an investigating committee, or creating a special committee to consider a special topic. The given structure will not satisfy some group, and there will be a drive to create a new committee. As a result of this process of creating the new and retaining the old, the number of standing legislative committees had by 1918 grown to 61 in the House and 75 in the Senate. They were cut back, only to bloom again. The Reorganization

Act of 1946 reduced the number of committees to less than a score in each House, but in the meantime there had been a mushroom growth of subcommittees, more than 60 permanent subcommittees having been created in each House.

The staffs of the committees should also be mentioned because of the significant part they play in supplying information to committees and acting as a conduit of communications between the committees and the outside world. From the nature of their office, the committee staffs are in a strategic position where they can provide the committee with material necessary for making a decision and perhaps influence attitudes as well. Although there is general agreement that all committees require staffs, and legislation so provides, there has been little examination of how the staffs operate or of the rationale developed of what might be called proper staff behavior. A wide variety of practices are found. Staffs may be recruited because of their competence in party tactics, in which case their function may be more related to securing support for policy (and for politicians) than to examining the content of policy. Or they may be recruited primarily because of their technical competence. Some staffs or staff directors are given a clear field to develop programs, question witnesses, write reports, and grant interviews to the press, while others operate as agents within the framework of the existing committee structure. The various possible uses of committee staffs add a new dimension to the legislative process, and especially so if they create in effect new structures of authority rather than limiting themselves to assisting the operation of the given committee process. The problem is essentially one of competence, control, and function. In what areas are the staffs competent? To whom are they responsible? What is their function in assisting legislators to make independent decisions or in making decisions themselves?

In all, the committees do a good deal of work—more, indeed, than is required, in that considerable attention is spent on items of a trivial nature; less, also, than may be required, for legislation may be inadequate or review ineffective. Some committees are relatively lethargic; some are most active and energetic. Whatever the product may be, the time and energy spent by the totality of committees during a session of Congress, or even during a single day, reach prodigious proportions.

SUMMARY

Once elected, the new legislator will be confronted with a pattern of organized action which will now govern much of his behavior. He is no longer on his own, an individual appealing for the support of his constituents, but a part of an involved and intricate legislative organization. He will find standards of rectitude which he is expected to adopt and of competence which he is expected to master. In making provisions for bringing in new members, Congress is continually faced with the problem of maintaining the continuity of the system and at the same time permitting all members to participate in the crucial phases of the legislative process.

The legislature itself is highly organized, with a number of concrete interrelated systems of authority and influence assisting Congress in carrying out the three principal facets of the process: the selection of the agenda, the deliberations, and the final decision. The member's office, with its manifold channels of communication, provides special facilities for relating government more particularly to the constituents. The two chambers, although organized slightly differently, perform essentially the same functions, and the political conflict over legislative policy occurs within their organizational framework.

Some of the political associations with which members identify are of a transitional nature, being concerned with relatively few topics for a short period of time; others are more highly organized, relatively permanent, and attract the continued loyalties and energies of the members. Of the permanent associations, the most significant are the political parties and the committees. The parties attempt to organize Congress by seeing to it that their own members are placed in positions where they can influence important aspects of the legislative process. The comprehensive controls which parties exercise over appointments make party membership virtually mandatory for anyone aspiring to an influential legislative career. The parties also influence other aspects of the legislative process, as will be seen subsequently, but the function they fill most completely is that of assigning their members to the positions of authority in the two chambers, the parties, and the committees. The organization of political parties creates something of a problem, for there is no agreed principle on who should have what type of authority. The actual formal structure may conceal more than it reveals, for the labels are not necessarily synonymous with influence and importance. In effect, the leaders must feel their way as best they can, relying on their knowledge of the situation and the personalities involved as a guide to action.

The organization of committees follows better-developed lines, but the constant problem of canalizing existing interest within the bounds of the prevailing structure of committees is difficult to solve. The general inflation in the number of committees or subcommittees which goes on continually is a reflection of the attempt on the part of those interested to gain further specific control over particular policy. Within the established committee structure, one can observe the four major organizing principles of limited and exclusive membership; relative party strength in allocating the membership between the two parties; seniority in appointment, rank, and selection of the chairman; and of major policy areas in determining the jurisdiction of the committees.

CHAPTER 4

The External System of Influence

CONGRESS IS NOT AN ISLAND UNTO ITSELF, SELF-sufficient, isolated, and unconcerned with the outside world. Its ability to regulate the behavior of others makes its actions the sedulous concern of many people, and a vast network of relationships flows in and out of Congress. The fact that Congress can make authoritative decisions results in the creation of a system of relationships through which other groups express interest in and attempt to influence decisions made by Congress; and Congress, in turn, is interested in or attempts to influence decisions made by other groups—and especially the governmental bureaucracy.

It may be useful to develop some general classifications to distinguish the various functions performed by those who bring information to Congress and who attempt to influence its actions. The term "expert informers" may be used to identify those who provide Congress with pertinent information useful in making decisions. Occasionally Congress is confronted with reluctant informers, where witnesses refuse to testify (a subject discussed later) but for the most part information is given voluntarily. One of the continuing problems facing Congress is the accessibility of unbiased, impartial, nonpartisan information from sources which have no immediate stake in the outcome of the decision. The need for supplying this type of information was a factor in enlarging the professional staffs of the committees in the Congressional Reorganization Act of 1946. "Persuaders" is a term which designate those who attempt to influence Congress to adopt a particular point of view. They may be letter writers, delegations who wait on Congressmen, lobbyists, or even the President. "Negotiators" are those who attempt to develop agreement on procedures to be followed or on the content of proposals and who may also attempt to arrange legislative combinations for accepting or rejecting a proposed course of action. Not infrequently, talent from outside Congress may be used in developing a consensus within Congress. "Opinion makers" are those who provide information on specific issues for the benefit of the broader public. In this regard, the total system of public communications is an important factor in legislative action, for it enables many people (including those in the legislature) to follow and perhaps to influence the development of policy. These functions are carried out by various individuals and groups, both within and without the government, so that, in fact, a complex network of influence, spreading over Congress from the four corners of the nation, may be assumed. Within this network of influence, the position of the President is especially significant, and one may find him playing all the functional roles enumerated above.

The inflowing stream of information provides Congress with some understanding of how proposed policy will be integrated with other activities, either in government or in the society at large. This information may influence legislative attitudes by showing whether a proposal is acceptable to the public as well as the degree to which individual members maintain the support of their constituents. In all, the inflow in information provides Congress with some awareness of how policy might be integrated with other activities, of the desirability of supporting or opposing specific proposals, and of the nature of the support being received.

Although Congress is autonomous, its relationship with the outside world is not static. Pressure groups, public opinion, political parties, and governmental bureaucrats are continually exerting influence over it, and these persistent demands may make it difficult for Congress to make a completely independent decision. One may well ask whether the stability and integrity of the legislative process may be endangered if, as is implied, so many people can influence Congress in so many ways. Can one be sure that malevolent influences will not seek to undermine the legislature or manipulate it for personal advantage? There is, of course, a possibility that outside influences might become so strong or so persuasive that the legislature could not retain its independence, and the outsiders may even try to abolish the legislature and usurp the government by a dictatorship. On the other hand, the legislature must not be so aloof that it is unaffected by political forces within society or not subject to constitutional restraints against arbitrary or illegal actions.

There is no single answer to the question of the proper amount of autonomy which a legislature should have, but the questions go to the heart of proposals for a stronger party system or for increased presidential leadership. The essential purpose of such proposals is to increase the internal cohesion of the legislature through the ability of some outside group to persuade or compel the legislature to act in a prescribed manner. In its structure and in its theories, Congress attempts to protect itself against "excessive" influence while at the same time utilizing the stream of information which flows into it. If Congress is not to be the pawn of the conflicting forces which themselves are to be controlled, it is necessary that it have some degree of independence, some autonomy of its own.

Congress has created a number of safeguards to protect itself against excessive outside interference, perhaps the most important of which is concerned with the integrity and continuity of normal operations. The usual accouterment of guards and doorkeepers are utilized to prevent forceful disturbances, and here the key legal concept is the word "contempt." Congress may punish certain types of contemptuous actions performed by members or even by strangers. The jurisdiction of the courts over some types of contempt, such as the refusal to give information, does not exhaust Congress' authority to protect its procedures from disruptive interference.

The right of access to the floor of the two chambers is sedulously guarded, and Congress has long feared that an increase in presidential influence would follow any provision giving cabinet members access to the floor. The President and other invited guests may address Congress by invitation only. Members of the cabinet have not participated in congressional debate since the days when Alexander Hamilton was Secretary of the Treasury, and while they may testify before congressional committees it is to be noted that these deliberations do not take place either in a chamber or during a legislative session. The extent to which Congress limits access to its deliberations is revealed in an incident after the last war when the attention of Congress was focused on the Army's plan for demobilizing troops. Although most members of Congress were obviously interested in demobilization, the required sanctity of the legislative chambers would not permit the Army to reveal the plans before Congress directly. They were revealed by General Eisenhower to members of Congress, duly assembled unofficially in the nonsacrosanct auditorium of the Library of Congress, a short distance from the capitol building.

Congress has also established safeguards to protect legislators from being corrupted through such devices as bribery, threats, and promises of rewards for satisfactory behavior. Bribery is deprecated because it wrests the effective decision from the member and gives it to an individual or group having an immediate stake in the decision. But other types of subtle and possibly effective influences, not covered by current regulations, may nevertheless raise questions of propriety and of legislative independence. Such influences illustrate the difficulties encountered in making regulations broad enough to cover all instances of permissible and nonpermissible influence. In a hypothetical case, a member of Congress belonging to a law firm having as a client an influential trade association or labor union sponsors legislation favorable to the client. Should the relationships among the member, the law firm, the client, and the proposed legislation be revealed? To

what extent should members be restrained from advancing publicly
certain private interests in which they themselves are to some extent
involved? In another hypothetical case, a member of Congress develops
expertness in a certain field of policy and is well informed on pertinent
administrative and legislative procedures. Because of his knowledge
and experience, the member is persuaded to resign his office and
accept employment at a higher salary as legislative expert for an
association directly interested in this particular field of policy. Should
the legislator have been forbidden to take such a job or at least have
been required to wait a period of time before accepting the new
employment? Might there otherwise be a suspicion that the legislator's previous decisions in Congress were influenced by the hope
of personal advancement in which there was a conflict of interest?

In an attempt to protect its own procedures, Congress has legally
restrained government agencies from spending public funds to influence legislation. Above all, Congress wishes to prevent government
agencies from engaging in propaganda undermining its actions by
asking the public to "write or wire your Congressmen" about particular legislation. The law provides that no money appropriated by
Congress may be used "to pay for any personal service, advertisement,
telegram, telephone, letter, printed or written matter, or other device,
intended or designed to influence in any manner a member of Congress, to favor or oppose, by vote or otherwise, any legislation or
appropriation by Congress." [1] However, government officials are
permitted to communicate with Congress directly in requesting legislation or appropriations "which they deem necessary for the efficient
conduct of the public business." These prohibitions against lobbying
are difficult to enforce and the infractions are difficult to define. In
appealing to a wide audience for the support of some particular
legislative program, such as farm legislation, what are the boundaries
of permissive governmental influence?

Restrictions are also placed on the use of propaganda. From time
to time Congress discusses the effect of the enlarged number of
lobbyists who attempt to influence legislation, and it has held several

[1] 18 USC §201.

inconclusive investigations. Here again it is difficult to draw a line between permissible and nonpermissible influence, and the current regulations are essentially an attempt to secure the facts on the nature and source of the interest. Those who are directly engaged in influencing legislation must file a report showing the name of the employee and the employer, the legislation with which they are concerned, the titles of the publications distributed, and the amount of money raised and spent in connection with lobbying activities. This type of information is potentially useful to Congress in identifying the witnesses before committees and in evaluating the political import of their testimony.

INFLUENCE: THE PRESIDENT

Although Congress and the President have independent authority, they must function as parts of a single system in performing such acts as making law, appropriating funds, and selecting certain types of personnel. Within this joint system, the authority of each is restricted by the consent given to the use of that authority by the other. Congress may become impatient with presidential action and, asserting its independence, attempt to strike out on its own. However, it cannot go very far on its own, for its structure is not suitable for administering the government, and presidential approval may be needed to validate many of its actions. Inasmuch as Congress and the President are in effect inseparable parts of the same system, it follows that each will be greatly interested in the decisions made by the other and on some occasions may attempt to influence these decisions.

The relationship between Congress and the President is close and continuous as well as frequently controversial. It is close and continuous because the President is a part of the legislative process, conceived as a complete whole, and it is controversial because both have restricted authority over the same areas of policy. The President is thus able to play a significant role in resolving conflict in Congress because of his position of authority in making law. He can exert considerable influence in suggesting what legislation Congress should consider and he may in effect determine what law is to be enacted because of his authority to sign or to veto legislation. Moreover, the President has considerable authority over appointments, although some of them must be additionally confirmed by the Senate. The President cannot compel Congress to take any specific action, but he can frequently prevent Congress from acting independently, thus placing him in a position to guide and lead.

For some types of action, the President becomes in effect the leader of Congress. He is compelled by the Constitution, by law, and by the nature of his position within the governmental structure to exercise some leadership, and he can exercise his veto to prevent Congress from going too far along an independent course without his consent. Within the limits bounded by suggestion and prevention, the President must determine the kind of relationship he intends to establish with Congress. He may wish to keep Congress on a tight leash, as it were, holding it close to his own program, or he may choose not to interfere with the prevailing system of congressional authority. In providing leadership for Congress, the President continually runs the risk of giving offense by failing to recognize prerogatives or to fulfill expectations and even by wounding the pride of Congress by exerting his leadership too strenuously.

The President, like Congress, is elected by the voters, but here, again, the method of organizing the electorate affects the nature of the representation achieved. The members of Congress are at least partially bound by the interests of the geographic districts they represent, but there are many members, with many interests and many groups represented. The President may theoretically be able to take a broader viewpoint than any one member, being somewhat freer to pick and choose between conflicting interests and to assume the leadership in promoting policies affecting many areas, but the President also may be restricted by commitments to specific groups whose favor he solicited in seeking nomination or election. However, from the nature of the whole selection process, the President represents many interests similar to those of his party in Congress, and he will be expected to speak forcefully on issues supported by his party and stressed in the elections. However, there are limitations on the continuity or identity of political influence; the political groups most influential in nominating or electing the President or who have his ear after he is in the White House cannot be perfectly equated with those who elect the congressional majority or who control the structure of authority within Congress. On some issues, one may anticipate that the President and the party organization in Congress will not see eye to eye.

The position of the President as leader of Congress has been advanced by several Presidents who enlarged the conception of their office; Jefferson, Jackson, Lincoln, Wilson, and the two Roosevelts, for instance, tended to increase the influence of the presidency. However, the assertion of new claims by strong Presidents is not the only explanation for the development of leadership within the presidency. It has also been promoted by Congress, which has often been willing to have the President assert some leadership in situations where it lacked the will, the wisdom, the foresight, or the ability to act on its own. Congress has expected Presidents to have a prepared policy for a variety of unanticipated events—wars, depressions, floods, pestilence, scientific discoveries, manpower needs, farm price maladjustment, labor disputes, and on and on. What solution do you propose, Mr. President? From the nature of his position, the President must be prepared to offer expert solutions on many subjects, but he may also wish to go beyond the role of expert adviser and become an advocate of the policies as well. However, the policy advocated by the President may not necessarily be acceptable to Congress, which may have some ideas of its own, and the President must, therefore, try as best he can to bring Congress along with him, or failing that, to arrive at an acceptable compromise.

There is considerable fluidity in the structure of the relationship between the Congress and the President. On some occasions, the leadership of the President is welcomed, if not demanded; on other occasions, it may be resented. This fluidity results in part from the changing concept of function which each President brings to his job as well as from the shifting nature of authority within Congress. The President has relations less with Congress as an entity than with small groups within Congress, each having well-developed expectations of the appropriateness of policy to be enacted or of deference to be shown. Not only does the composition of these groups change constantly, but new groups may develop out of nowhere, as it were, and demand to be heard. The relationship between the President and Congress varies with the time, the issue, and the men concerned.

The President's relations with Congress may be divided into those categories which are mandatory, those which are permissive, and those which, though not actually proscribed, may nevertheless be resented by Congress. In the mandatory category one may place the actions of the President which are considered to be acceptable, legal, and necessary and about which there is now little or no question of appropriateness. As the administrative head of the government, the President is expected to develop legislative and fiscal policies for Congress to consider. The proposed legislative policies are for the most part contained in the President's State of the Union Message, delivered annually at the opening of Congress, and in a series of special messages on particular legislation. The proposed fiscal policy is in part contained in the budget message submitted to Congress annually; according to law, the budget is to contain the President's estimate of the appropriations believed necessary for the support of the government as well as the amount of anticipated receipts. As we shall see, however, the President is limited in the extent to which he may take additional action to ensure the adoption of his proposals.

The mandatory category also includes the President's authority to appoint officials, ranging in rank from the heads of departments to the postmasters of small villages. However, the extent of the President's control over appointments is to some extent balanced by the influence which members of Congress, and especially Senators, may also exercise over them. The President is ordinarily permitted to select his chief administrators with no more than token opposition, but the members of Congress may have more influence in his selection of other types of appointments.

The mandatory category of relationship also encompasses the variety of reports which the President must submit to Congress, in-

cluding those on economic conditions as well as on the operation
of various specific policies; in addition, departments and agencies
must also submit periodic reports. The President ordinarily submits
his reports in writing, rather than making them orally to Congress,
but an exception was President Roosevelt's report to a joint session
of Congress in January, 1945, on the results of the Yalta Conference.

The frequent complaints that Congress is not fully informed, or
that heads of agencies are not entirely frank, or that information is
being purposely withheld, indicate that Congress might welcome an
increase in the extent of presidential reporting. An increase in quantity only, however, might give little satisfaction, for Congress has not
yet fully determined the type of information it wishes to receive, or
who should receive it, or the nature of the action which should be
taken subsequently. Congress is continually creating investigations to
ferret out facts, but once the action has been taken it may be too
late for Congress to do anything positive about it. The many questions
relating to the supply of information which Congress receives will be
discussed subsequently in the chapters on control.

In the mandatory category one would also place the President's
authority to sign or to veto legislation. Although the right of the
President to veto legislation is no longer controversial, for half a
century Presidents believed that they should veto legislation only in
the event it was thought to be unconstitutional, not simply undesirable.
This belief is no longer held, and the ability to veto legislation gives
the President continual influence over many decisions made by
Congress.

In some areas of policy, the President is required to submit his
proposals to Congress before they become effective. After a law is
enacted, the supplementary orders are subject to further consideration
by Congress and may be approved or disapproved. This device is
widely used in plans for reorganizing government agencies and, to a
lesser extent, in plans for the development of atomic energy for com-
mercial purposes, the sale of surplus property, and the deportation
of immigrants.

The permissive category of relationships encompasses the various arrangements developed by Presidents for establishing effective communications with Congress, its committees, and its members. These arrangements are ordinarily quite flexible and may change with the personnel involved. Some of the more important channels of communication are the consultations on policy which the President holds with various congressional leaders. The President's task may be more easily accomplished if the groups in Congress responsible for the policy are clearly distinguishable and do not object to such conferences because of the inference that the President would do all the suggesting and the leaders all the listening. When Speaker Cannon was the accepted spokesman for the House of Representatives, he was consulted regularly by President Theodore Roosevelt, although toward the end of that Administration the relations cooled and the conferences were less frequent. Senator James E. Watson, of Indiana, the Senate Leader during President Hoover's tenure of office, has written that a private telephone to the White House made him constantly available for consultations with the President. In the past 25 years, the practice has developed of the President's meeting weekly with the political leaders of the House and Senate although, as has been suggested earlier, the political leaders cannot speak definitely on all legislative matters.

It might appear that the President's task of establishing effective relations with Congress would be easier if he engaged in more congressional conferences, but the pitfall here is that the President has additional functions to perform which compete for his time and attention. The President may also feel that consultation with legislators whose advice he does not intend to take is a waste of time and that in any event he would be criticized for consulting the wrong people or ignoring others. Moreover, conferences are not always successful. In July, 1919, for instance, President Wilson invited the Senate Committee on Foreign Relations to the White House for a discussion of the Covenant of the League of Nations, which had just been drafted in Paris. The meeting failed to quell senatorial doubts or allay opposition. Again, in the spring of 1939, President Roosevelt invited a bipartisan group of congressional leaders to the White

House for a survey of the increasing military tensions in Europe. The supposedly confidential remarks of the President were soon public knowledge, with headlines appearing on the streets proclaiming that America's frontier was on the Rhine.

The President may also consult members of Congress about personnel appointments, public works projects, and other matters in which both share some common interest. He may entertain some members, showing overt signs of recognition and approval, and even permit his favorites to announce their political intentions from the steps of the White House. President Coolidge entertained Congressmen at a series of breakfasts, but "entertained" seems hardly the correct verb inasmuch as the breakfasts were said to be more on the order of the Coolidge receptions where, as someone once remarked, water flowed like champagne. The President may emphasize the importance of a message by delivering it personally before a joint session of Congress. In the hundred years between the presidencies of Jefferson and Wilson the custom fell into desuetude, but it was revived by President Wilson and has been used by subsequent Presidents for the annual message on the State of the Union.

Presidents might consider addressing Congress more frequently, appearing not only to request but to inform. The willingness of Presidents to submit to questioning by the press correspondents indicates that there is a legitimate area of public interest about the President's activities. However, both Congress and the President have been reluctant to make too many demands on one another. Each stands on its dignity and its rights, having considerable respect for the prerogatives of the other, and if the President appeared more frequently before Congress, the latter might fear that its independence was being threatened. The President, also, might believe that too frequent appearances before Congress might result in a kind of familiarity where contemptuous remarks might lessen the dignity and prestige of his office.

Alas for Presidents! There is also a category of relationships with Congress that they are well advised not to enter, however much they may be blandished or tempted against their better judgment to do so.

Relationships in this area may lead to some unpleasantness, with the advice of the President ignored and his intervention resented. The President may be entrapped into stating a preference in a contest for authority within Congress, such as that for Speaker of the House, or the post of Majority Leader, or even for membership on an important committee, under the thin pretext that otherwise there would be endless wrangling and dissension within the party. He intervenes at his own peril. It has already been mentioned how President Roosevelt was caught up in the snarls of senatorial politics when he expressed a preference in 1937 for Senator Barkley over Senator Harrison as Majority Leader.

Presidents may also be inveigled into commenting on legislation currently being considered by Congress—again, a type of intervention likely to be resented. Inasmuch as the President can suggest legislation and veto legislation, it might appear that he should also be allowed to comment on legislation when it is being considered in committee, on the floor, or in conference. Presidents have indeed made their comments from time to time, but only at the risk of being charged with exerting improper influence. For example, in 1942 President Roosevelt protested against Congress' considering legislation to prevent the Commodity Credit Corporation from selling its surplus holdings at prices below parity. The Senate passed the bill, 50–23, despite the President's objections, but Senator Gillette (D., Iowa) questioned whether it was "proper procedure" for the President to send a letter to the presiding officer of the Senate "to influence our action in a matter which is before us." [2]

President Roosevelt was also criticized on an earlier occasion when he used injudicious words in seeking support of legislation to regulate the bituminous coal industry. His views were contained in a letter to Representative Samuel B. Hill (D., Wash.), a member of the Ways and Means Committee, which was considering the legislation. After stating that the courts would ultimately determine whether the legislation was constitutional, the President expressed the hope that the

[2] *Congressional Record*, February 25, 1942, pp. 1596, 1598.

committee itself would "not permit doubts of constitutionality, how-ever reasonable, to block the suggested legislation." [3]

The President may also find it perplexing to know how far he should go in attempting to influence the vote of a member of Congress. Should he maintain his silence while lobbyists and other persuaders attempt to tell the Congressmen how to vote, or should he also exert influence? On some issues the President cannot well remain indifferent if he believes that a defeat in Congress would be calamitous for the nation, the party, and his own political fortunes, as in the vote in August, 1941, on extending the draft, which was carried in the House by the narrow margin of 203–202. In such cases he may attempt to mobilize his party, thus indirectly persuading his fellow partisans in the legislature to follow his leadership. But presidential intervention in mobilizing votes cannot go very far without develop-ing resentment.

Still another controversial relationship stems from the President's constitutional authority to convene either or both Houses "on ex-traordinary occasions" and to adjourn Congress in the event of dis-agreement between the two chambers "to such time as he shall think proper." The President has frequently used his authority to convene Congress—or frequently the Senate alone—for special sessions, but he has never intervened in an adjournment controversy. President Truman was criticized for calling Congress into session in July, 1948, after his nomination, but Congress, controlled as it was by Mr. Truman's political opponents, was in no mood to enact the addi-tional legislation requested and it adjourned within two weeks. On adjourning, it took the unusual course of authorizing its several political leaders, "all acting jointly," to reconvene Congress "when-ever, in their opinion the public interest shall warrant it." [4] This was an attempt to permit Congress itself (through its leaders) to deter-mine whether it should be reconvened at some future date and not allow the decision to be made by the President alone. When the

[3] *Congressional Record*, August, 23, 1935, p. 14363; letter dated July 5, 1935.
[4] *Congressional Record*, August 7, 1948, p. 10247; H. Con. Res. 222.

Democrats did not include a similar provision in the resolution of adjournment two years later, the Republicans objected on the grounds that it "would preclude any reassembling of the Congress . . . except by Proclamation of the President." [5]

DEPARTMENTS

The heads of the major governmental departments are not elected by and directly responsible to the voters—a practice followed in state governments—nor are they selected from and directly responsible to the legislature, as in parliamentary governments. Nevertheless, the governmental departments do have an interest in many phases of the political process, especially in appropriations and legislation, just as Congress has a corresponding interest in how the departments administer the law. The Department of Agriculture, for example, has many obvious political and economic interests, often well organized and identifiable, and the Department, of course, would be concerned with whatever farm legislation Congress was currently considering. Governmental interest in particular facets of legislation extends throughout the governmental bureaucracy.

We are concerned here with the manner in which the bureaucracy advocates and defends its interests in Congress even though it is not directly represented there. How can it persuade Congress to accept its viewpoint? What channels of communication are open to it? The relationship between the departments and Congress has been a contentious point since the beginning of the Republic, the problem being that of allowing the departments full opportunity for being heard without, at the same time, giving them an inordinate amount of influence over the actions of Congress. As Secretary of the Treasury, Alexander Hamilton was permitted to appear on the floor of the House to advocate legislation, but this practice was thought to give Hamilton too much influence. It has fallen into disuse, although the law still provides that the Secretary of the Treasury "shall make report and give information to either branch of the legislature in person or in writing, as may be required, respecting all matters referred to

[5] *Congressional Record,* September 22, 1950, pp. 15635–56.

him by the Senate or House of Representatives, or which shall appertain to his office." [6]

The biblical injunction that no man can serve two masters needs slight modification to fit the case of department heads who must please the sometimes conflicting wishes of the President and Congress. Although department heads are appointed by and can be removed by the President, they must also build up some support in Congress if they are to secure the desired legislation and appropriations and maintain public support. The departments and agencies must, in other words, make some provision for establishing continuing relations with Congress, and many special units for congressional liaison have been created for this purpose. The liaison unit many encounter resistance within its own department, as well as in Congress, for some bureaucrats may resent the suggestion that they discuss questions of policy with congressional committees. A bureaucrat trained to operate within a chain-of-command type of authority may feel that his responsibility is to his superior, not to a group of politicians on the Hill.

Regardless of the resistance within the bureaucracy itself, departments have found it advantageous to establish a continuing relationship with Congress, and a few agencies—the Veterans' Administration, Civil Service Commission, and the Army, Navy, and Air Forces—have been given office space in capitol buildings. These liaison units have little actual authority in their own right; they do not control administrative or fiscal policy within the departments nor, of course, do they control congressional proceedings. These units must build support as best they can, and they too may be affected by an election or change in committee personnel which may alter the nature of the support that has been received.

The relationship between Congress and the civilian bureaucracy varies with the committees, the departments, and the personnel concerned. The Reconstruction Finance Corporation under the chairmanship of Mr. Jesse Jones maintained exemplary relations with Congress, which treated the agency with awed respect and responded favorably

[6] 5 USC §242.

to requests. Later, the RFC lost its coveted position as the white-haired boy of Congress; Mr. Jones was no longer chairman, the legislative friends of yesteryear were no longer in positions of authority. The agency was criticized, investigated—it was during an inquiry into the operation of the RFC that the gift of a "royal pastel mink coat" to a presidential stenographer was revealed—and at last liquidated.

There is no single precept to follow in attempting to influence Congress; departments must do as best they can without having a formula to fit all cases. The requests of departments for new legislation may be contained in a routine annual report, but their ability to persuade Congress may be increased if the President also includes the request in his annual message to Congress. During the Second World War, Mr. Henry L. Stimson, the Secretary of War, and several other administrators attempted to persuade the President to give his support to the enactment of National Service Legislation (compelling everyone to work or fight). Mr. Stimson thought that the attempt had failed, and he has written of his surprise on finding that the President had supported the proposal in his State of the Union Message in 1945.

The departments not only advocate legislation but they also assume some of the burden of explaining and defending the legislation. When Congress is considering an important bill, many units within the departments may play a role in the legislative proceedings, being called on to testify before committees, to "brief" committee members, to prepare reports and perhaps amendments, to supply information for debate, and to develop political support.

THE STATES

The states do not have the same kind of direct representation which existed, say, under the government of the Articles of Confederation (preceding the present Constitution) or which the German states had in the Weimar Constitution and now have in the Bonn Constitution. Under the present system the state electorate, not the government of the state, selects the representation in the American Senate.

The states would have direct representation if the governors or other officials sat in the Senate, and one may presume that a Senate so composed would have a somewhat different type of interest than under current representation practices. Of course, the ideology of a federal system of government is brought out in some policy debates, such as those concerning the poll tax, or regulating insurance rates, or using federal funds for education, but the defense of the federal system is often limited and associated with particular points of view. However, the states are not directly represented in those areas of policy where they may have considerable interest—appropriations (with federal strings attached), taxation, and regulation.

The states, then, not participating directly in making policy decisions in Congress, must behave like any other group in seeking to influence policy or in appealing to the House or Senate for support. A closer relationship existed between state legislatures and Congress before the Seventeenth Amendment, adopted in 1913, substituted popular election of the Senate for the older method of election by state legislatures. In the former period, state legislatures would "instruct" the Senators and "request" the Representatives to take certain action, but now that their influence over Senators has been reduced, the state legislators can do little more than submit petitions for action. Congress does not cringe when a state legislature breathes fire; the petitions are received with little excitement, and they are likely to be treated routinely—recorded, referred, and forgotten. If several legislatures send in petitions worded identically, it will perhaps indicate no more than the activity of some pressure group in persuading the various state legislatures to support its cause.

The Governors of states may be in a somewhat better position to influence Congress, for they are organized and can speak unitedly through the Council of State Governors. The State Attorneys General are also organized, and so, too, are the mayors of large cities. One can say, then, that although the states have no direct representation as organized institutional entities, they may be able to exert influence unofficially on legislative policy in which they are especially concerned—flood control, taxation, labor disputes, offshore oil, regulation of insurance and public utilities in general, grants-in-aid for a wide number of causes, including education, and the maintenance of the National Guard.

THE COURTS

The federal court system is also a constituent part of the total governmental structure, but it does not ordinarily play a conspicuous part in formulating legislative policy. However, the court system exercises covert, subjective, and indirect influence in delineating methods and content in the action taken by Congress. In an earlier discussion of the relationship between legitimacy and authoritative action it was indicated that the actions of Congress are confined by the judicial requirement for making "good law." This sets the bounds in which Congress can act. The court system, like Congress, is engaged in resolving conflict, but there is some difference in the types of conflicts considered and in the procedures followed in resolving them, the interest of the courts being directed more toward controversies between two sets of claimants than in adjusting the behavior of a number of interested groups.

Although differing in procedures and in jurisdiction and being autonomously independent of one another, Congress and the federal court system nevertheless share some common interests. The most obvious common interest, where they participate in the same process, occurs during an impeachment trial when the Senate, acting as a court, is presided over by the Chief Justice of the United States. Congress has shown some willingness to give the courts additional duties, but on the whole the courts have opposed going beyond the functions clearly prescribed in the Constitution. The courts have refused to give advisory opinions or to serve as election judges, although three justices of the Supreme Court were members of the Electoral Commission which decided the results of the Hayes-Tilden election in 1876. The most penetrating influence of the courts over legislation concerns the judicial review of the Acts of Congress to determine their constitutionality, a precedent set in 1803 in the case of *Marbury v. Madison.* In other words, although Congress may enact legislation creating the judicial system and prescribing its jurisdiction, the courts may in turn review Acts of Congress.

Congress accepts the decisions of the courts on the constitutionality of legislation and it tends to support the position of the courts in reviewing the legality of administrative decisions. In the nineteenth century the debates of Congress were frequently concerned with issues of the constitutionality of legislative proposals, but the interpretation of the Constitution has been so broadened in recent years that few legislators resort to constitutional arguments as convincing reasons for adopting or rejecting legislation. Although Congress accepts the right of the courts to determine the constitutionality of legislation, it will not necessarily consider the judicial decisions to be final. Indeed, in many cases Congress will seek to enact legislation to restore the equilibrium upset by the judicial decision. Many of the laws enacted under the aegis of President Roosevelt's New Deal Administration which were found to be unconstitutional were later reënacted, with Congress resting its authority on different clauses of the Constitution.

PRIVATE GROUPS

One may make the general assertion that individuals associate together in groups to accomplish various purposes and that these group associations have varying degrees of interest in legislative policy. A group organized primarily for recreational purposes would have limited political interests, although it might be concerned with policy relating to parks, streams, fishing, and the like, and in the case of organized baseball, with antitrust legislation. A professional group composed, for example, of medical doctors might have somewhat wider interests, including the protection of its professional standards through licenses issued by the government and extending perhaps to questions of public health and medical insurance. Members of various groups affected by legislative policy may wish to express their views when that policy is being developed and they also may base their attitudes toward legislators on the latters' stand on that particular policy.

Since 1946, groups which attempt to influence the passage of legislation have been required to file certain information with officials of
the Senate and the House listing the object of their interest and the
amount of money spent in pursuing their objective. The list of registrations reveals the extent to which groups are organized to influence
legislation. The thousand or more lobbyists now registered represent
a variety of group interests ranging from those of trade associations
and patriotic organizations to those of Indian tribes. Although the
salaries of some of the lobbyists appear to be in the $50,000 a year
category, the information filed is not sufficiently complete to round out
the picture of the total income of all lobbyists, whether or not they
are registered. The registrations show only the amount of compensation allocated to the legislative account; attorneys who give legislative
advice to clients but who themselves take no direct part in legislative
activities are not registered. A number of former members of the
House and Senate are registered as lobbyists, and still others are employed as consultants.

The lobbyists provide a link between various autonomous groups
and the legislative process and to that extent act as a further conduit
of information running into and out of Congress. They may also
exert influence at strategic phases of the process and thereby expedite
the process of enacting legislation. For instance, the lobbyist may be
interested in all phases of a particular bill, extending from its initial
consideration to the signing of the bill by the President, and from
there the interest will carry through to the administration of the law
by some governmental agency. In the course of the bill's passage
through Congress, the lobbyist may draft bills, prepare reports, give
testimony, suggest amendments, solicit speeches, and request votes.
He acts as an expeditor, a proponent, and a purveyor of information.

The lobbyist may have no direct sanctions over legislators, but he
is frequently in a position where his influence is respected. The great
associations interested in public policy are frequently organized on a
national basis, and their members are not only voters but also influ-
encers of opinion in the communication network. Political recrimina-
tion is always possible and may be feared by legislators, but lobbyists

and the associations they represent do not necessarily engage directly in partisan political activities. Nor do voters at election time necessarily cluster together in the same pattern as the groups who, after the election, are interested in specific policy. The influence of lobbyists over the electorate is frequently more subtle than direct political appeals. For example, a lobbyist may advocate the adoption of an amendment regarding a tariff on watches. Jewelers throughout the country will be requested to wire an appropriate message, and the members, duly impressed by the mounting pile of telegrams and letters, may be spurred to take appropriate action. The associations also have access to channels of public opinion, although it is difficult to generalize on the effectiveness of this type of indirect sanction, and it is not always effective. For a number of years after the war, the railroads and theaters carried on general agitation to persuade Congress to repeal excise taxes levied during the war, without being wholly successful.

SUMMARY

In view of the fact that the actions of Congress affect other people, it is natural to find a network of relationships existing between Congress and those affected by but not part of the legislative process. Outside groups have no direct authority within Congress, although they may attempt to influence congressional action in a variety of ways, and in so doing function as expert informers, persuaders, negotiators, and opinion makers. The fact that outside groups can influence congressional action raises the question of the need for Congress to maintain its autonomy in making decisions. Attempts are continually made to force Congress to make decisions on particular issues, or, alternatively, to prevent an issue from being considered by Congress and to direct it into other channels. Safeguards to protect the autonomy of Congress relate to contemptuous action, the protection of proceedings against intrusion, prohibitions against corrupting influence, restrictions on government propaganda, and provisions for disclosing lobbying activities.

In the hierarchy of influence surrounding Congress, the position of the President is paramount. Indeed, for some purposes the President may be considered as an extension of the congressional system itself in view of his power to veto legislation, make reports, propose legislation, nominate officials and negotiate treaties, and his position as leader of his party gives him additional influence over legislative action. However, the President must treat Congress circumspectly: some relationships are mandatory, some are permissive, and some are inadvisable. The mandatory class of relationships includes that prescribed by law and by the Constitution. The permissive class includes the various devices which Presidents develop for establishing effective communications with Congress and its leaders. But the President may not go too far. He engages in disputes within his own party at the peril of his reputation and he comments on legislation under consideration at the risk of giving offense.

Government departments are likewise interested in the legislative process, and they may be called upon to participate in a type of parallel action in all of its phases. They help select the agenda through their comments on proposed legislation; they assist in the deliberation through hearings and by supplying members with speeches and arguments; and they help determine the final vote by mobilizing supporters for the crucial decision. All these activities take place, however, in relation to and not as a constituent part of the congressional organization. Similarly, the states are interested in some phases of legislative policy, but they are not represented directly as policy-forming entities. The courts, also, are influential indirectly through their power of judicial review, but they have resisted playing a more direct part by giving advisory opinions on the constitutionality of legislation before its enactment.

The fact that government control exists in so many areas of life results in the organization of groups to protect the various interests which develop in each of these control centers. The groups which are affected by government controls will, at the very least, wish to avert the possibility of adverse decisions being made. So they organize, partly to find out what is happening and partly to influence action favorably through whatever means are called for—including the possibility of mobilizing opinion to influence elections. The question whether lobbies effectively represent all groups has no very clear answer. In effect, the question is bypassed by a policy which permits free and unlimited organizational activities to go on, providing only that a public record is made of the source of funds and objects of expenditures and that the influence exerted neither corrupts the legislature nor undermines its autonomy.

CHAPTER 5

The Process: Analyzing the Problem and Raising the Issue

THE DISCUSSIONS UP TO NOW HAVE CONSIDERED CER-
tain factors which affect the organization of Congress. These include
the representative system of selecting members, the various units
within Congress which are concerned with making policy or establishing controls over the legislative process, and the external units
which seek to influence congressional action. We have now reached
the point where we can examine the process by which policy is made.
We can, so to speak, put in motion the various units which have been
discussed heretofore, showing the part they play at the several stages
of the process and observing how they interrelate with each other.

One might here make a useful distinction among various categories
of congressional behavior. The full scope of congressional activity
can be seen when Congress creates the legislative instrument known
as an Act. The total organization of Congress is involved in making
an Act, which becomes legitimate only after receiving the attention
and consent of the various constituent parts. However, other activities
of Congress not culminating in a law may nonetheless affect the
content of policy. The enactment of new legislation is ordinarily

cumbersome compared to the relative simplicity of influencing policy by other means, so that a considerable amount of congressional action is expended on activities not directly relating to enacting legislation. The following discussion encompasses all categories of legislative action, whether or not they culminate in a law, but Congress distinguishes between the legitimation of action by law and the pursuance of activities which may merely influence policy without creating legislation.

ANALYSIS OF THE PROBLEM

Let us take up initially the intellectual considerations that are involved when Congress makes a policy decision. The process of making policy in Congress is different from that followed by a government agency or a court, but in what way is it different? What special conditions are imposed by the fact that there is a continual turnover in membership, that the deliberation and the voting take place in public, that members speak with the aim not only of informing but of convincing, that membership itself depends on the acceptability to others of speeches and votes, and that decisions affect people, processes, and situations about which the legislators themselves have no personal knowledge or even any direct personal interest? What type of mental activity is required of all members before there can be any form of corporate action?

Congress is not able to concern itself exclusively and continuously with any single, specific policy such as would be the case if it were administering an Act. It must necessarily move from topic to topic as it proceeds to create different types of policies affecting a variety of situations. This limited concern, this restricted attention, also affect the manner in which Congress considers an issue. Under ordinary circumstances, Congress does not start with a clear slate which will permit an unlimited number of alternatives. Rather, Congress cuts in at some point in a system of action already established, for which an existing policy (however inadequate) may already exist, and which may be administered by a bureaucracy with its own ideas on what should be done.

The fact that Congress often enters a field where policy already exists may raise presumptions on the type of decision which it should make as well as limit the type of decision which it can make. The intellectual leeway, as it were, in making policy may be greatly affected by conditions over which Congress has little control. In developing an understanding of how past events have shaped current policy, Congress will be assisted by having access to the historical record of the issue under review. It is here especially that legislative and committee continuity is useful in providing an institutional memory so that new decisions can be related to what has gone on before. Without such a background, the legislature runs the risk of developing policy without regard to past events or even to present expectations. What is needed, essentially, is for Congress to build up over a period of time a series of standards for various types of policy. These standards would encompass the nature of the administrative discretion which may be permitted, the goals to be achieved by the legislation, the controls to be exercised, and the need for review and revision. This would not preclude change or a new assessment of existing policy. As time passes, differences may develop where once there was agreement; new members may have attitudes different from their predecessors, and the bureaucracy, too, may change. In the legislative deliberations, these divergences should be brought to the fore, debated, resolved, and a firm decision made on the new policy. However, the debates will be clarified if they take place against a background of standards generally agreed upon, so that everything does not have to be decided anew whenever a change is made.

In analyzing political problems, Congress must be interested in the content of a proposal as well as in the manner in which the proposal may be integrated with the various elements of society; and in the deliberations, it may change the content to secure consent or perhaps to develop a better integration with other activities. Whatever the extent of the disequilibrium which led to demands for some legislative adjustment, the new policy will have to be integrated with these other systems of action already in existence and which may be affected by any change. In considering a proposal to build an atomic reactor in a submarine, for instance, the legislature would want to know the feasibility of such a scheme in addition to the effect of the proposal on the recruitment of personnel, the budget, national commitments, protection of secret equipment, and so on. If a government agency makes the proposal, the procedure followed for most important legislation, Congress has the responsibility of making certain that the officials concerned have gone through a certain intellectual process in developing the proposal. The officials will be asked to explain their reasoning and justify their decision, indicating the alternatives that were examined and why they were rejected, and the limitations placed on their choice by factors which they do not control. If Congress itself chooses to develop the policy, it needs to acquire, order, and interpret the appropriate information and raise similar types of questions.

The consideration of foreign policy by Congress raises special issues which do not arise in considering domestic legislation. In foreign policy, where one is dealing more concretely with relationships between governmental systems than with the interrelationships within the domestic order, the authority of a government extends to but one side of the equation. Influence may be exerted on the party of the second part, and force may even be used at times, but conflict between governmental systems is not controlled by a single set of laws or a single system of authority. Now the question arises, what significance has this for Congress?

The fact that foreign policy treats of people and institutions which are outside and beyond the jurisdiction of American laws restricts the use of legislation in formulating policy and, to that extent, limits the authority of Congress. A treaty, a conference, even a statement to the press may be the vehicle for enunciating foreign policy, but some of these techniques are beyond the competence of Congress to utilize. The nature of foreign policy also affects its execution, which is often highly proceduralized and requires special technical ability in such fields as diplomatic and military careers.

In considering the competence of Congress in making foreign

policy, the following questions seem pertinent. What kinds of foreign policy decisions are most adaptable to public debate by a legislative assembly such as Congress, as opposed to those which can best be decided by generals and diplomats? What kind of administrative structure is demanded? What type of legislative accountability can Congress rightly expect from those who have direct authority in foreign affairs? What is the function of Congress in explaining foreign and military policies to the constituents and in defending or opposing these policies at elections? Granted that a legal case can be made for Congress having considerable influence in shaping foreign policy, how competent is Congress from the point of view of experience, ability, and knowledge?

There is an area of foreign policy where the authority of Congress does not reach through law and where the authority of the President and the relevant departments is predominant. Although domestic policy is developed in the form of law, Congress cannot so readily formulate civil and military foreign policy in strictly legal terms. The development of such policy may require some secrecy, in order to avoid premature commitments, as well as technical information which Congress does not necessarily possess. Moreover, it may be necessary to make decisions more quickly than is possible through the leisurely congressional timetables.

Congressional law may determine the structure of the administrative organization for carrying foreign and military policy and, broadly, the functions to be performed, but it may not always be able to develop a standard by which policy issues are decided. For instance, the policy followed by the American government in the protracted negotiations for an armistice in Korea was not, and could not well have been, determined in advance by law. At an earlier date, the decision to divide Germany into military zones of occupation was not based on legislation. Likewise, the initial decisions to aid Greece and Turkey, to promote the economic revival of Europe, and to rearm Germany and Japan were not made by legislation, however much it was necessary to use legislation for implementing these decisions.

Moreover, the process used by Congress in resolving domestic conflict is not necessarily appropriate for developing foreign policy. Domestic policy is developed through negotiation and compromise, with an attempt made to balance the various interests. The decisions may be made after a sharp debate conducted in part for partisan advantage. In foreign policy, however, all the interests to a dispute are not so clearly represented. In addition, the facts necessary for making a decision may not be suitable for public debate, and prudence may require appropriate restraint in expressing opinions on the behavior of other nations.

Whether Congress is dealing with foreign or domestic policies, the desirable end would be the creation of an internal organizational structure that would encourage the examination of crucial issues as a matter of course. Questions would be raised which clarify methods and goals, which demand planning and foresight, which motivate administrators to perform a high level of inspired service, and which develop standards of excellence. In areas of policy requiring secrecy, strictures on communications may prevent the ordinary procedures from being followed, and Congress may have difficulty in learning what the existing policy is, let alone examining it from the point of view of its acceptability or modifying it to secure integration. However, legislatures are adaptable, and it is possible to develop general policy through debates even though its current development is not openly discussed. In some areas of secrecy, as in the development of nuclear energy, congressional scrutiny tends to be exercised by a joint committee, which in effect acts in the name of Congress.

Some may think it desirable that Congress, with the assistance of policy specialists, know as much as any of the groups affected by legislation, but such an ambitious goal is ordinarily not necessary in order for the legislature to be effective. Such a gross amount of information would raise additional problems of the actual location of authority in making decisions because of the new element introduced in the relationship between the specialists and the legislators, and it might also increase the difficulties of Congress in making decisions as a corporate group.

It is the special merit of Congress that it is an integrative body, not simply a group of specialists, and its *forte* is knowing how specific policy will coördinate with other interests. Congress should raise the significant questions already mentioned, establish clear policy directions and goals, and retain strategic controls over the administration of the policy; the inundation of the legislature with facts and specialized knowledge might defeat these broader goals.

RAISING THE ISSUE

If one thinks of Congress in terms of an organization which can create a product from the nature of its procedures, it may be said that Congress creates public policy, usually stated in terms of law. The total legislative effort is so organized that some type of collective action is possible, and this is accomplished by bringing along those members and units who are legally concerned with the process to the point where they will approve or reject the proposal.

We have dealt so far with the general considerations facing Congress in making policy decisions. The actual process of making these decisions may for the sake of convenience be divided into the three stages of raising the issue, considering a proposed course of action, and approving, modifying, or rejecting the proposal. The right to participate in these stages is highly coveted, with competitive influences in Congress attempting to exercise effective control over them. Although each of these three stages can be readily identified in a deliberative body, it is possible to telescope the process so that everything occurs practically simultaneously. This was the case, for instance, when the Roman Tribunes would pose the question and, without debate, the plebeians would shout back their answer. Nor are the three stages equally emphasized in dictatorships where a legislative shell survives; there the legislatures are hurried along to acknowledge their consent and get on home, without debating the proposal or changing its content. It is obvious, of course, that such precipitate action fails to meet the requirements of an autonomous legislative body.

In considering policy at the three procedural stages, Congressmen assume what amounts to different functional roles. The nature of the function being performed requires differentiated types of behavior on the part of the members and, in some cases, the development of additional skills. The various roles, and the identity of those who play these roles, are determined not only by the structure of authority within Congress and the requirements of the process but also by the interpretation of the individual member of the kind of behavior required in the particular situation. A member may not always have a clear choice in the role he is to play, his particular action being determined, perhaps, by his position on a committee. Or he may have a choice. In considering some issues, a member might be highly motivated and wish to persuade others to accept his point of view, while on other issues he might prefer to hear more evidence before he reluctantly makes up his mind.

The name of advocate may be given to those who raise an issue in support of some particular policy. The advocate need not be a member of the group which deliberates and makes the final decision, and he may appear before the group for a limited purpose without being a part of it. The role of an advocate before a court, for instance, is highly proceduralized, as it is also—although to a lesser extent— before government agencies and congressional committees. Members of Congress may themselves act as advocates before committees to which they do not belong, and they may also represent their constituents before government agencies (but they do not receive a fee for such services).

In locating the first phase of the legislative process, that of raising the issue, we may have to go beyond the physical confines of Congress. This is understandable enough inasmuch as the need for legislation to adjust conflicting interests and develop patterns of ordered behavior would ordinarily arise outside the halls of Congress. The declaration of the intention to seek legislative action may occur in a variety of places, ranging from the debates of political campaigns to the more tranquil proceedings of a governmental bureau. The electoral contest itself gives some indication of the type of political issues which Congress will consider, and so does the distribution of authority within Congress. Evidence of the existence of competition in Congress over what legislation is to be considered may be found by contrasting the thousands of bills which are introduced annually with the relative handful which Congress actually enacts. The ability to select the issue on which a legislative decision is to be made is, of course, half the battle won. However, no one person, no single political group, has full command over the docket of Congress, and there is continued political conflict in deciding what topics are to be considered. The standing committees of both Houses as well as the Rules Committee of the House of Representatives have considerable influence in making a choice, and so, too, have the political leaders and even, occasionally, the majority of members. Inasmuch as legislative authority is widespread and decentralized, topics may be considered by some of the required units but fail to command the support of Congress as a corporate entity. Legislation may be initiated at one of several points, with the advocates pushing the measure as far as they can—perhaps as far as a hearing, or through a committee, or through one or both Houses—and hopefully reaching the point at last where the President affixes his signature to a bill.

Legislation is not entirely on a push-or-pull basis, however, for there is considerable order in the manner in which Congress proceeds with its work. A session of Congress develops a certain rhythm from the fact that governmental business is conducted on an annual basis and that elections are held every two years. Congress convenes in January and remains in session for at least six months, and there are always a number of specific items—fixed items, occasional but continuing items, emergency items, and items arising from special situations—which demand attention.

The most important of the fixed items is the granting of the annual supply of money for the government. The prolonged process of appropriating money and reviewing past performance receives the intermittent attention of Congress during the first six months of each session. It may also be necessary for Congress to consider legislation which terminates at a specific date, and the Senate will be confronted with a continuous flow of nominations. In addition, Congress must review the performance of the various agencies, spending some time each session in regularizing the accounts of fiscal officers, receiving reports, conducting hearings and investigations, and making presentations to departments.

The list of occasional but continuing items includes issues concerning existing policy which need not be reformulated every session of Congress. In such policy areas, the political equilibrium may have been adjusted sufficiently satisfactorily to continue for some time without any major changes. Policy toward labor, agriculture, taxation, or the merchant marine would ordinarily fall in this category. On the other hand, rumblings of discontent may surround any policy, with changes being proposed and amendments offered, but new legislation will not be considered until the factors of unrest reach greater proportions. Of course, when a large number of adjustments become manifestly unsatisfactory at about the same time, as in March, 1933, the result is politically chaotic, but in more normal times the legislature can be somewhat selective in choosing its agenda. Some legislators may prefer not to make a decision on some topics, however much they are importuned to do so, and will attempt to prevent the issue from coming to a head. Examples falling within this rubric would include the Townsend pension plan, the payment of bonuses to veterans, and certain proposals which historically have been opposed by Southern members—force bills, antilynching bills, repeal of the poll tax, and fair employment practice legislation.

Legislation of an emergency nature may call for new decisions on new subjects, and the necessity for quick action may upset congressional timetables by speeding up the more leisurely methods of deliberation. Congress was asked to act quickly on new issues which developed during the depression, the First and Second World Wars, and the postwar period, in the latter instance on policy relating to military and economic assistance to foreign countries and domestically on strike legislation. Very frequently this emergency legislation has been pressed on Congress under conditions which have not permitted adequate deliberation. Some of the more mischievous aspects of such legislation could be averted by improved planning, coördination, and foresight on the part of legislative and administrative leaders.

The final category of legislation relates to issues developing from special situations—from events which are not repetitive since they occur only once. Such legislation is designed to correct a particular situation which, once resolved, is unlikely to require further settlement. Falling in this category would be claims bills and private bills of various kinds.

Who raises the issues in Congress? What is the essential link between the disequilibrium which exists in some part of society and the intention of Congress to consider a remedy? The fact that the decisions of Congress are largely concerned with the action of other people suggests at once the significance of the channels of communication between Congress and the outside world. Who has the ear of Congress? What type of information does Congress need? How can Congress make sure that its actions will be received sympathetically and obediently? How will the new equilibrium created by the legislation affect various groups? What controls can Congress establish for guiding, constraining, and restraining action? Political decisions, a scarce commodity, are in demand because of their potential utility in improving the relative position of the people affected, and the demand for legislative attention is considerably greater than the available supply of political nostrums. The selection of the political issues for Congress to resolve is, as one might expect, a matter of considerable controversy. Continually, competing groups with rival proposals attempt to secure the attention of Congress.

In identifying those who raise issues for the consideration of Congress, one may look first of all at the President, who may assume the leadership in dramatizing the attractiveness or urgency of proposals on which he would like legislative action. Specific proposals for action may be found in his State of the Union address as well as in periodic messages which he sends to Congress, although the general trend of the proposals will have been shaped by campaign speeches and promises, by statements in the party platform, and by the nature of the political alliances which elected the President. Declarations to "seek legislation" will also be made by a variety of other individuals, both in and out of government. Department and bureaus may indicate in their annual reports the legislation they favor; the State Department may ask the Senate to ratify a treaty or ask Congress to enact implementing legislation; Congressmen may introduce legislation to satisfy commitments they have made to their constituents; and various types of private groups—labor, agriculture, manufacturers, oil producers, cattle raisers—may propose specific legislative action.

Control over the legislative agenda is widely scattered within Congress. The final product is developed from the impact of many forces operating at various stages of the process. In any session there is considerable jockeying for position, with disputes occurring over what subjects will be considered, by whom, and when. There is no master plan for a session, no agenda on which all will have agreed although, as has been mentioned, some items—such as the budget— will be considered as a matter of course.

The political leaders have limited control over the agenda; they can negotiate, suggest, request, and coördinate, but they cannot command. They may discuss the legislative program with the President, with committee chairmen, or with partisan committees, but they have no authority themselves to make independent decisions on the nature of the agenda. The legislative leaders may plan the agenda of legislative sessions from day to day, and, with some margin for unexpected developments, from week to week. Planning the agenda for an entire session, however, can go little further than jotting on the back of an envelope the items which it is hoped will be considered. A proposed program may be upset by such events as a message from the President, the failure of a committee to report legislation, or the success of an interest group in forcing Congress to consider some preferred proposal.

Legislative leaders cannot go faster than the committees permit, and the committees do not like to be prodded. The sparseness of the legislative program at the beginning of a session can be illustrated by remarks once made by Representative John W. McCormack (D., Mass.) while serving as Majority Leader. There was nothing before the House for the balance of the current week, Representative McCormack said, and he knew of no program planned for the following week. There was a possibility that a bill extending the Rubber Act, which expired in June, would be ready, but he had been advised by the chairman of the committee that they would not take it up next week. "Of course, there will be some messages here. If anything is to come up I shall give the House advance notice." [1] Toward the close of a session, however, the legislative calendars are crowded, and there is not sufficient time to consider all the items reported by the committees.

The official legislative units involved in making policy decisions have been discussed previously: They are the committees, subcommittees, and the two chambers, these formal groups having an underlying structure of partisan alliances. In the consideration of any particular policy, membership on the committees is fixed in the sense that the current membership takes up whatever questions are referred to the committee, without having members especially assigned for considering any particular issue. However, as has been mentioned, members tend to gravitate toward committees having jurisdiction over policy in which they are especially interested.

The fact that the composition of committees fluctuates and that the committees themselves attract different types of membership suggests that the chances of legislation being favorably (or unfavorably) reported are affected by the nature of the committee to which the bill is referred. The considerable control of committees over legislation has, in the past, led to a gradual expansion in the number of committees and subcommittees. A new legislative unit is created if a given committee is not quite trusted, or is not especially interested or competent, or is otherwise busy. The expectation is that by decentralizing consideration of policy, by organizing committees around decreasingly small spheres of interest, the locus of control will become more certain. Those having a continuous interest in certain legislation might prefer a decentralized organization where there would be a limited and known number of people to persuade and inform.

Although bills are often referred routinely, controversy over the jurisdiction of legislation may flare up between two or more commit-

[1] *Congressional Record,* January 16, 1952, p. 252.

tees because of different interpretations of the precedents as well as different attitudes toward the legislation. There may, indeed, be an open clash between committees for the right to consider particular legislation, with a vote of the parent chamber being required to decide the issue. A jurisdictional controversy developed during the latter years of the Second World War when special postwar committees were created to develop a unified program for transforming the wartime economy to a peacetime basis. After the postwar committees entered the field, a number of standing committees claimed that they, too, had legitimate authority over such legislation so that in the end more committees, rather than fewer, were concerned with postwar policy. The surplus property bill, to take one example, was the concern not only of the postwar planning committees but also of the Judiciary, Navy Affairs, and Military Affairs Committees. Another dispute arose in Congress in 1947 over the proper committee to consider the legislation placing the armed forces in a single department, with the legislation referred to the Committee on Armed Services in the Senate and to the Committee on Expenditures in the Executive Department in the House. The political as well as military aspect of General MacArthur's removal in 1951 were recognized in the Senate, with hearings on the incident being conducted jointly by the Armed Services Committee and the Foreign Relations Committee. A lingering conflict, varying in intensity but continuing from session to session, exists between the appropriations committees and the legislative committees. A basic, unresolved difference remains inasmuch as the extent to which a program authorized by law can exist in fact may depend on the amount of funds appropriated.

Committees have commanding control over bills once they secure jurisdiction, and they report back to the parent chamber no more than a fifth of the bills and resolutions referred to them. The government agencies have some influence in selecting legislation for further consideration, for they, as well as the Bureau of the Budget, are regularly consulted by the committees on the merits and desirability of the proposed legislation. Bills having the approval of the departments and the Bureau of the Budget are in a preferred category, whereas disapproval may presage a future presidential veto. However, raising the issue is not confined to introducing the central proposal; amendments may be offered in committee or on the floor which will change or modify the content of the proposal.

Committees may show considerable independence in reporting legislation, even at the risk of a possible presidential veto; in the past, committees have proceeded against presidential advice to consider legislation affecting say, labor, veterans, and farmers. On revenue measures, the Treasury Department customarily has but moderate influence over the fiscal committees of Congress, and these committees are not necessarily deterred by vetoes or threats of vetoes or signs of displeasure on the part of the Treasury officials.

Committees may proceed to consider legislation on their own initiative, as it were, even though it is unlikely that the legislation will be enacted or even reported out. Committees may hold hearings, for example, on monopolies or political ethics or the price of silver or patent discrimination, with few prospects that such legislation will be currently considered by Congress. This behavior may be explained by the fact that favorable committee consideration is part of the long process of securing the consent of the corporate whole; any indication of approval or even of attention by a committee might be considered to be one more step toward the final goal. Members of the committee may also feel that they can enhance their own political support by listening to, even while rejecting, proposals which have not yet developed broad popular support.

Our discussion up to now points to the conclusion that the issues raised for consideration in the Senate and House must first secure the consent of the appropriate committee. This fact suggests additional questions. If the parent chambers do not consider all bills reported back by committees, who then decides which committees, or which legislation, will be given priority? Conversely, what recourse has the parent chambers in the event the committees fail to report back legislation, nominations, and treaties? Can the committees be relied upon to report back all legislation which the party platform calls for, or the President wishes, or the leaders expect, or the party majority favors?

An awkward political situation may arise if the House or Senate wishes to consider legislation which remains bottled up in a committee. Or it may even be amusing as on the occasion when the Senate Foreign Relations Committee lost control of a treaty and was unable either to consider it further or to report it back to the Senate. This treaty, creating an inter-American bank, had as a matter of courtesy been submitted for comment and advice to Senator Carter Glass (D., Va.), the chairman of the Committee on Banking and Currency. Senator Glass, finding the treaty to be at odds with his own theory of the proper role of government, did not return it with appropriate comments to the Foreign Relations Committee but, instead, referred it to a subcommittee of which he named himself chairman. There the treaty stayed, and the obstreperous Senator was unwilling either to report it back to his own committee or to return it to the Foreign Relations Committee. Senator Glass was then in his eighties and his frequent illnesses often kept him from the Senate chamber for months at a time. It happened, also, that on matters of foreign policy generally, Senator Glass supported the Foreign Relations Committee. The treaty matter was not pressed, for it was thought imprudent to test Senator Glass's remarkable temper on a matter of no great urgency. The treaty remains unratified.

Legislation can be dislodged from a committee in several ways—although the necessity for such action might be averted by raising the issue through some other channel. Such was the case, for instance, when Congress enacted strike legislation during the Second World War. A measure controlling strikes in war plants was passed by the House and then referred to the Senate Committee on Education and Labor; there it stayed. The committee, not liking the proposal, hoped to kill it off by sheer neglect. The War Labor Disputes Act was eventually enacted by circumventing the reluctant committee. The legislation was considered by the Military Affairs Committee in the House and the Judiciary Committee in the Senate on the ground, in the first case, that it affected the production of military equipment and, in the second case, that it amended the criminal code. In effect, then, the labor committees were forestalled by withdrawing from them their exclusive jurisdiction over labor legislation. Committees may also be circumvented by offering the proposal as an amendment to some other bill; this is especially the case in the Senate where the rules for proposing amendments are often broadly interpreted and unevenly enforced.

The problem of securing legislation held by an obdurate committee may be met head on by moving to discharge the committee from considering the legislation further. Motions to discharge are made with caution, however, for the irritations of the moment may be endured more easily than the antagonisms which may plague future relations. A Senate committee can be discharged from further consideration of a bill by the passage of a motion requiring the support of a simple majority. Discharging a House committee is more cumbersome. After the House reduced the authority of the Speaker in 1910, control over legislation was more firmly placed in the committees, but a counter-balancing force was given to the House membership in the form of a discharge petition. This petition requires the signature of a quota of the members, but controversy develops periodically over the optimum size of the quota. The Republicans were initially reluctant to lower the quota to a simple majority lest effective control would then rest with a combination of Democrats and insurgent Republicans. The Democrats, on the other hand, were willing to set the quota at less than a majority to prevent a combination of Republicans and conservative Democrats from blocking petitions. On organizing the House in 1931, the Democrats lowered the quota requirements to less than a majority, but their own liberality proved an embarrassment when legislation opposed by the leaders and the President was brought before the House by means of the discharge petition. They raised the quota to an absolute majority, where it has remained. Although a score or more of discharge petitions are filed every year, few acquire the requisite number of signatures. The discharge petition may be considered to be an emergency measure for separating a committee from a bill rather than a routine procedure for establishing the agenda.

Although some committees may fail to report bills which might otherwise be acceptable, the general practice is for committees to report more legislation than the parent chamber is willing or able to consider. In one recent year some 84 House measures and 78 Senate measures, reported from committee, were not acted on by the parent chamber. In such a situation, committees compete with each other for a place on the agenda, and provision must be made to decide which committee or which bill will be given priority. In the Senate, all legislation is placed on a single calendar, with separate calendars being used for treaties and nominations. Ordinarily the legislation is taken from the calendar on the motion of the Majority Leader or some other properly designated person. Objections are infrequently made, but they may lead to a roll call vote or even to a filibuster. These relatively simple procedures for selecting legislation are accompanied by informal negotiations and conversations on the part of the party leaders, the committees, and the special groups concerned, with the negotiations capped by a unanimous consent agreement. These agreements are the customary method of proceeding, not the exception. The procedures for selecting legislation in the Senate place a considerable burden on the leadership of both parties, who, in reaching an understanding, must continually be sensitized to the various extant interests, anticipations, and expectations.

The independent attempt to bring the Fair Employment Practices bill before the Senate in January, 1946, without a unanimous consent agreement having been worked out previously, illustrates some of the difficulties which may be encountered when the usual procedures are not followed. The motion to take up the bill caught the leadership by surprise, for they had not anticipated such action, but the motion was nevertheless adopted by a vote of 49–17. The motion to call up the bill was made independently, with no forewarning given the leaders, on the initiative of Senator Dennis Chavez (D., New Mexico). Some Senators opposed to the bill were absent from the chamber at the time, and Senator John H. Bankhead (D., Ala.), an opponent, told the Senate subsequently that "assurances had been given" that the bill would not be called up that day. Then a filibuster began on the question of correcting the journal of the prior day's business, which prevented either the Fair Employment Practices bill or any other legislation from being considered. The filibustering debate continued for some three weeks, but a cloture motion to limit the debate failed to secure the necessary two-thirds majority—the vote was 48–36. Once it became clear that the proponents of the FEPC legislation were not strong enough to end the filibuster, the FEPC legislation was dropped. The Senate proceeded to a different topic and made no further attempt to consider FEPC legislation that session.

Whereas the Senate relies on a system of personal negotiations carried on by the trusted leaders in selecting bills for consideration, the House places greater reliance on formalized procedures. In the latter chamber, bills reported from committee are initially placed on a calendar, from whence they are removed by the operation of a priority system. The system includes the Union Calendar, to which are referred all bills for raising or spending money or those "directly or indirectly appropriating money or property"; the House Calendar, for public bills not related to revenue; the Private Calendar, for bills of a private character; and the Consent Calendar, to which are referred, on request, certain bills from the House or Union Calendar.

At the end of the spectrum of priority preferences are found the committees whose reports are privileged in the sense that the House will proceed to consider this legislation at once, without the further consent of anyone being required. Appropriation bills fall in this preferred category. Most committees, however, not having such a privileged position, must secure for their important bills a rule indicating when and how this legislation will be considered by the House. The Rules Committee has considerable authority over the agenda by virtue of its right to formulate rules. It can recommend what legislation the House should consider, the time to be consumed in deliberations, the type of amendments which may be offered, and the degree of control which the committee may exercise over the legislation.

For example, three recent rules permitted debate for two days on a bill reducing excise taxes, debate for a day on a foreign aid bill, and debate for two days on a bill amending deposit insurance legislation. No amendments were permitted to the tax bill other than those proposed by the Committee on Ways and Means. In the other two cases, amendments were permitted to be offered by any section of the legislation.

The legislative committees are not necessarily given a rule merely because they have reported legislation back to the House; they are forced to queue up and wait their turn much as Congressmen must do in waiting for favorable committee assignments. During a recent period of two years, the House adopted rules for considering more than 200 bills and resolutions; some 14 additional bills and resolutions remained in the Rules Committee without having been given a rule. The Rules Committee has been criticized frequently because of the discretion it exercises in failing to report some bills or in compelling other bills to be amended before they are given a rule. The fact that the Rules Committee holds hearings on the substantive content of legislation shows that it conceives its function to be broader than that of regulating the flow of business. For periods during the decades of the 1930's and 1940's the effective control of the committee was in the hands of Republicans and Southern Democrats, who occasionally formed a majority at odds with the political leadership of the House. The chairman of the committee during part of this period, Representative Adolph J. Sabath (D., Ill.), was more than once embarrassed by being directed to report rules which he neither favored nor advocated, and on one occasion, in asking that greater restraints be placed on the committee which he headed, Sabath referred to the "coalition of six or more members of the Committee on Rules who might arrogate unto themselves the power to determine what vital legislation should or should not receive consideration by this great legislative body." [2]

Although there is occasional grumbling about the authority exercised by the Rules Committee, its actions are rarely overruled, partly

[2] *Congressional Record,* January 2, 1951, p. A8012.

because its judgment may conform to the effective majority in the House and partly because the committee is in a strategic position to grant future favors. Occasionally, however, it is rebuked, as in 1944, when it reported a rule on the Price Control Act which made it permissible to offer amendments from another bill developed by an investigating committee. This went too far to suit many Representatives, Republicans and Democrats alike, for it posed a threat to the continued exclusive jurisdiction exercised by legislative committees. The Speaker himself, Representative Sam Rayburn (D., Tex.), denounced the Rules Committee from the floor and asked that the offending provision be deleted. The Rules Committee, said Rayburn, "was never set up as a legislative committee," and he did not want the Committee on Rules "to take away the rights, prerogatives, and privileges of other standing committees." [3]

Representative John J. Cochran (D., Mo.) went on to complain that on numerous occasions the Rules Committee "required a legislative committee either to strike out certain provisions of a bill or agree to certain amendments before the rule would be granted. In other words, it has set itself up as a superduper committee assuming control over the various legislation committees of the House." He predicted that if the practice did not stop, "there is going to be another revolt." [4] On this occasion the Rules Committee suffered one of its few setbacks, and the offending portion of the rules was deleted.

The revolt predicted by Representative Cochran did not materialize until 1949, when the House changed the rules to provide for alternative procedures if the Rules Committee took no action on legislation for 21 days. If the Rules Committee failed to report a rule during the three-week period, the chairman of the legislative committee concerned was empowered to bring the bill before the House, and the Speaker was directed to recognize him for that purpose. On a test vote, the proposal was adopted by a vote of 275–143. Ironically, the liberals who forced the change in the rules reversed the trend of the revolt of 1910; they were now willing to place effective legislative

[3] *Congressional Record,* June 7, 1944, pp. 5465 and 5471.
[4] *Ibid.,* pp. 5469–5470.

control in the hands of the Speaker and the committee chairmen, rather than in an independent Rules Committee of which the Speaker was not to be a member. During the subsequent session, the new rule was used some eight times, and the Speaker recognized committee chairmen for the consideration of legislation relating to the poll tax, flood control, United States participation in international organizations, statehood for Alaska and for Hawaii, the National Science Foundation, mining, and a veterans' hospital. In the following Congress, however, the rule was repealed.

SUMMARY

The congressional system is characterized by the multiplicity of conduits for raising an issue, and no one person, no one group, controls the agenda for all of Congress. There are many advantages to this free-flowing system, although there is also a price to pay which may prevent the maximum use of the manifold talents of Congress. The great advantage is that it permits extensive deliberation, often by lay specialists, of a wide variety of subjects. The broad, almost uncanalized agenda permits deliberation on a wide variety of matters and need not be squeezed into a limited amount of time controlled exclusively by party leaders. Such an extensive access to legislative authority has considerable advantages in a free society such as ours. The many facets of organized life which come in some contact with government often require a forum, however informal, for reviewing the nature of this relationship. There is, of course, the possibility that particular issues may fall under the scrutiny of unrepresentative legislative groups more anxious to expose or to punish than to exercise the qualities of deliberation. But here, too, the very fact that a multiplicity of conduits exists makes it possible to transfer the locus of attention so that a more productive consideration of the topic can be achieved.

Two of the major weaknesses of decentralized control over the agenda are not so serious that they cannot be corrected. One weakness is that a proposal which is "rigged" in some controlled group, such as a subcommittee, is not given adequate attention subsequently in the whole legislative process. The proposal is carefully guided, with further steps being purely procedural and lacking in substantive content. It seems to me desirable that the corporate idea of making congressional decisions be maintained in substance (and implemented where needed) and that these various specialized groups within Congress, however meritorious their deliberations may be, should not be given the last word in making policy.

The second weakness is that the decentralized development of the agenda may permit some topics to be ignored which ought to be considered. If Congress is to have greater control over delegated legislation, if it is to give increased attention to the development of military and foreign policy, it should be able to control its agenda sufficiently so that all topics in which it has an interest can be considered. Important aspects of policy making should not be permitted to go by default merely because no legislation has been introduced or no pressure group brings the situation to the attention of Congress. This calls for closer legislative coördination and planning. Additionally, some provision might well be made for the regularized consideration of policy questions which do not fit the ordinary pattern of legislation.

CHAPTER 6

The Process: Deliberation and Final Decision

IN THE SECOND PHASE OF THE LEGISLATIVE PROCESS, where the issue is considered, the significant activities which take place may be identified as the examination of the content of the proposal and the control of action toward the end that a final decision may be made. Special legislative roles are required in carrying out these functions: Deliberators are needed to examine the issue and regulators are required to control the proceedings. In the subsequent stage, that of making the final decision, proponents and opponents, mediators and neutrals are required to mobilize support. The second phase of the process is something more than an intellectual exercise where pure reason prevails, and something less than a manifestation of power politics where the decision is given automatically to the side with the largest battalions. So many things must occur during this phase of the process and so many functions must be performed that the effective consideration of legislation becomes a highly developed skill. None of the essential activities can be overlooked; none can be pressed forward to the exclusion of others.

In providing for legislative deliberation, an assumption is made that certain conditions exist which will permit the process to operate. At the initial stage of the process it is assumed that not everyone is committed to being a proponent or an opponent and that enough questions remain unanswered and doubts unresolved to permit some deliberations. This assumption is not always merited. When the G.I. bill was introduced in the Senate in 1944, for instance, it was sponsored by more than 80 Senators. Objections were made to this type of mass sponsorship because some thought that precommitting the Senators on such a vast scale made additional debate unnecessary. The 80 Senators were in a position, if they wished, to prevent any deliberation at all, and their mass sponsorship of the legislation implied that none was needed. They had closed their eyes and ears in advance to possible criticism of the legislation, or suggestions for improvement, and in effect approved the legislation before it was debated. In this case there were too many proponents, too soon. (In the House, where there was no mass sponsorship, the bill was debated fully.)

In creating the conditions of deliberation, it is also assumed that an advocate who is also a legislator has no undisclosed stake, certainly no special economic stake, in the results of the decision. Advocates having a special interest in the outcome of a project cannot be relied upon to ask pertinent and essential questions relating, say, to costs, or the possibility of developing alternative programs, or the integration of policy, or the effectiveness of provisions for legislative control. One would not want the members of a city council, for example, to give contracts to themselves, nor would one want labor policy determined exclusively by labor representatives or maritime policy by members with seaboard constituencies. If the advocate is personally involved in the results of a decision it may be desirable for him to declare his interest and perhaps even withdraw from the deliberation. There is perhaps less declaration of interest within Congress than there might be, for members are not prone to indicate publicly their possible association with special legislation. Such declarations would not necessarily decrease the effectiveness of members as advocates although it would provide safeguards for other members as well as for the public.

The burden of examining the content of a proposal is played by members who act as deliberators. Their function is to think through the ramifications of the proposed policy and to raise questions of purpose, of implementation, of feasibility, of results, and of the relations of the proposal to the interests of other groups. In the full consideration of a proposal, the locus of deliberations may extend beyond the legislative buildings, for legislators may study the subject at home during the evenings or talk it over with friends in other places. In many, perhaps all, situations some deliberations may take place outside the legislative chamber, and these outside deliberations may be so extensive that the function of the legislature is reduced to authenticating, or legitimizing, an agreement reached elsewhere. Whatever the extent of outside deliberations, the legislative ideal assumes the desirability of some exchange of views within the congressional establishment itself, with members meeting, exchanging thoughts, informing others of the product of their cogitations, and announcing publicly the reasons for making a particular decision. It is presumed, in other words, that even in cases where the deliberative process is reduced to that of authenticating decisions made elsewhere, the reasons for this authentication will be placed on record for public inspection.

Legislative deliberations are used for developing an understanding of an issue and in arriving at an eventual consensus. The proponents of a course of action must be prepared to explain and defend their proposals, and the issue will be rigorously analyzed during the ensuing discussions. Questions may be raised, doubts expressed, and anxieties quelled or accentuated. The deliberative process may seem to have some strange characteristics, for the legislators are expected to carry on an intelligent and persuasive discussion in public about technical matters on which there may be conflicting and contentious opinions. Newspaper correspondents in the press gallery report the debates to newspapers throughout the nation, and shorthand reports on the floor record the discussion for posterity—and for the possible use of political opponents.

The deliberative process seeks to accomplish the twin functions of explaining and of persuading. It is not enough that a member understand; he must also make up his mind. Inasmuch as persuasion may result from factors other than a mastery of the contents, extraneous matter may enter the debate, so that deliberations may range from intellectual exercises of a high calibre to noisome party bickerings. Some might wish things were otherwise than they are, that debate would always be pertinent, and that legislators would take a more detached approach to the subject. However, the fact should not be overlooked that the legislature is resolving real conflict in society and that it becomes possible to resolve such conflict by transforming it, as it were, into a partisan debate conducted under rigid proceduralized safeguards. In the legislature, the conflict is restrained and kept in bounds, with opportunity provided for a consideration of the issues in an atmosphere that will permit free discussion.

Although Congress talks a good deal during its deliberations, it is more than a debating society inasmuch as the debate is not an end in itself but a part of the long process of resolving conflict and making an eventual decision. Congressional debate utilizes the partisan spirit and the partisan organization for developing and resolving controversial issues, and all debate takes place against a backdrop of partisan organization. Not all subjects are equally saturated with political interest, but the partisan organization is always available for whatever displays of partisan strength or partisan opinion may be required. The deliberations take place under rules which compel the partisans to be effective and persuasive.

Political strategy in the sense of making an assessment of the advantage of proceeding in a particular fashion or of raising particular issues is required at each step of the process. Continually the partisans must determine how their own interests may be advanced or retarded in considering legislation. It is necessary to make decisions on the content of the legislation, on the proper time for its consideration, and on calling for a vote. The partisans must also estimate the possible sources and strength of the opposition as well as of their own following. They must also secure proper clearance from influential sources; they must inform those who have some interest in the legislation of current developments; and they must deter possible opposition by anticipating objections and explaining in advance questions which might be raised. In considering major legislation, issues of political strategy arise at every step of the process.

Within Congress, the locus for considering legislative proposals is ordinarily found within the committee structure and the two chambers. This does not exclude the possibility that events elsewhere may influence the nature of this deliberation. The preliminary examination of the content of a proposal is frequently made in the committee hearings. These hearings, which are ordinarily open to the public, perform the function of bringing to the committee the pertinent information necessary for making or for justifying a decision. The hearings also provide a communications link with the external groups affected by legislative action, and spokesmen for these groups are frequent witnesses before committees. With the right to command the appearance of witnesses and the production of papers, the committees have considerable resources for marshaling evidence. The hearings are ordinarily so popular and provide such an abundance of informative material that the problem commonly faced by committees is not that of compelling testimony but how to keep the testimony within sufficiently manageable bounds to evaluate its content. The legal limitations on the authority of a committee will be discussed later, but these limitations do not ordinarily affect the general ability of Congress to mobilize information through hearings.

In determining the nature of the testimony to be given at hearings, essentially the same problems arise as in controlling the procedures of Congress itself, for the committee must determine the nature of the witnesses who will be invited to testify and the length of the testimony. In some cases, the spokesmen of particular interest groups seem to have developed a presumptive right to testify before committees, in which case the hearings may be used as a platform for enunciating points of view rather than as a forum for examining the content of a proposal. Inasmuch as testimony given before congressional committees has some value in the world of publicity and public relations, spokesmen of special groups may persistently demand to be heard for the benefit of themselves if not of the committee. The long parade of witnesses may be less an indication that the committees have considered a proposal thoroughly than that they have been lenient in permitting the hearings to be used for propagating ideas of private groups. The numerous witnesses, having special points of view and perhaps being more anxious to persuade than to deliberate, may affect the hearings in other ways. Their testimony may engender a bickering, partisan spirit, with sharp questioning followed by partisan retorts. Congressional committees are under constant pressure to conduct extensive hearings, not only to examine the content of a proposal but also to promote the publicity needs of various groups; the fact that hearings are held at all may be the first rung of the ladder in getting proposals adopted.

Hearings have the virtue of informing Congressmen by the spoken rather than the written word inasmuch as few Congressmen have time, or take time, to carry on extensive independent research through library resources. The hearings are often extensive and intensive, with oral and written statements offered by witnesses variously representing the government, special interest groups, nonpartisan specialists, and even Congressmen. It is not unusual for a hundred or more witnesses to testify, and for additional statements, documents, and exhibits to be inserted in the record. Although some hearings are relatively short, lasting no longer than three or four days, others are more extensive and may continue through a session or even longer. The Senate committee investigating organized crime (the Kefauver Committee) heard testimony from more than 600 witnesses in 14 cities, and it compiled a score of volumes of hearings containing more than 13,000 pages.

Extended hearings may be more impressive than useful. Their value may be restricted if they are conducted by subcommittees with limited membership or if there are frequent absences. Prolonged congressional hearings might be compared with a Chinese melodrama which goes on for days, with no action omitted or proceedings telescoped and members of the committee attending as time permits. Although the hearings may contain a vast quantity of useful material, they are not ordinarily processed in such a fashion that their usefulness is maximized. No systematic attempt is made to edit and condense the hearings, separating the significant from the irrelevant, for the benefit of those not present in person. It is unrealistic to expect members, however earnest, to read voluminous volumes of hearings conducted by committees to which they do not belong. The reports of committees, however valuable in themselves, are essentially explanations of the legislation rather than synopses of the hearings. All things considered, it is pertinent to ask whether hearings are conducted or their findings presented in such a way as to be of the greatest use to Congress in considering the content of a proposal. The examination of policy content does not necessarily require the appearance of an extensive number of witnesses, and the witnesses who do appear could be more carefully selected, with the committee staff assisting by sharpening up the issues which need to be examined. The same criticism cannot be made against the commission form of inquiry, such as those on government reorganization conducted under the direction of former President Herbert Hoover. The commissions have made a greater effort to assess evidence, to pose alternatives, and to lead one's thoughts beyond the anarchy of unprocessed testimony one finds in congressional hearings.

In listening to witnesses the committee members adopt an attitude compounded of curiosity, skepticism, and frequently impartiality. The physical facilities of some committee rooms, where the members sit at elevated semicircular tables, accentuate the mood of sobriety and thoughtfulness rather than that of political oratory and partisan strife. The members of the committee assume an attitude of restrained impatience, and witnesses are expected to make a convincing case. Partisanship enters from time to time, however, often to the accompaniment of sharp comments and leading questions; witnesses may be helped over some of the rougher passages by friendly members who conveniently suggest the right words for replying to an embarrassing question. After the hearings, the committee reconsiders the legislation in the light of new evidence presented at committee hearings; this reconsideration takes place at closed meetings, with no record published of the deliberations. However, the report accompanying the legislation often contains a remarkably full account of the history of the bill, pointing out what amendments were excluded or included, the reason therefore, and the probable effect.

The defense of legislation is ordinarily considered the responsibility of the interested departments, with witnesses from other groups supporting or rebutting the testimony. Some departments—and especially those having established a basis of confidence with committee— may also assume the leadership in developing political support for the proposal. They will be expected not only to defend the legislation at the hearings but also to assist in preparing the report of the committee, to provide information to members and even prepare speeches for them, to give advice on the acceptability of proposed amendments, and to expedite the legislation at the various stages of the process.

Hearings may be conducted simultaneously by several committees, making it virtually impossible for even the best-intentioned legislator to keep informed of all legislative developments wherever they occur. The representatives of special groups keep informed, however, and so do administrators. This decentralized and somewhat informal method of deliberation may not result in the public's securing a very wide knowledge of the proposal, and even in Congress detailed knowledge will ordinarily be restricted to a relatively small group. However, within smaller orbits, some members of Congress may be very well informed indeed and if they are successful in building up tenure on a committee they may have as much knowledge of the subject as an administrative expert. The continuity of committee membership makes it possible to relate a current crisis to past policy and the reasons which led to making the policy initially. Committees with a relatively stable membership can perforce build up a body of knowledge—an "institutional memory"—but it will be less able to do so if its membership is constantly changing. An experienced staff can also assist a committee in relating past experience to present needs.

DEBATE

A group of key figures predominates in every floor debate. If the debate is highly organized, the leadership of the deliberation is assumed by representatives from the committee—often the chairman and the ranking member of the minority party. Under their aegis, the debate proceeds apace, and although these proponents and opponents may wear partisan tags, the ensuing debate may be of a high calibre with partisan overtones minimized. And so the debate proceeds, first one speaker, then another, but the high standard of objective explanation set by the committee leaders may not be sustained throughout the debate. Or again, in a less formal debate, the initiative in developing a point may be assumed by any member who can secure recognition.

In addition to the committee leaders, who act as policy proponents and opponents, the deliberations require the services of the partisan proponents and opponents, the leaders of which are the respective legislative leaders of the majority and minority in each House. The majority leaders are in general charge of the legislative program, and within the limits imposed upon them they coördinate the actions of committees, determine political strategy, make numerous decisions, and mobilize the partisans for the various votes. The minority leaders attempt to protect the exposed position of the minority, constantly raising questions about the propriety of the procedures being followed. As experts in the art of being meticulous, they continually call attention to ostensible procedural irregularities, indignities, and inconveniences. They raise the point or leave the impression that the minority has somehow been slighted, that a different order of business was expected, that insufficient time was allowed, that printed hearings were not available in advance of the debate, or that certain interested members are absent. Such protests are made continuously: they are often *pro forma,* regularly expected and easily adjusted, but they serve the purpose of keeping the majority alert to its responsibilities for maintaining the requisite procedures.

An example of sagacious legislative leadership overlayed with a touch of devilment may be found in the story of the round robin resolution, which Senator Henry Cabot Lodge (R., Mass.) brought up for consideration in the Senate on March 4, 1919. Although the Senate did not vote on the resolution, the strategy of Lodge was such that the action was considered equivalent to a vote, with the result that the world public believed the Senate to have threatened the position of President Wilson as an international leader. The Lodge resolution was brought before the Senate during the period when President Wilson had returned to Washington briefly from the Paris Peace Conference in order to be present for the closing days of the congressional session. President Wilson hoped during this short period to develop support for the League of Nations, which was part of the treaty. Senator Lodge, with other ideas, wished to make it appear to the world that the Senate would not approve the treaty President Wilson was then negotiating.

The vehicle for Lodge's scheme was the round robin resolution, mentioned above, which stated that the present form of the proposed treaty was unacceptable to the Senate. Senator Lodge baited his trap skilfully. In the closing hours of the session, which was due to end on March 4, Lodge asked the Senate for immediate consideration of his resolution, surely knowing that the automatic response of the Democratic leader would be to object to considering a resolution so clearly out of order. Objection having been made, Senator Lodge went on to say that if a vote had been permitted, the 38 Senators whose names he read would have supported the resolution. This was more than the one-third required to defeat the treaty. The world may have received the impression that the Senate was opposed to the League of Nations, but in truth the round robin resolution was only a ruse, skilfully executed. In gathering names, Senator Lodge had included Senators who would assume office on March 4 as well as those who were going out of office on that date; all the Senators whose names were read could not have voted at the same time. The one-third majority had been artificially contrived, but it appeared to the public that President Wilson had been challenged by a group large enough to defeat the treaty.

In the process of deliberation, it is necessary that controls be placed over the amount of time used and over changes in the content of a proposal. It is necessary to allocate time in such a fashion that the subject is roundly debated and to control the content in such a fashion that the areas of dispute are continually narrowed. It is also necessary to terminate debate at some point; otherwise, continued uninterrupted talk might prevent a decision from being made. The allocation of time and the establishment of controls over the scope of deliberation are determined by procedures and by the presiding officers as well as by the legislative committees, the political leaders, and the House Rules Committee. In the Senate, to a surprising extent, they are determined by unanimous consent agreements.

We are here concerned less with the units which exercise this authority than with the standards used in resolving possible conflict between various claimants. There may be conflict, for instance, between those who wish to continue the debate and those who wish to end it. There may also be conflict between those who wish to consider amendments and those who want to accept or reject the proposition as a whole. In allocating time it is also necessary to provide safeguards against any temptation to award time to one's friends and to muffle one's opponents.

Time is a scarce commodity, and control over its use is the major device through which authority is exercised in legislative deliberation. The business of the House is conducted in units of time, a specific number of minutes, hours, or days being allocated for particular purposes. The House, more than the Senate, operates under the assumption that the time available for debate must be regulated, even curtailed, if the legislature is to act. The time available for debating major bills in the House is specified in a special rule, or in the standing rules, with the control over the time further devolved to the chairman and ranking minority member of the legislative committee, who in turn reallocate it to the various members. When the bill is being read for amendment, the prevailing limit for speeches is five minutes, but it can be extended. General debate is limited to one hour, although a special rule may extend this to a longer period, and debate under the so-called suspension of the rules is limited to 40 minutes, the time being divided between the majority and minority. There is a small degree of elasticity in the use of the units of time, with extensions occasionally granted when the debate is running well, but these exceptions do not undermine the general rigidity of the time schedule.

The careful allocation of units of time in the House results in a certain degree of precision in the deliberations; once a bill is brought before the House, a final decision will be made within a prescribed period of time. This is not equally true of deliberations in the Senate. The control of time in the House makes filibustering difficult, although one may gain short delays by insisting on lengthy and repetitive roll calls. The control of time in the House relates to deliberations on a single measure, not to the total amount of proceedings, and toward the end of a session the House calendars are often crowded with legislation awaiting action. This pell-mell rush at the end of a session is a result of the lack of central control or coördination of the various committees, who, after prolonged deliberations of their own, may delay the report on their legislation until the session is far advanced. Even so, the careful control of time permits the House to enact a considerable amount of legislation very quickly, but this is possible only by limiting debate even more stringently than in normal periods.

The rigid allocation of time does not necessarily result in good debate, which depends on other factors. But if there is no special enthusiasm or verve for debating a particular subject, and if the allotted time must be consumed nevertheless, the debate may be perfunctory, wandering, and even irrelevant. On the other hand, the requests for time to debate some subjects will exceed the supply available. What happens then? The demand may be satisfied, after a fashion, by the peculiar custom of revising and extending remarks, which are then included in the *Congressional Record* as if the remarks had actually been made on the floor during debate. The single merit of this otherwise appalling custom is that the constituents are thereby apprised of the attitude of their Representative; but the material appears without challenge, without the necessity of being defended, and contributes nothing to the deliberations.

The Senate controls time less rigidly than does the House, the general rule of free and unlimited debate being modified by whatever agreements seem necessary to bring debate to a close. Even the orderly rules of Senate procedure, such as the proper time for introducing legislation, submitting reports, and holding executive sessions, may be suspended by a unanimous-consent agreement. In the ordinary rhythm of Senate proceedings, the extremes of no control and total control are seen constantly. On the one hand, debate will proceed for as long as anyone wishes to talk; on the other hand, procedures will be foreshortened by unanimous-consent agreements which bind the actions of everyone. Unanimous-consent agreements are used for adjournment, introducing and considering bills out of order, accepting nongermane amendments, addressing the Senate during the speech of another Senator, suspending present business in order to consider other business, and even limiting debate. They are just as binding as a rule in the House—with the proviso that they may in turn be modified by another unanimous-consent agreement. As an illustration of its use, the unanimous-consent agreement for considering the Displaced Persons Act set the time when the debate would begin, limited debate on amendments to one hour and on substitute amendments to two hours, placed the control of the time in the hands of two Senators, one opposing and one supporting the bill, and prohibited amendments which were not germane. But consent is not always given to proposed agreements. After the debate on the offshore oil bill had been running for some three weeks, Senator Taft attempted unsuccessfully to secure a unanimous-consent agreement limiting debate to half an hour for each Senator. An objection was made, and the proposal was lost.

The rules of debate in both Houses provide a number of safeguards for the expression of individual opinion, and most noteworthily in the Senate, where a Senator may talk until he has exhausted himself, his subject, and his audience. Debate on some types of legislation continues on and on, and at times it may be difficult to terminate it. The Southerners have perhaps the greatest reputation for filibustering, especially on topics relating to the franchise and nondiscriminatory employment practices, but other regions of the country also produce long-winded orators. The latest record for continuous talking was set on April 24–25, 1953, when Senator Wayne Morse of Oregon held the floor for 22 hours and 26 minutes in a remarkably coherent speech on the offshore oil bill.

Why do Senators talk at such length? Why does a small group carry on a dreary, inconclusive, repetitive, and often ungermane debate for a prolonged period of time? In such prolific outbursts of verbiage, talk is more than an aspect of deliberation; it is also an instrument of political tactics designed to delay or even prevent a vote. Senator Morse wanted to delay the vote, hoping that during this respite the opponents of the offshore oil bill could mobilize public support against the legislation. In 1950, some Senators wished to delay action so that public opinion could be rallied to sustain the President's veto of the Internal Security Bill. Although postponing action overnight, they could not enter into a prolonged filibuster because they were bound by a unanimous-consent agreement to adjourn Congress. Again, in 1947, the Senate was held in session through the Friday night of June 20 and on through an all-day session on Saturday by a group which hoped to delay action on the President's veto of the Taft-Hartley Bill long enough for public opinion to crystallize. On Monday, however, the vote was taken and the veto overridden. The long overnight filibuster of Senator Huey P. Long (D., La.) on June 12, 1935, was more a demonstration of Long's showmanship than of purposeful legislative tactics, and the Senator apparently had no more in mind than offering himself as a rival attraction to the Shrine Convention then meeting in Washington.

Those who carry on a filibuster against specific legislation hope, of course, that demands to consider other legislation will become so great that the offending legislation will be dropped. When there is competition for definitive action to be taken within a limited amount of time, something has to give way, and filibusters can be used most effectively under such conditions. These conditions were present in the so-called "lame duck" session of Congress which ran from December until March every second year. It was during such a session in 1917 that the famous and successful filibuster took place against the proposal to arm merchant vessels, enabling them to defend themselves from attack by German U-boats. The lame duck session was abolished in 1933 by the Twentieth Amendment, and there is now no prescribed length for a session of Congress.

Filibusters such as that on the Armed Ship Bill raise the question of the responsibility for governmental action in cases where authority is exercised procedurally, as it is in Congress. Through the happenstance of being able to filibuster against arming merchant vessels, Senator Robert La Follette (R., Wis.) was able to influence foreign policy although La Follette and his group were not otherwise directly responsible for making foreign policy. President Wilson, annoyed by the action, called the filibusterers a band of "willful men" who, representing no opinion but their own, had made the government of the United States "powerless and contemptible." As it turned out, however, the government was not as powerless as the President had suggested, for other legislative authority to arm the ships was found. Indeed, one of the results of filibustering, of making Congress unable to act, may be to encourage the development of other more reliable procedures—and in this case to permit the President to extend his authority where the law was not clear.

The discomfiture caused by the Armed Ship debate led the Senate to adopt a cloture rule for ending debate by the vote of a two-thirds majority. However, the cloture rule has not been popular and has been used only four times since 1917, whereas some 17 motions to end debate have failed. Cloture was used to end debate on the Treaty of Versailles in 1919, on the World Court in 1926, and on a banking bill and a government organization bill in 1927. The reluctance of the Senate to use cloture has resulted in proposals designed to make cloture easier to apply, even to the extent that a majority be empowered to stop debate. However, when the cloture rule was reconsidered in 1949, a proposal to end debate by a simple majority was defeated 80–7, indicating that there is no considerable support in the Senate for strengthening cloture. On the contrary, there is a good deal of latent pride in the tradition of permitting unlimited debate, which is considered to be most desirable if all Senators behave as Senators should. The rhetorical views of Senator Millard E. Tydings (D., Md.) on the evils of cloture express the sentiments of many Senators. "Cloture is predicated upon the theory that the majority can do no wrong," Senator Tydings said; "cloture is predicated on the assumption that might makes right; cloture is predicated on the idea that the voice of the individual, for which this country was founded, for which the Constitution was written, for which the Bill of Rights was brought into being, is to be set at naught. It was cloture that crucified Christ on the Cross; it was cloture that put to work the hangman on a thousand gallows through all the Dark Ages. No, the right to protest is one of the strongest guaranties of human rights and liberty left in this or any republic." [1]

The cloture rule, last revised in 1949, now requires the support of "two-thirds of the Senators duly chosen and sworn," with the proviso that cloture cannot be applied to a debate on the standing rules of the Senate. In other words, any future debate on a change in the rules could not be ended by applying cloture. The new rules were supported by more than two-thirds of the Senate, the vote being 62–23. Some discussion of the need for liberalizing the cloture rule occurred during the political campaign of 1952, but, unfortunately for the reformers, the new session of Congress began with a debate over the disposition of the offshore oil lands. During the long, repetitious dispute, there was more than a hint that a filibuster was taking place, engaged in, ironically enough, by members who had condemned filibustering in the preceding campaign.

The legislative committees bear the main responsibility for organizing and developing the debate in the respective chambers. The debate ordinarily begins with a statement on the purposes of the legislation made by the member of the committee—often the chairman—who

[1] *Congressional Record,* January 22, 1946, p. 203.

has been given the responsibility for managing the bill in the floor proceedings. Following the introductory statement, a member of the minority party on the committee gives his interpretation of the bill and indicates the parts to which he takes exception. In the House, the debates will proceed apace until the allotted time is consumed. It is then in order to consider amendments, and the bill is read, line by line, for this purpose. Here the House operates under the five-minute rules, the theoretical limit of the length of speeches permitted at this stage of the proceedings.

The House rules assume that debate will follow the prevailing political alignment, with allocations of time controlled by the partisans. In reality, however, debate does not necessarily follow party lines so strictly; bipartisan majorities and minorities may develop, and even the chairman of a committee will be found supporting the position of the nominal minority (which may have become the temporary majority). This fluidity of party alignment during debates may result in an opponent of a measure having to secure speaking time from a proponent. The following colloquy during a foreign policy debate illustrates the plight of a member, wanting more time, who is out of sympathy with the stand of both the majority and minority party.

Mr. Gearhart (a Republican who opposed the resolution): "Mr. Chairman, may I have some additional time?"

Mr. Eaton (the ranking Republican on the Foreign Affairs Committee): "I am sorry; I cannot yield or I would impinge on eternity."

Mr. Gearhart: "Can the gentleman from New York let me have any additional time?"

Mr. Bloom (the Democratic chairman of the Foreign Affairs Committee): "I am sorry, but I have none available."

Mr. Gearhart: "I know how sorry the gentlemen are. Unfortunately, I am against the resolution passing. Strange how much time there is for those who are for it." [2]

The Senate procedure is much the same in giving the committee members the primary responsibility for developing the debate. How-

[2] *Congressional Record,* January 21, 1944, p. 575.

ever, except in cases of unanimous-consent agreement, there is no
time limit on speeches and ordinarily no time limit for considering the
entire bill. Moreover, the consideration of amendments is less formalized.

Some committees are more successful than others in protecting
their legislation from being seriously modified or even destroyed when
it is considered in the parent chamber. To begin with, all committees
do not command the same degree of respect from nonmembers, and
if in addition to a lack of status, its views are not representative, it
may have difficulty in protecting its bills from unwelcomed amendments or even from defeat. The opposition may choose to concentrate
its attack by offering specific amendments to the legislation, hoping
to modify a part of the bill if it cannot influence the whole.

The procedures of both chambers are such that it is not too difficult
to amend legislation from the floor. When the House debates legislation in the Committee of the Whole, the presence of 100 members
satisfies the requirements of a quorum. The amendments agreed to
under these procedures are tentative, in the sense that a roll call vote
may later be requested, but in fact the bulk of amendments adopted
in the Committee on the Whole are retained. Representative John J.
Cochran (D., Mo.) once remarked on this phenomenon, saying that
"Members will add an amendment in the Committee of the Whole,
and when a special vote is requested in the House a sufficient number
of members would refuse to stand up to provide a roll call so that a
record vote could be taken on the amendment." [3] The proponents of
the legislation have the onerous burden of maintaining continually a
majority of supporters during the proceedings. They depend, of
course, on the party organization to see to it that a sufficient number
of members is present to defeat unwanted amendments. But the
opponents may also be able to mobilize their forces quickly. In general, the proponents must have a majority readily available at all
times; the opponents need to recruit what they hope will be a majority
only when particular amendments are being considered.

The amending process may be used to "test" political strength as

[3] *Congressional Record,* June 7, 1944, p. 5470.

well as to change the content of legislation. Amendments may be offered to sample attitudes, and, on the basis of the votes, a compromise will be offered to satisfy the various factions. Again, the main controversy may be centered on an amendment, and it is not uncommon for bills to be adopted unanimously after amendments have been voted up or down. In order to secure the adoption of a bill, the proponents may be forced to accept amendments which they do not want and which, if they pushed the matter, they might be able to defeat. The leaders must continually consider the advisability of accepting amendments, for in the long run the friendship and good will of the opposition may be more valuable than securing a legislative victory—even with the votes on hand.

On one occasion when the Senate was considering legislation providing for the adjudication of claims of private American citizens against the Republic of Mexico, Senator Bennett Champ Clark (D., Mo.) expressed some divergent ideas concerning the category of claims to be adjudicated and the type of tribunal to be created. Clark, clearly in the minority, was the only defender of his particular point of view, although in a vote he might have been able to persuade six or eight of his fellow Senators to support him. Neither the Foreign Relations Committee nor the State Department went along with Clark. However, Clark was adamant, he was obviously informed, he had thought through the problem, and he could support his point of view rationally in public debate. The committee amended the legislation to meet some of the objections, after which Senator Clark supported the bill. By modifying the legislation, the Foreign Relations Committee was able to present a united front on the Senate floor, and it was more influential than if it had been divided in its advocacy of the legislation. It may also have built up strength and influence, for the committee would continue its existence on into the future, when there would be new issues to be decided long after the Mexican claims controversy had passed into history. The committee would perhaps be a happier and more effective unit with Clark's good will and coöperation than if he had remained obdurate and unreconciled.

The content of congressional debate varies greatly; sometimes it is informative, pertinent, and even witty, while again it may be heavy, ridden with platitudes, and not to the point. This lack of sprightliness may result from the fact that relevancy is neither insisted upon in the House nor required in the Senate. Once control over debate has been established in the House, there is a propensity to allow a member to say what he wishes during the time at his disposal, and the point of order is seldom made that a speaker has wandered from his subject. The practice in the Senate, which has no rules on relevancy, has been described by Senator Kenneth McKellar (D., Tenn.), who as president pro tempore of the Senate was in a position to know the precedents: "Under the rules of the Senate," he said, "it is not required that any speaker speak to the question before the Senate. He may speak on whatever subject he chooses. That is both the written and unwritten law." [4]

In defending the Senate practice, a witness once told a Senate committee that he was "not at all convinced" that a rule of relevancy should be enforced. For a hundred years, he said, the Senate practice has been "that you can't tell whether a subject is relevant until you have heard it," and he had been "very strongly impressed with that argument." [5] This seems equivalent to saying that no one but the Senator who is speaking knows what he is saying! Of course, in practice, the expectation of rational discussion on the part of one's colleagues and the presence of newspaper reporters in the galleries tends to produce a degree of pertinency in debate.

Congressional debate may appear to be inconclusive, especially if an attack on government fails to point up or resolve an issue. If a partisan attacks a government department in somewhat extravagant terms, the chances are good that the charges will not be answered and the words will be lost in space. Why? Other members may lack the necessary knowledge or be unwilling to assume the responsibility for making an answer; time may not be available to consider the

[4] *Congressional Record,* January 23, 1946, p. 234.
[5] Senate Committee on Expenditures; Hearings: *Legislative Reorganization Act of 1946,* February, 1948, p. 191.

issue further; and the administrators directly concerned may have no suitable forum for making a response.

Another characteristic of congressional debate is its discursiveness, although this is perhaps more true of the Senate than of the House. Senate debate proceeds by stops and starts, a result of the common practice of temporarily laying aside current legislation for the consideration of other items. A recapitulation of the debate during a single day, taken at random, emphasizes this point. After the routine morning business, the Senate resumed its consideration of a bill to amend the Legislative Reorganization Act. Debate was interrupted while a message was read informing the Senate that the House had passed certain bills. Following the interruption, the Senate heard a speech on the role of the United Nations in the Tunisia crisis and a second on the threatened steel strike. The latter speech, in turn, was interrupted by a unanimous-consent request to reconsider a motion, passed the prior day, designating the Senate conferees on the offshore oil bill. The request was granted, the motion adopted, and the speech on the steel strike was resumed. Then the Senate returned to the Reorganization Act, and when general debate on this measure was ended a quorum call summoned members for the subsequent votes on proposed amendments. Before the voting on amendments could begin, Senator Burnet R. Maybank (D., S.C.), interrupted the proceedings to make a speech on the steel strike, justifying his action by stating that he wished to speak on a subject "which is of far greater importance than the passage of this bill." The Reorganization Act was again taken up and, following a quorum call, was passed. At this point various requests were granted for inserting material into the *Congressional Record,* much of which would appear in the Appendix, the latter containing an agglomerate of political desiderata, ranging from bad doggerel to reprints of speeches of nonmembers, editorials, letters, articles, and documents. The Senate then went into executive session and quickly confirmed presidential nominations to the Securities and Exchange Commission, the American delegation to the United Nations, the Department of State, and the Diplomatic and Foreign Service.

In examining foreign policy, Congress may be especially concerned with the effect of the proposal on the internal domestic economy. The members of Congress come from areas where economic dislocations may be felt, and it follows that in discussing foreign policy these dislocations may be emphasized. The fact that congressional discussions of foreign policy may revolve around local interests may give the debate an element of parochialism, but the fact is, of course, that foreign policy is not an abstraction unrelated to domestic events. The concern of Congress for local interests is not in itself an undesirable or unnecessary action, for foreign policy, like other types of policy, must somehow be made to blend with the type of action currently being carried on. The test is not the emphasis on parochial interests but the degree to which such emphasis may distort the possible harmony of a broader plan of action.

Nevertheless, the actions of Congress in dealing with foreign policy may often seem mystifying to those without an awareness of the crosscurrents of conflict that pervade Congress. The main issue may be accepted inferentially and the debate rage on some apparently minor point. Great armies and navies may be authorized, but members of Congress may also wish to make sure that a harbor will be built in City *A* or a military camp located in State *B*. Acts of generosity may be conditioned by provisions of obvious assistance to some domestic group, such as the legislation for UNRRA and for aid to Europe which contained provisions for quota purchases of American commodities, some of which were then in surplus supply. A Senator may oppose certain policy because no Foreign Service Officers have been appointed from his small Western state. Ideas may be introduced which run counter to the desires of the international negotiators, as when Congress included provisions for extending military aid to Spain at a period when other nations did not want to include Spain in a defense organization.

The parochialism of Congress, sometimes annoying, vexing, and meddlesome, may lead to proposals for extending presidential discretion in foreign affairs. However, the extension of discretionary power to the President would not remove the pressures themselves but merely change the locus of their effective operation. It can be argued that the President and the bureaucracy can resist pressures more easily than Congress in that all factors of a situation—domestic and foreign—will be considered. Nevertheless, one cannot ignore the fact that the President, also, is a political figure, interested in his own future and that of his party, and that favoritism and special protection may exist even though not blatantly written into the legislation. Indeed, the pressures on the President and the bureaucracy may be harder to detect and easier to conceal, and the action may be authorized by the President through some euphemistic reference to the public interest and the national welfare. In addition, individuals within the bureaucracy may be in a strategic position to make preferential judgments without any effective, self-correcting methods of review. Such was the case uncovered in the MacArthur hearings, when it was revealed that a relatively obscure official in the Department of Commerce had vast discretionary powers over domestic exports which he was using in a questionable manner.

JOINT CONFERENCE AND PRESIDENTIAL SIGNATURE

A word should be added about the function of the joint conference committee in resolving legislative differences between the two Houses. The fact that conference committees may have considerable latitude in developing a new synthesis agreeable to both Houses, added to the prevailing custom of meeting in secret with no records preserved other than the final decision, has led to charges that the conference committees are "too powerful." However, it is apparent that there must be an adjustment of views if both Houses agree to a common instrument. An examination of the function performed by the joint conference committees provides some justification for the influence they command and some rationale for their behavior, including that of holding their sessions in secret.

The function of the joint conference committee is to work out a solution for areas in dispute in order that both chambers can agree on an identical legislative instrument. Its interest in the content of legislation is limited to developing a formula that will be agreeable to the respective chambers. At this phase it is accountable directly and solely to the two parent chambers, the members of the conference committee being in effect negotiators interested only in reaching a common agreement. It is not necessary at this stage that the conference group attempt to mobilize public support, and indeed such a course might prove embarrassing. The support of the public will be secured through regular congressional channels rather than through the committee conferees. The conference committee, not being a continuing body, has no interest in preserving its identity as such or in bolstering its authority with groups outside Congress.

The content of the bills in dispute may vary considerably, thus giving the conference committee a wide choice in arriving at a new synthesis of views. The rule restricting the jurisdiction of the committee to the material actually in dispute may, in effect, be modified in practice. Indeed, it is not uncommon for amendments to be added by one or the other House merely to give the committee greater flexibility in creating workable legislation—and perhaps to give one set of conferees additional bargaining power in their negotiations. Flexibility is also provided by the practice of considering identically worded passages to be in dispute if they occur in different sections of the bill. If the conferees go beyond the areas in dispute, the new legislation is technically subject to a point of order, but with agreement reached, the point of order might not be raised.

An example of the joint conference committee going beyond the areas in dispute may be found in the history of the Surplus Property Act of 1944. Both Houses adopted an amendment which provided that funds from the sale of surplus property should be deposited with the Treasury "to the credit of a special fund which shall be used exclusively for the reduction of the public debt." No point of order was raised when the conference committee deleted the amendment, and the provision did not appear in the final Act. The conferees claimed that the amendment was superfluous, being a device which would result only in creating more work for bookkeepers. If Congress appropriated more funds than there was revenue available, the money used for retiring the debt would have to be otherwise supplied by additional borrowing. If a point of order had been raised, the presiding officer might have held it inapplicable because the amendments were found in different sections of the bill. Actually, however, no point of order was raised, for apparently no member wished to assume responsibility for delaying action of the legislation or even jeopardizing its passage completely by forcing further meetings of the conference committee.

The selection of the membership on conference committees is fairly stylized, the custom being for the chairmen of the committee handling the legislation to suggest the names of the conferees to the presiding officer, who actually makes the appointments. The requirements for membership are either seniority of service on the committee or special familiarity with the legislation through service on a subcommittee. Conferees are selected from both parties and theoretically represent the decision made by the chamber, regardless of their own particular preferences. As Senator Tom Connally (D., Tex.) once put it, "to all reasonable extent" the conferee should represent "the views of the body that appoints him." Any other rule "would be contrary to established parliamentary usage and the highest parliamentary ethics." The conferees should be resilient, however, and the Senator added that it seemed to him that "both sides should not stand out like stone walls, in which event there is no occasion to have a conference." [6] On the other hand, there may be those like Senator Robert La Follette (Prog. Wis.) who would prefer not to serve on a conference rather than advocate a point of view they do not support. On one occasion Senator La Follette found himself "so out of sympathy with the action taken by the Senate" on a tax bill that he asked "to be relieved from service on the conference committee." [7]

The conferees meet behind closed doors, with no record kept of the deliberations, and Congress is informed officially only of the decisions reached. The reports tend to be factual and technical, listing the amendments on which there is agreement or disagreement, and they may be difficult to follow without referring to the legislation in dis-

[6] *Congressional Record,* February 10, 1944, pp. 1521–1522.
[7] *Congressional Record,* May 14, 1943, p. 4458.

pute. Each set of conferees has the same voting strength, although the number of conferees from each chamber may differ. In the conference deliberations, various alignments may develop: It may be the House against the Senate, or one party against the other, or a recalcitrant individual or group holding out for a particular point of view. In the conference on the Ruml Tax Bill in 1943, for instance, the deliberations lasted some three weeks, and in the long deliberations there was never a unanimous vote and only one—the last vote—which commanded a majority.

The conferees may bolster their bargaining position by securing special instructions from their parent chamber, and with these special instructions they will be less likely to retreat from a position previously held. During the consideration by the conferees of the War Mobilization and Reconversion Bill in 1944, for instance, Representative Robert L. Doughton (D., N.C.) asked the House to reaffirm its opposition to paying transportation costs for returning war workers or to including federal employees in unemployment insurance benefits. The Senate had included these provisions in its bill. The House voted to continue its opposition to these provisions and they were not included in the final conference compromise. On the other hand, the reaffirmation of a position previously taken may not always be convincing to the conferees. In 1943 the Senate was asked to express again its opinion on removing three federal officeholders—the Dodd-Lovett-Watson case—and it maintained its position by a vote of 69–0. The House conferees nevertheless insisted on retaining the amendment, and later the House reaffirmed its previous stand; after rejecting the amendment five times, the Senate finally capitulated and adopted the conference report.

Conferees face the twin difficulties of arriving at an agreement which will not only satisfy themselves, as conferees, but will also satisfy the House and Senate as well. It may be necessary in some cases to reach the final agreement by stages, taking a few hard cases at a time and continually narrowing the material in dispute. In defending the agreed results before the parent chamber, the conferees may have to fall back on their stock of rhetoric, especially if they have conceded an issue on which their colleagues may have strong feelings. The conferees may stress the extent of their own victories, where the agents of the other chamber gave way, and will pass over more lightly the sections of the bill where they themselves agreed to yield.

The conferees do not always find it easy to persuade their colleagues that the right course has been taken. On one occasion when the conferees deleted an amendment which he had sponsored, Senator Raymond E. Willis (R., Ind.) said that the Senate was confronted with a situation "in which an amendment agreed to by a vote of nearly three to one in the Senate, and supported by the three Senate conferees, is blocked by a vote of three members of the House. That certainly is a perversion of the democratic process." [8] On another occasion, when the Senate was on the point of rejecting a conference report, Senator Kenneth McKellar (D., Tenn.) complained that "as a member of the organization" he thought he had "a right to expect that when the conference committee brought in a report we would receive help for the organization on our side of the Senate," [9] and he threatened to resign as a conferee if the report was defeated.

Some bills are lost because the conferees fail to agree or because one of the Houses fails to approve the report. During the closing months of World War II, for example, the Senate rejected the conference report on national service legislation, and the bill was never again considered. On the whole, however, the bulk of the conference reports are accepted with little or no debate and without a roll call vote.

If the President signs a bill passed by Congress, the last step in the legislative process has been taken, but if he vetoes the bill, Congress must take further action. The Constitution provides that all bills must be presented to the President before becoming law, that the President must sign the bills he approves and, with objections noted, return others within ten days (Sundays excepted) to the House where they originated. The bills then become law if approved by two-thirds of both Houses. Bills do not become law, however, if an

[8] *Congressional Record,* March 21, 1944, p. 2804.
[9] *Congressional Record,* June 29, 1943, p. 6730.

adjournment of Congress prevents the President from returning them within the required time period—the so-called pocket veto.

Although the provisions of the Constitution apply to all types of bills, the veto is, in fact, used differentially. For some types of legislation, the veto is not effective; for other types, the veto is final; for still other types, the veto is controversial. The President is compelled to accept some types of legislation, rather than risk the failure of Congress to pass more suitable legislation within the time required. The President would rather accept the evils of unwanted amendments than face the prospect of securing no legislation at all. Most Presidents are reluctant to veto tax bills or appropriation bills, for instance. Congress and the President frequently play a game of cat and mouse, and Congress might secure legislation which otherwise might fall by amending a bill which the President would be loath to veto. During World War II, Congress wished to repeal an executive order which limited net salaries, after tax payments, to $10,000. The limitation was based on authority delegated to the President, and while the provision was not popular in Congress it would no doubt have been supported by enough members to uphold a veto had Congress tried to repeal the provisions directly. At that particular time, it was necessary to authorize an increase in the debt limit, and the Treasury was then preparing a new bond sale. Given the urgent need for more funds, the debt limitation bill was the type of legislation which the President could not prudently veto. Congress took advantage of the President's position by including in a single bill the item raising the debt limit and the item repealing the limitation on salaries; the President was effectively blocked from using his veto.

The bills where the President's veto is final consist primarily of private bills and of those supported by interest groups whose strength is not great. Half a hundred or so of this type of bill are vetoed every year, and little or no attempt is made to override the veto. Other things being equal, Congress must feel strongly on a subject if it overrides a veto, and it is not easy to develop such feelings on minor measures. When such bills are passed initially, they may be shepherded through Congress by a few interested members, and no procedural objection will develop. It is another matter, however, to develop an affirmative and extraordinary majority on such measures at a time when the attention of the public is focused on Congress.

The third category of bills contains those where the President's veto is controversial. The President's influence over this type of legislation may be felt even if the veto is not actually used, and the procedure in Congress may be governed by the known willingness or unwillingness of the President to veto particular bills. In a way, of course, the entire scope of legislative business is conditioned by the presumed response of the President, and, negatively, it can be said that the probability of a veto prevents Congress from consuming time on legislation which has little likelihood of final approval. In some areas of policy, however, the possibilities of eventual success may seem great enough for Congress to proceed with legislation, even at the risk of a veto. In this category may be placed veterans' legislation, farm legislation, and labor legislation—all subjects of continuing controversy between the President and Congress.

THIRD PHASE: THE FINAL DECISION

The examination of the content of a proposal proceeds simultaneously with the attempt to mobilize support for an eventual decision. Both phases of the process are necessary in developing ultimate agreement, but, as may be apparent, it is possible to distort the process by placing too great an emphasis on one or the other phases. In order to accomplish both purposes, the chambers and committees are polarized in two directions, one relating to the party and the other to policy. This dual polarization may be seen when Congress considers a controversial measure, at which time the partisan proponents and opponents as well as policy proponents and opponents will emerge. In the latter stages of the process, the partisan and policy proponents may often be identical, but in any event, the function performed by each is carried on by a somewhat different internal organization. In the formal consideration of legislation on the floor, the political organization and the policy organization can be identified. There is, of course, a close working relationship between the two groupings, but they are not identical; if they were identical, no purpose would be served by examining the content of the policy. A partisan vote would suffice.

It is also true that partisan alignment may condition the attitude of a member toward a proposal, and the member may be expected to identify himself as a political proponent or opponent without having any special knowledge of the particular policy in question. But partisan attitudes are not necessarily so frozen in advance that no deviation in developing policy or in expressing attitudes on it is permitted, although, regrettably, some members prefer partisan clichés to constructive thinking. However, the partisan organization is always present in periods of tranquility to provide leadership and a semblance of order, and in periods of strife and storm to provide strength through unity and victories through majority votes. In the committees and in the chambers, the partisans cluster together in propinquity, arranged in mock battle formation, with one group of leaders assuming the burden of advocating and another group of opposing. But, as has been said earlier, the deliberative process assumes that everyone does not make up his mind too soon, at least to the extent that a decision is demanded at once, and in theory at any rate (and very frequently in practice), some members of the chamber will not yet have identified themselves as proponents or opponents of a policy.

In the deliberative process it is necessary that some action be taken to persuade neutral members to make up their minds and join one side or the other, for the process is incomplete if it is left in a disarray of divergent and indifferent attitudes. Members have to be asked, or persuaded, or otherwise moved to make up their minds so that a decision can be made, even though the neutrals may have no significant influence in shaping the content of a proposal for which their approval is nevertheless required. Of course, if these neutrals are staunch party men, the vote is already in someone else's pocket, but lacking this they may be open to persuasion and capable of being something more than pawns in the hands of the political leaders. We may also introduce at this point the members who act as mediators and whose function it is to arrange some acceptable agreement between the proponents and opponents, for at some point these rivals must stop asserting positions and attempt to secure agreement.

All who exert influence in the legislative chamber are not necessarily permitted to vote. The right to participate in approving or rejecting a proposal is restricted to members of the legislature—to those who, by law, are permitted to make authoritative decisions. A fundamental distinction is made between those who are and who are not members of Congress, and within Congress a further distinction is made between members and delegates, the latter being permitted to participate in raising the issue and in examining the content of a proposal but not in making the decision on approving or rejecting the proposal. A further distinction is made within various units of the internal organization of Congress, there being strict regulations concerning those who are permitted to vote in committees, subcommittees, conference committees, and the like. The select group which can make the final decision is limited in number and the participants known in advance. The names of those who vote may also be known to the public, the Constitution providing that "the Yeas and Nays of the members of either House on any question shall, on the desire of one fifth of those present, be entered on the journal."

The method of expressing consent or dissent, of approving or disapproving legislation, is overt and highly proceduralized. The physical conditions of Congress are designed to prevent possible interference with the actual casting of a vote, and the Constitution further forbids interference with members attending a session. The assembly remains moderately quiet during the process of voting; no demonstrations are permitted, no shouting, no parades, and no derisive remarks. Members who participate in making the decision may be subject to political reprisals on the part of outside groups, but the members themselves cannot be sued for their action, nor can they be bribed, promised rewards, or be given benefits which will advance them socially or economically. No reprisals are permitted against the legislative body itself.

In the process of making a final decision, usually expressed by a vote, an attempt is made to transform the variety of individual opinions into a concrete expression of the corporate group. The decision is that of the whole body, not a part thereof or of the in-individual members. In the actual process of voting, the position of the individual members, even of the legislative leaders, is subsumed in the totality of the membership, for the concern of the process is now with quantitative values expressed by gross numbers rather than with individual expressions of opinion by those having positions of status or authority. However, this is not to suggest that an individual member may not influence the voting of others if, for example, he is thought of as a specialist, a wise politician, or a member whose judgment one respects.

Here one should mention the significance of the concept of the majority as a procedural device for making group decisions. With the exception of a few types of action, decisions which are considered legitimate and binding are made by a majority of those voting. (It does not follow that any decision made by a majority is, therefore, *ipso facto* legitimate and binding.) At the several phases of the legislative process, the political controversy is directed toward the eventual goal of mobilizing a majority for an eventual decision, and it is here, in making the final decision, that the concept of the majority has its greatest usefulness. And it is here also that a vote may be required to determine whether a majority does in fact exist, as well as to determine the nature of its composition. The concept of the majority is useful in recording attitudes but it is less useful, say, in determining the subject of deliberation—although in the latter case the majority (of some group) may select representatives to speak in the name of all, and even the rule of seniority for determining committee rank has the legal support of a majority decision. Nor is the concept of the majority especially useful in legislative delibera-tions, although it may be utilized to determine time limits of debate. Indeed, legislative deliberations should not be considered as a process subservient to the "will" of "the majority" but rather as a process for permitting a majority opinion to be formed.

The use of the word "majority" may be somewhat misleading,

especially if it carries with it moral overtones of authority which, in any situation, would permit the greater part of a given group to impose its "will" on the smaller part, or, in popular parlance, would always permit the majority to "rule." The meaning of the word might be clarified if one thought of the majority as being a part of a process rather than a concrete entity which is everywhere and easily identified with peculiar characteristics of its own and which by definition is always right. Within Congress one might say that a majority "emerges" for certain purposes and that it is not a constant, concrete entity. The final legislative decision by a majority is only part of a longer process which encompasses the selection of members, the allocation of internal authority, the representation of interests, the selection of the agenda, the preservation of the integrity of procedures, and the development of opinions through open deliberation.

Used in its proper context, the concept of the majority has considerable significance in making legislative decisions. Ready-made majorities do not necessarily exist and may have to be developed by various, frequently temporary alignments of groups, blocs, and partisans. A number of majorities will be formed in the total process, rather than the single monolithic entity implied in the term "majority rule." A more accurate term to describe what occurs is that of "multiple majorities." The picture of a permanent majority, continually outvoting a permanent minority, is an inaccurate description of voting in Congress, for the composition of majorities fluctuates constantly as the locus of debate shifts from place to place and the attention of Congress from topic to topic. Several varieties of majorities are involved in making all the decisions necessary to reach final agreement. Members will be found on the winning and losing sides of many questions, and over a period of time it would be difficult to find any large identifiable group which is always voted down.

The majority, considered as part of the process of making legislative decisions, is restricted in what action it can take, being limited by the Constitution as to the type of question it can decide, by various procedural rules, and by the purpose of the whole process. Special types of majorities may be required for different types of issues: An extraordinary majority is needed for passing legislation over the veto of the President, for proposing amendments to the Constitution, for suspending the rules, and for removing members from Congress. Sometimes the action of only one chamber is sufficient, as for treaties or impeachments by the Senate (with an extraordinary majority), or for negating an Executive Order by the House or Senate. The taking of a vote may be delayed, even though a majority is present, because absent members would like to participate in the voting. One can say, then, that the right of the majority to make decisions is restricted by the function it performs and the type of decisions it makes. The majority considered as a device for measuring attitudes quantitatively is a procedural development and not a mystical repository of truth.

Although legislative bodies are so organized that they can eventually come to some conclusion, the decision is made not only because the conscience of the members is pricked but also because the members are persuaded, maneuvered, and organized in such a fashion that the decision can be made. Pressures are brought on the members from various sources both within and without Congress. The President may ask his followers in Congress, and even members of the opposition, to support some proposal, and the possibility of gaining patronage and other favors which the President has to bestow may serve to bolster the claims of an otherwise good argument. The departments may be persuasive also, although they are prevented by law from asking the public directly to exert pressure on Congress. Lobbies certainly are active, and their techniques include not only the direct approach but also the indirect approach, where the constituents who are also members of the interest group in question are encouraged to persuade Congress to vote correctly.

Incidents where faked telegrams have been used in propaganda campaigns and other attempts to bring extraordinary pressure on Congress suggest the significance of the question of permissible and nonpermissible influence. The minimum rule is, I believe, that pressures should not be such as to prevent an independent decision from being made by Congress, and this would exclude such reprehensible and obviously deleterious actions as bribery and deception, while not preventing citizens from petitioning Congress in accordance with their constitutional rights. Of course, the independence of Congress might also be threatened in other ways which have nothing to do with corruption, a topic which will be reverted to later.

In examining voting behavior within Congress one can discover patterns of influence and types of alignment with which legislators identify, either consciously or unconsciously. An examination of these patterns may be a useful first step in analyzing legislative behavior, although there is no simple answer to the question of what influences a legislator to vote as he does. One might be able to make a satisfactory explanation in any particular case, given sufficient information, but one would hesitate to generalize on the basis of much of this evidence. The motivation may be the influence of some individual, or committee, or party, or some other grouping—all in turn affected by external associations and anticipations.

Individual leadership still counts for something. It has been noted that in state legislatures especially, where parties are frequently less well organized than in Congress, an individual member with a reputation for integrity and intelligence may influence the votes of those who follow him on the roll call. On one occasion in Congress a Senator who was making a determined effort to prevent the confirmation of a presidential nominee was having no success in convincing members of either party. A colleague who was impressed with the effort if not with the argument told the protesting Senator that he would vote against the nomination because he admired the fight he was making. The support was rejected, the Senator being told that if he hadn't been persuaded by the argument he shouldn't vote against confirmation. "I have concluded," the first Senator said, "that friendship should never be the basis on which a Senator casts his vote."

The influence of the committees varies considerably. In general, the leadership of the committee is accepted if its membership is broadly representative and if the subject matter is not especially sensitive politically. However, if the committee is not representative, or if the subject matter is of considerable public interest—relating, for example, to veterans' legislation, or labor legislation, or foreign policy—the attitude of the committee may not necessarily be of commanding importance. The labor committees, especially, seem to have considerable difficulty in persuading the parent chambers to adopt the legislation they had reported. However, no committee is always in favor with its colleagues, and sometimes some surprising reversals occur.

The President may undermine the influence which a committee might otherwise have by making his views known and even by sending a message (and messengers) to Congress. In 1953, for instance, the tax reduction proposed by the Ways and Means Committee was opposed by President Eisenhower, and that normally influential committee found itself at cross-purposes with the leaders of the Republican party. Moreover, committees may run counter to the position of strong interest groups, who will attempt to mobilize support for defeating the committee. If the issue becomes contentious, the members may be guided less by the views of the committee than by the views of the broader public.

An examination of the voting behavior of Congress reveals that clusters of members are found supporting various types of issues. Time, also, is a factor, and the period before elections, for instance, may have a considerable impact on voting propensities and alignments. In the voting process, combinations of members are found to develop for one issue and then disperse, realigning themselves in a somewhat different pattern on other issues. Some members belong to groups which cluster together on many issues; and some issues result in alliances from dispersive groups. An analysis of voting forms an ever-changing mosaic of groups and individuals, with similar patterns forming and reforming on the various categories of issues.

The pattern of party voting is readily identifiable, and one can say that, while there is an element of partisanship in every vote, the significance of the element varies. Some issues divide the membership along strictly party lines; other issues have less partisan appeal. Some members tend to vote with what might be called the party position. Others tend to vote with the winning side, or the losing side, regardless of party. In addition, one can find many types of alignments on various issues: the States' right Southerners, and, on some issues, all Southerners; liberals; urban representatives; city organizations; and regional representatives.

The making of a legislative decision frequently has a therapeutic effect on the membership. After the controversy and the tension, the decision is made, and members can then relax, reassess their strength, and redetermine their political bearings. It may not always be easy to accept a decision as final, but this must be done inasmuch as the usefulness of a member and of Congress too depends on the continued integrity of the legislature as an institution which can make binding decisions.

In making a decision, it is often necessary to mollify the constituents, for their confidence in the member, or even in the legislature itself, may be shaken if it appears that a decision has let the group down. In making a compromise, the legislator may be compelled to accept less than his supporters would have liked or he himself would have preferred, and such a compromise may result in charges that the legislator has given in, or sold out, or been a traitor to his cause or his class. One may note, for instance, the reaction of John Greenleaf Whittier, who believed that Senator Daniel Webster had compromised his principles in supporting the Fugitive Slave Law. In the poem, "Ichabod," Whittier expressed his anger at Senator Webster's position, saying in the last stanza:

> All else is gone; from those great eyes the soul has fled;
> When faith is lost, when honor dies, the man is dead!
> Then, pay the reverence of old days to his dead fame;
> Walk backward, with averted gaze, and hide the shame.

In order to secure the acceptance of a legislative decision by the most obdurate members of the community, it may be necessary to provide additionally some sort of enforcement procedure, which may include the use of duress to compel individuals and groups to adjust their behavior in accordance with the new law. However, duress in itself will ordinarily not be considered sufficient inducement to secure the acceptance of a law. Congress will continually wish to justify its decisions by broad appeals to the public, and the insertion of remarks in the *Congressional Record* may be interpreted as fulfilling this function. This is supplemented by various devices for appealing to the public such as weekly columns to the editors of the newspapers; television and radio programs; public speeches, and the like. Moreover, Congress will wish to know how effectively the administration of the law is resolving the conflict, and it will develop methods of being informed. These methods will be discussed in the following chapter on control.

SUMMARY

From the very nature of a legislature, the deliberation tends to be stylized, bound by procedures, and directed toward the end not only of informing but of arriving at some definite conclusions. Within this rather limiting strait jacket of controls, it is necessary to develop whatever intellectual resources can be mustered in examining the content of a proposal. The examination covers many facets, including the way in which the proposed course of action will blend with other given patterns, but in the last analysis it involves a judgment on the part of the members of the desirability of the proposal.

In view of the fact that the attention of the legislature proceeds from topic to topic and is not confined to any one proposal, it follows that the legislature must be continually supplied with a stream of information which will not only acquaint the members with the critical areas where there is conflict but also with objective and dispassionate analyses which will assist their thinking. This presents a challenging demand which is met in part by the operation of committees and committee hearings although, as organized, the opportunities for partisan or specialized preferment may overshadow the quest for carefully evaluated information. The debates on the floor are frequently instructive and penetrating, showing considerable zeal on the part of the members to master difficult material, but the main function of debate may be distorted by competitive claims for the floor, by rambling and even irrelevant discussions, and by the failure to point up more clearly the major issues to be decided.

In casting the vote, it is necessary for Congress to protect itself from overt and disruptive outside interferences, although from the nature of the relationship with external institutions it can be expected that various types of influences will be brought to bear on Congress. The extent to which external influences are permissible is directly related to the need for maintaining the integrity and independence of Congress. The decentralized system of authority within Congress combined with the ease of access to the members provides a voting pattern of great flexibility and diversity. Party voting is pronounced but it by no means commands a uniform response from its members, and one can further detect in the voting behavior in Congress the geographic locus of many of the various issues with which it is confronted.

CHAPTER 7

Control: Direction and Review

A LEGISLATIVE BODY SUCH AS CONGRESS WILL NOT BE content with making policy decisions and letting things rest at that point. It will also wish to make sure that its expectations are fulfilled with some degree of adequacy. Once a particular policy has been put into effect, a cycle of continued interrelationships is established between Congress and the bureaucracy. On its side, Congress is continually giving direction to the bureaucracy as well as reacting to what has been done, and the bureaucracy, in turn, is continually informing (or not informing) Congress of the nature of the action it has taken and the reasons therefor. The circle continues: Directions are given, action is taken, policy is reviewed, new directions modify existing policy.

Some may ask why Congress should attempt to control policy after legislation has been passed, raising the question whether this activity falls within the proper competence of Congress. If the President as head of the Administration is enjoined by the Constitution to see that the laws are faithfully executed, why should he not be permitted to assume full authority at this point? The fact is, of course, that Congress cannot ignore its interest in how policy is actually carried out unless it chooses to abdicate its authority. Giving directions to guide administrative action and reviewing the performance thereof cannot be separated completely; the one is a necessary facet of the other. Whenever Congress passes a law creating, say, an agency, it must perforce do something more than give specific directions on what legal power the agency is to have; it must also indicate the nature of the future obligations owed to Congress and to other institutions. It may state whether the courts are empowered to review the rules made by the agency; whether personnel can be hired at whatever salary the agency wants to pay; whether the agency can have all the money it thinks it needs; and whether it need tell anyone what it has been doing. In other words, Congress cannot avoid the question of establishing controls whenever it authorizes the government to take any kind of action.

Controls are also needed to preserve the integrity of Congress itself. To put the situation in as extreme a manner as possible, if controls were not exercised it might otherwise be possible for Congress to delegate all of its authority to the government, which henceforth would make the effective political decisions. Something like this happened in the Roman Empire, when the Senate and other deliberative assemblies in effect delegated in perpetuity all their authority to the Emperor. Nor does Congress operate in the fashion of a constituent assembly which is dissolved after creating a governmental structure. Rather, as a permanent body, it has a continuing interest in how policy is carried out.

In reviewing policy, Congress has the burden of making sure that legal instructions have been complied with. If the laws are not obeyed, if the bureaucrats pay no more attention to an Act of Congress than to the resolutions of a debating society, it would be clear that Congress was not an effective body able to secure acceptable responses from the agencies it attempted to control. Compliance introduces the perplexing problem of establishing responsibility. A theory of responsible government assumes that those in authority should be held accountable for their actions to some other group or person or standard which they themselves do not control. Accountability may be exercised through such various channels as the restraints found in the Constitution, systems of fiscal accountability, electoral systems, and the obligations assumed by a morally integrated individual whom one can "trust." It follows that those to whom an official is responsible may also need some authority themselves if their controls are to be effective, and they in turn will be responsible to still others for their behavior. The situation in Congress is something like this: Congress gives directions to guide the action of government officials and it may also attempt to influence their action after a law has been passed. It also created procedures by which those in authority can be held accountable not only to Congress but also to other institutions. The chain continues. As individuals, the members of Congress are responsible for their actions —internally to the membership and externally to other groups, including the electorate—and Congress as a corporate body cannot go beyond the constitutional provisions. Lord Acton's aphorism that all power corrupts may be somewhat of an exaggeration, but it would not be far from the mark to say that all power is subject to abuse. Controls, then, are set up to prevent the abuse of authority by providing effective restraints on its use.

Review also assists Congress in making certain that the existing policy is continually adequate. When enacting the legislation initially, Congress supposedly attempted to integrate various purposes and to adjust various ends. However, the fact that a particular agency was created with jurisdiction in a certain area and the ability to regulate certain types of action would not necessarily resolve the conflict permanently or exclude the legislature from having any further interest. The problem may not be solved, with the legislation accomplishing little more than transferring the locus of pressures to the bureaucracy. Or if solved initially, the effectiveness of the solution may be modified with the passage of time, changes in the membership of the legislature and the bureaucracy, and variations in the substantive nature of the conflict. The legal solution might be less satisfactory than was hoped initially, and the course of action now followed may no longer meet the expectations of the members of Congress or of those most closely affected by or interested in the policy. Controls are created in part to assure Congress that policy is adequate and it is for this purpose that attempts are made to regularize the review of policy decisions. If the policy is no longer believed to be adequate, appeals will be made for Congress to inject its influence at some point. There is no disagreement on the proposition that Congress, and only Congress, has the authority to enact new legislation when the old modus vivendi is no longer satisfactory, but there is less agreement on the extent to which Congress may intervene in administrative matters when there is need only for adjustments which do not require the reconsideration of the policy in its entirety.

Review is also necessary in order to maintain the continued support of policy on the part of Congress and the public. At the minimum, some public knowledge of what is being done is required in order to avoid suspicion and to establish confidence, and if the action requires the expenditure of funds, demands will be made for a periodic review. The whole process of elections and lawmaking is posited on the belief that the government requires the support of the public and that through such processes the direction and purposes of the government can be controlled. An absurd situation would develop if the control of elected representatives over governmental agencies were to be broken just at the point where it would be effective. Congressional interest in any particular policy continues after the passage of legislation, and it extends—often in an ill-defined and irregular fashion—to the execution of all laws. Any Congressman ignores at his own peril the manner in which the government is administered, or who administers it, or the costs involved, for there is, in fact, a close interrelationship between the manner in which the government operates (especially in certain sensitive, politically volatile areas) and the election of members to office.

When the question is raised of the type of control over policy which Congress can best exercise, one encounters a deficiency in theory, which is reflected in practice in considerable unevenness in the nature of the directions given and the type of accountability expected. The theory of congressional controls is not sufficiently explicit to be a completely useful guide for congressional action. The essential problem is perhaps first that of determining the purposes of controls, of deciding what kind of controls might best accomplish specific ends. If there were agreement on the nature of what might be called a model government agency, on the location and use of authority, and on the nature of the accountability owed to Congress, many of the subsidiary problems of control would resolve themselves by falling within the rubric of this larger framework.

Without a guiding theory, control may easily get out of hand; some aspects of governmental action may be neglected and others will confront Congress with more detailed information than it requires. It is obviously physically impossible for all members of Congress to watch over all acts of government all of the time, but short of this point of supersaturation Congress may nevertheless be inundated with issues of varying degrees of pettiness. But where to draw the line? What of greater importance should be included and what of lesser importance should be excluded? A combination of detailed directions and strict accountability would, if wisely used, contribute to the strength and stature of Congress, while a combination of broad grants and indifferent accountability would soon lead to the withering away of effective legislative control. Congress actually follows a variety of practices, some adequate, some quite inadequate, for in these matters Congress is often the heir of its history when, in times past, strict controls were established or loose controls permitted.

One may note several possible positions that Congress may take in establishing controls. Legislative directions may be precise, clear, and unambiguous, or, conversely, they may authorize action under some ambiguous standard such as "the public interest." The accountability prescribed may be strict, continuous, rigorous, and effective, or it may be so vague that Congress forfeits any opportunities for exercising further control over policy once legislation has been passed. Various combinations of direction and review are, in fact, utilized. The traditional method of authorizing legal action through detailed specific directions may give way to broad grants of authority when Congress is confronted with the crisis of a war or when, in a new policy, the standards of action have not yet been clarified. So, too, with review. New agencies, or those which have exhibited some unsettling form of behavior, may be kept on a short leash, and if established procedures for review appear inadequate, it is ordinarily possible to create an investigating committee.

STRUCTURAL LIMITATIONS ON CONGRESSIONAL CONTROL

In establishing controls over the government, Congress is confronted with the doctrine of the Separation of Powers under which the President is directed to "take care that the laws be faithfully executed." If Congress is also to exercise controls, one may assume that officials may be held accountable to more than one institution. Is this possible, or if possible, desirable? It is surely possible, for responsibility is many-sided and is by no means restricted to a monolithic chain-of-command type of structure. Any federal official is accountable in varying ways to the President, Congress, the courts, the General Accounting Office, and other groups both in and out of government. The constitutional structure makes officials responsible both to the President and to Congress, but the nature of the responsibility differs. The question, then, is not whether such a system is possible (for it is possible); it is not whether such a system is desirable (for it exists, will continue, and has great strengths); the question, rather, is how the required legal and political standards of official performance can best be met through this duality of controls. The fact that there may be disagreement between Congress and the President as to whether these standards have in fact been met is in itself no argument against the system, for a theory of responsibility presumes that there may be disagreement on the adequacy of certain types of action. If one were absolutely certain, as an item of knowledge requiring no further information, no review, and no controls, that all officials behave correctly on all occasions, that all standards are met without question or doubt, there would be no need to develop systems for holding officials accountable (and we would be living in a totalitarian thought-controlled society). This assumption is not tenable, however. Systems of accountability are created in order that other institutions with an interest in the action taken may learn what was done and why it was done, and in addition have some opportunity for adjusting conflicting standards. What is done, essentially, is to abstract certain phases of action —for example, those relating to personnel or finance or purchases or law or general policy direction—and provide for review and control over those aspects of the system by external specialized groups.

In general, those addicted to the administrative point of view would like to limit the function of Congress to formulating objectives broadly, giving the administrators considerable leeway in finding the means to reach those objectives. They would also maintain that the responsibility of the administrators is primarily (if not solely) to the President. The theory of presidential supremacy may at times be pushed to extremes, as when its advocates would expand the prerogatives of the President and create a mythology of his omniscience. It is found in claims that personnel appointments and dismissals are beyond the competence of Congress, that the President alone should have authority in foreign affairs, that administrative decisions should not be reviewed by the courts or by Congress, and that the internal organization of departments is not properly the concern of Congress.

Those who are more alert to bureaucratic shortcomings would increase the scope of legislative supervision. This view, also, can be pushed too far, and perhaps many of those who advocate certain kinds of control are not aware of the type of legislative structure which would be required to accomplish their ends. Proposals to place such presidential staff agencies as the Bureau of the Budget under the control of Congress fall in this category. The assumption seems to be made in some congressional hearings that the existing administrative structure need not be considered in establishing accountability and that each individual bureaucrat is directly responsible to Congress in the first instance. Moreover, some Congressmen in positions of influence are not reluctant to make direct suggestions to bureaucrats on matters of policy or personnel. The failure of Congress to do everything it sometimes tries to do or some people expect it to do adds to the sense of frustration which many Congressmen feel.

Although Congress and the President are autonomous, they are nevertheless part of the same broader system of providing orderly government, with neither one able to exist independently of the other. Their relationship might be better understood if described in terms of a process which performs certain functions than in terms of the rivalry which exists between competitive institutions. Both Congress and the President must perforce be interested in resolving social conflict, in integrating purposes and ends, and in securing public support. Once an Act is passed, Congress does not somehow lose all interest in the policy. Rather, it becomes the vehicle for proposing new combinations of adjustments or revealing new discontents, and, if it is believed necessary, it can reconsider the policy by enacting new legislation. Before things reach that extreme, Congress will be interested in applying less drastic controls where directions can be given, integration achieved, and support indicated. Congress—if it is to remain a Congress—surely does not turn over to the President the full authority for resolving conflicts, raising funds, selecting personnel, and maintaining the political support necessary for carrying out policy. This continuing interest in how government is carried out makes it likewise necessary for Congress to establish continuing relationships between itself and the bureaucracy.

These relationships must be established within the limitations implicit in the separation of powers. This, in itself, would be enough to prevent Congress, or a representative group thereof, from administering the government directly. On the other hand, the whole theory of constitutional government would be subverted if the doctrine were permitted to develop that the President has prerogatives that enable him to act independently, on his own right, without a legal base developed from the consent of Congress. It might be well if the distinction between policy based on the law and that based on some vaguely stated, incompletely defined prerogative of the President were reconsidered. In all important cases of policy development, it seems to me that the President should attempt to take

Congress along with him. This is desirable not only because all policy is very much interrelated but also because of the function of resolving conflict and providing support which Congress can perform so well. The development of policy through discussion, with opportunity given at many points for the injection of thoughtful analysis, may indeed be preferable to relying on the happenstance structure of authority and influence surrounding the President. If the theory is not modified that, in many areas of policy, the President alone is competent to speak, if the President's prerogatives are permitted to grow, we shall surely have a government based less on law than on the machinations of those who gain access to the President or who speak in his name. It may, of course, be inconvenient for Congress to debate all pertinent subjects or to formulate all significant policy, but the presumption should prevail that Congress should have an opportunity to do so, not that it is an interloper if it attempts it. In point of fact, everyday policy must be carried out at all levels of government, but the possibility of reviewing this policy by Congress should always be present and encouraged. The President cannot—or should not—go beyond the law, and the law can determine the nature of the standards to which government agencies are expected to comply and the nature of the accountability which government agencies owe to Congress. In other words, the controls by Congress over the government can be established through devices which fall within the constitutional framework, the doctrine of the separation of powers, and the autonomous position of the President. What is needed is not so much the will or the desire to establish controls but the development of a useful theory in which the purposes, values, methods, and limitations of control will be clearly understood.

In establishing controls over policy, that is, in giving directions and establishing procedures for review, a two-way set of communications must be developed between Congress and the bureaucracy. The bureaucracy would in the natural course of events be apprised of directions given in the form of law, but it must also be alert to additional signals of expectations or dissatisfactions given in the form, say, of resolutions or debates or legislative riders. It needs to interpret the meaning of such signals and, after interpretation, to decide whether existing policy should be modified.

On its side, Congress is also interested in the communications received relating to performance of the bureaucracy. However, there is some uncertainty concerning the nature of the communications which would be of most assistance to Congress in establishing satisfactory controls. What information, from whom, is required? Who is to give the information? Who is to receive it? Some types of communications between the executive branch and Congress are regularized, such as the provisions for annual reports, the budget message, and information on the State of the Union. Some types are not, and where communications are not regularized, information may be requested in the hearings, in debate, by mail, or even over the telephone. If the request is not complied with, Congress may use extraordinary measures to compel performance, even to the extent of subpoenaing witnesses to testify or requiring the production of papers. In addition to the communications received from the bureaucracy, Congress will of course receive information on the operation of the bureaucracy from nonofficial sources.

The question might well be raised whether effective congressional review is possible so long as partisans control the organization of Congress. Might not the majority party, identifying itself with the Administration, refuse to hold hearings or to create investigations or to permit relevant questions to be discussed? Although it is true that the minority may not always be able to go as far as it might wish to go, for example, in creating investigating committees, it is by no means excluded from participating in the review of government action. In addition, the partisan member of the majority party himself has some interest in having controversial material resolved (even unfavorably), rather than having to defend incidents cloaked with innuendo and suspicion. During the Second World War, for instance, there were repeated demands on the part of a congressional minority for an investigation of the military disaster at Pearl Harbor. At the close of the war, when an investigation was feasible from the point of view of military security, the investigative proposal was sponsored by members of the majority and approved unanimously in both Houses. It was to the advantage of both parties to have the facts on the record and clear away any suspicions. In congressional hearings, members of whatever party may play the role of conscientious questioners, and even strong partisans may wish to be personally convinced before giving a proposal their support. There is no long-time advantage to any partisan in committing himself blindly or in permitting mischief in his own party to go undetected. To some, it may appear anomalous that, on some internal issues, partisans struggle for supremacy while, on other issues, perhaps relating to the behavior of the government, Congress stands as one. The fact is, however, that Congress itself has interests (with which all members identify) which may transcend other interests, including those of party. The autonomous position of Congress as a body capable of making independent decisions is respected and preserved.

The most important techniques of control utilized by Congress relate to law, to administrative structure, to finances, and to personnel supervision, in addition to controls exercised through reporting, debates, and, in some cases, accountability extended to other groups. Methods for controlling policy in the fields of foreign and military policy are perhaps less well developed than for other fields, and congressional control may be weak where policy cannot be quantified in terms of monetary units or closely prescribed in terms of law. There is not always a clear-cut answer to the question of the nature of accountability owed to Congress, for in reviewing government action Congress may act less in its corporate capacity and more as an aggregate of groups and individuals. Indeed, in reviewing policy Congress tends to splinter its action and to multiply its interests.

LAW AND TREATIES

Law is perhaps the most important technique in the arsenal of controls used by Congress in regulating the actions of the government. The all-embracing premises of this type of control are that officials acting in the name of the government must do so within terms and conditions prescribed by law, that no illegal action may be taken, and that the officials who take the action are legally competent to do so. An official who goes beyond the bounds of his competence is still under the law and may be held accountable to the courts for his illegal actions.

The significance of law as a method for providing standards for action and controls over action cannot easily be exaggerated, and even without other forms of control the restraints and constraints imposed in the law go a considerable distance toward establishing responsible government. The catch phrase that our government is one of law and not of men has real meaning; it does not exclude the significance of men in operating the government, but it does mean that the authority exercised by men rests on law and is not the capricious, arbitrary, or willful invention of men operating outside the law.

This broad theory of government of law is still maintained in principle, although its utility in supplying standards has some limitations in those areas where policy cannot be closely defined by legislation. In such cases, the Administration may have considerable latitude of choice, with Congress relying on other techniques to establish accountability. Another difficulty of relying only on the law as a method of control is that, with the broad delegation of authority to government agencies, there may be a good deal of discretion as to what law means. Modern administrative law is often more complex than a general rule, applicable to all, which legitimates some ancient custom. It may be less concerned with specific legal restrictions than with developing a pattern of ordered relationships which will permit groups having conflicting interests to work together harmoniously. In enacting complex legislation of this type, Congress is, in effect, transferring the locus of conflict to some administrative agency, under whose aegis disputes between groups are resolved.

Legal standards for controlling administrative action may, therefore, be vague because Congress cannot anticipate what type of action might be required in the future or because no single rule would fit the multiple number of cases coming under the law. In such instances the law may contain some vague standard such as the "public interest" to give legal sanction to administrative action, but the content of this standard will be developed gradually through cases, regulations, and carefully devised procedures. When Congress began to regulate railroads, it believed that it was not itself able to determine the components of a "fair rate" for all types of tariffs, and discretionary authority was delegated to the Interstate Commerce Commission. Or again, the Secretary of Agriculture has authority to prevent the "disorderly marketing" of sugar, the Federal Communications Commission to grant broadcasting licenses "if public convenience, interest, or necessity will be served thereby," and the ICC to regulate terminal facilities, if found "to be in the public interest and to be practicable." Neutrality legislation was to go into effect if the President found "that there exists a state of war between foreign states." [1]

In order to maintain the supremacy of law in controlling administrative action, it would seem advisable for Congress to review periodically the use made of broad grants of authority and, to the extent feasible, rewrite these legal standards with the increased precision which experience should provide. Of course, a type of supervision is exercised inferentially in that groups which are dissatisfied with administrative decisions will appeal to Congress for assistance. They will want Congress to investigate some administrative inadequacy, to amend the law, or to remove personnel in charge of some controversial program. However, it would seem desirable to place policy on as firm a legal basis as possible, so that important policy would be less infrequently subjected to change by pressures, influences, and inconsidered interference from outside sources.

In some areas of policy, it is difficult for Congress to lay down standards of any sort. The recognition of foreign governments now seems to be the prerogative of the President (although at an earlier date Congress authorized the extension of recognition through a

[1] 7 USC 1115; 47 USC 307; 49 USC 3; 22 USC 441.

joint resolution). Congress exercises little control over troop and ship movements, although troop mobilizations and naval demonstrations may affect foreign policy. Foreign loans may be a significant part of our foreign policy, but it is not usual to control them in any detail by law, and of course Congress exercised only the most general type of control over our postwar policy toward, as examples, West Germany and Austria. It is not here argued that in these areas Congress should attempt to define policy by law, but rather that it is difficult or impossible to do so. This barrier to establishing legal controls, however, does not lessen (and it does not necessarily satisfy) the concern of Congress in such policy.

If for some reason policy cannot readily be encompassed in the form of law, Congress may indicate its attitude by enacting a resolution containing various suggestions as to what might be done. The status of such resolutions is inconclusive in the realm of policy making, for they fall midway between the sanctity of law which must be obeyed and the inspiration of a debate which may be ignored at will. A resolution expressing what is known as the "formal opinion" of each House, or of both collectively, may provide a political if not a legal justification for the Administration in taking a certain course of action. In 1943, for instance, the resolutions passed by Congress advocating the creation of some type of postwar international organization tended to provide some political support for the State Department as it proceeded with its plans for creating the United Nations. To cite another example, the passage by the Senate in 1948 of the so-called Vandenberg resolution, advocating that the government proceed to create "regional and other collective agreements" led to the creation of the North Atlantic Treaty Organization. Other examples of resolutions introduced (but not necessarily passed) encompass such diverse proposals as encouraging "a peaceful, prosperous, and United Ireland," clarifying responsibility for acts of aggression, assisting India by sending food, opposing the seating of Red China in the Security Council, and invoking the President's "national emergency powers" in a coal strike.

Once a law has been passed, does Congress have any further

control over its contents, short of offering amendment or repealing the legislation in its entirety? It does in some cases through the terminal provisions or the review of orders made under the authority of the legislation. The law may expire within one year, two years, three years—some convenient date which will enable Congress to reconsider the controversial policy at relatively short intervals. Such a device may be used when Congress enters reluctantly into a new area of policy and where precedents are not sufficient to provide Congress with the confidence it might wish for enacting permanent legislation.

A more drastic form of control gives Congress alone the power to terminate an Act by a simple majority, with the approval of the President not being required. This innovation developed during recent periods of emergencies, depressions, and wars as a technique for making certain that legislation would, indeed, be temporary. An example of the use of terminal provisions is found in the Selective Service Act of 1945 which provided that the legislation could be terminated at the earliest of four dates. They included (1) a specific time for the Act to terminate, whatever the circumstances; (2) the date on which the President determined hostilities had ended; (3) the date on which Congress determined hostilities had ended; (4) the date on which Congress terminated the law by passing a concurrent resolution.[2] The opportunity for testing the constitutionality of such repeal provisions has not yet arisen, inasmuch as Congress has not yet exercised its option of repealing a law in such a fashion.

In a few instances, Congress exercises further control by reviewing administrative orders before they become operative. These instances relate primarily to government organization, the present procedure permitting Congress to approve or disapprove the proposed order before it goes into effect. Here is an area where Congress might well expand its control by reviewing additional categories of orders made under the authority of delegated power. The review would attempt to make certain that the agencies concerned had made defensible decisions, that all pertinent evidence was considered, that

[2] 59 Stat. 166, May 9, 1945.

special groups were not favored, and that substantial justice was achieved. More than this, the review of orders by Congress would assist in integrating the decision with other aspects of society; the decision would be more binding and perhaps less capricious or arbitrary. The increased opportunity for congressional review would not necessarily increase the opportunities for special interest groups to be effective, but it would provide a public forum in which the various interest groups could be identified and their position explained and defended.

The fact that authority is based on law gives the courts some control over the actions of the government. The courts may be called on to determine whether the action complained of was authorized by law, whether it was within the constitutional prescriptions, and whether administrative procedures have met the requirements of due process. In general, Congress has been willing to grant the courts the right to review administrative action. This is explainable in part because of the legal background of many legislators, but also because Congress has not itself developed satisfactory methods for reviewing governmental action. As interpreters of the law and of the Constitution, the courts provide a kind of control over the bureaucracy which is not otherwise provided by legal stipulations or by the political surveillance of Congress.

In times past, the Senate's participation in the treaty-making process has been considered one of the most effective controls exercised by Congress over foreign policy. The constitutional provision requiring the advice and consent of the Senate in making treaties has placed the Senate in a strategic position for influencing some types of policies. It is obvious, of course, that treaties encompass a limited number of subjects in foreign policy, a fact which has meant that the Senate, after feeling ignored or kept at arm's length on some issues, is suddenly brought into the thick of the fight when there is a treaty to discuss. The exercise by the Senate of its authority over treaties has occasionally been contentious, in part because of the partisanship and subsequent frustration engendered by the requirement of a two-thirds majority for affirmative action. The partisan spirit may be greatly stimulated if one party must resort to sheep stealing in order to mobilize the extraordinary majority. In the late nineteenth century, the close division between parties, which was reflected in Senate voting on treaties, caused Secretary of State John Hay to predict that the Senate would never again approve a major treaty. His prophecy was not fulfilled, although the treaty with Spain settling the war over Cuba was passed with but two votes to spare, and the Treaty of Versailles (which also contained the Covenant of the League of Nations) was twice defeated.

The dissatisfaction with the Senate's role in the treaty-making process has produced many proposals for reform. Some would give the President greater authority in foreign policy by augmenting his position as Chief of State and Commander-in-Chief, increasing the use of Executive Agreements which do not require legislative approval, and even permitting him to "pack" the Senate with men who would support his policy. A second group would decrease the control of the Senate by making foreign policy the province of both Houses, with treaties subject to the approval of a simple majority of both chambers. A third group, which supports such proposals as the Bricker Amendment, would restrict both the authority of the President and the scope of treaties by increasing the procedural difficulties of making foreign commitments.

On other than treaty matters, the organization of Congress for making foreign policy and military policy differs little from that employed in making domestic policy. Although it may be argued that congressional procedures were not designed for diplomatic or military debate, it is nevertheless true that Congress has considerable authority over some aspects of foreign and military policy. Not only must the Senate give its advice and consent to treaties and nominations, but Congress as a whole can enact laws embracing foreign and military policy, create administrative structures, and establish personnel recruitment practices. Some areas in foreign and military policy are not reached by legislation, but there many areas indeed where the law makes or influences foreign policy. The extensive concern of Congress with foreign and military policy is due partly to the fact that an increasingly large number of foreign activities are carried on by government agencies which require legal authorization and fiscal support, both of which come within the legal province of Congress.

The general lack of firm and full control over foreign policy has fostered the development of certain attitudes widely shared in Congress. Perhaps the most pervasive of these attitudes is the mistrust of the President in foreign affairs, an attitude which extends as far back in our history as the administration of President Washington. When the argument that the President has an independent position in carrying on foreign policy is combined with assertions that foreign and domestic policy are indistinguishably intertwined, the President emerges as a very powerful figure capable of dwarfing the significance of Congress on all fronts.

There is often a feeling of apprehension in Congress that the President, by acting alone, may adversely affect the autonomous position of Congress or even of the United States. Commitments might be made which Congress must accept although it had no part in their making. The fear that the President might act independently in foreign affairs has some basis in fact. The device of the Executive Agreement has been developed, and although some of these agreements are clearly based on law enacted by Congress, others seem to be based on something less specific, such as the "inherent power" of the President. In fact, of course, the President may have some choice in determining whether an agreement should be in the form of a treaty or in some other form where the unpredictability of the Senate would not be a factor to be considered.

The possibility that the President might act on his own, without consulting Congress, has provided the theme for many congressional debates on foreign policy, and it entered into the lengthy debates over neutrality legislation in the 1930's. In that legislation Congress attempted to limit the discretionary authority of the President to declare embargoes and to protect American vessels sailing in belligerent waters. Without such restrictions, the neutralitarians felt, the President would make decisions which would "drag us into war." During the Second World War, Congress was uneasy and disturbed by the specter of the President making postwar commitments without its consent. It was feared by some in Congress that the President would act on his own initiative in dictating the terms of the peace settlement, redrawing the boundaries of Europe, committing the United States to membership in some international organization, and removing restrictions on imports and immigration. In the several debates on lend-lease legislation, Congress attempted to find some formula for restricting the power of the President to make postwar settlements.

The proposal of the State Department in 1943 to establish American membership in the United Nations Relief and Rehabilitation Administration (UNRRA) through an Executive Agreement seemed to many Congressmen a confirmation of their fears. After the war, anxiety was expressed over wartime agreements which had been made by the President alone, such as those at Yalta and at Potsdam. The various accumulated fears that foreign policy could be made without congressional approval found an expression in the Bricker Amendment to restrict the treaty-making power, which came within two votes of receiving the approval of two-thirds of the Senate in 1954.

THE STRUCTURE OF THE BUREAUCRACY

Controls are also exercised by Congress over the bureaucratic structure of the agencies that administer the law. It is customary for Congress to give direction on the nature of the organization of the agency as well as on the agency's legal authority, its relationship with other governmental units, and its responsibilities to Congress. In creating administrative structures, Congress has not always provided uniform procedures for exercising accountability, and the actual legal relationship between the agency, the President, and Congress may vary considerably. One may contrast, for instance, the respective legal position of the Director of the Bureau of the Budget with that of the Secretary of the Treasury. The former, appointed by the President alone, without the advice or consent of the Senate, is directed by law to prepare the budget "under such rules and regulations as the President may prescribe." The latter, appointed by the President with the advice and consent of the Senate, is directed to "give information to either branch of the legislature in person or in writing, as may be required, respecting all matters referred to him by the Senate or House of Representatives." The General Accounting Office is even more removed from presidential supervision, the law describing it as being "independent of the executive departments." During periods of emergency, Congress has permitted the President to create new agencies and abolish functions of old agencies, only to reverse its policy during more tranquil periods by insisting that all agencies be created directly by law and restricting the President's authority to reorganize the bureaucracy. In delegating authority, Congress may permit agencies in which confidence has been established to have considerable discretion, but it will be stricter with newer, more controversial agencies.

Congress also has an interest in the adequacy of the administrative structure for carrying out policy—its internal coherence, its personnel, and its relationship with other units and with the public. It will wish to know whether the administrative structure is adjusted, internally and externally, so that it can fulfill its function, and in the event of some internal dispute, Congress may exercise temporary but strict supervision while new lines of internal authority are being established. If the agency is plagued by conflict with other agencies, where there is lack of coördination or duplication of effort, Congress may attempt to make whatever adjustments seem to be required.

The enabling legislation will ordinarily contain more directions than the administrative pattern to be followed and the functions of the various units thereof. Provisions will also be made for internal fiscal controls, including the review of the monetary requirements by the Bureau of the Budget and of expenditures by the General Accounting Office. The recruitment of personnel will ordinarily be undertaken by the Civil Service Commission, although other recruitment systems are also used, including for some positions presidential appointment with the advice and consent of the Senate.

Specific provisions for reporting to Congress on the part of government agencies may be found in the basic legislation. These requirements may go beyond the traditional annual report—frequently a valuable repository of information—and extend to particular types of action on which information must be given. The Mutual Security Act of 1951, for instance, directed the President to notify four congressional committees when countries not parties to the North Atlantic Treaty were to receive military aid; it also directed him to notify the same committees concerning certain transfers of appropriations. To take another example, the Selective Service Act of 1943 instructed the Director of the Selective Service System to report information on deferment "to the Senate and House Committee on Military Affairs monthly or at such intervals as the committee may designate from time to time."

In the actual execution of the law, Congress may develop direct and continuous relations with the bureaucracy, for the latter must work out policy in such a fashion that a pattern of ordered action emerges which will "work." Legal penalties may make it advisable for people to obey the law, but in addition it is expected that the law will blend into the situation as given and create the least disturbance in the existing arrangement of affairs. Congress may act as an informant, as a link in the chain of communications between those affected by government action and the governing agent itself, and it may itself have additional comments on how effectively it thinks the policy is being developed.

It was said previously that Congress has never determined completely the nature of the continuing control which it should exercise over the bureaucracy or the manner in which the bureaucracy should be held accountable. Congress has not decided, for instance, whether it should develop policy through debate and legislation, providing a clear line of action for the bureaucracy to follow and establishing clear channels of responsibility, or whether it should follow an alternative course of proffering suggestions at various levels of the bureaucratic hierarchy, although often permitting major policy decisions to be made by default and without congressional direction. Congress cannot do everything. If it enters the field of active and extensive review, it soon becomes so waterlogged with detail that it has little time left for giving generalized directions and establishing goals. In creating administrative structures, the goal for Congress should be the development of agencies with built-in and self-correcting systems of account-ability in which the lines of authority are clear. It should make certain that the organization as a whole is able to operate smoothly, that it will follow legal directions, and that it is accountable for its actions in a manifold variety of ways. Investigations, hearings, and the like may be necessary when there is unsatisfactory performance of func-tion, or a lack of understanding, or a failure to fulfill expectations, but the end of these controls in the reëstablishment of an equilibrium within the bureaucracy so that responsible action will result without excessive external supervision. The effectiveness of control bears no special relationship to the amount of time spent in examining details of policy.

CONSULTATIONS, HEARINGS, AND INVESTIGATIONS

If Congress thinks that the directions contained in a law are in-sufficient as a guide for policy, it may insist on being consulted further before official action is taken, and it has provided for consultations on policies relating, for instance, to the conduct of war and of foreign affairs, the negotiations of treaties, and even the disposal of surplus government property to private individuals. Although formal repre-sentation is not given to Congress when administrative decisions are made, informal conversations may be conducted in an attempt to keep Congress informed and to secure a kind of extralegal approval. The question of who in Congress is to be consulted may raise again the question of the allocation of congressional authority inasmuch as the organization of Congress is designed for securing agreement, not for delegating authority to individuals or groups who can speak for the total body. The committee chairmen are frequently consulted, per-haps even the minority leaders as well, and occasionally the entire committee. Such consultations may be used for developing an in-formed following in Congress, as was the case during the Second World War when the State Department included congressional leaders in the confidential deliberations which led to the creation of the United Nations organization. The record is less clear on the degree to which members of Congress are consulted on other types of foreign and military policy, and Congress has no representation, for instance, on the National Security Council, which attempts to coördinate policy commitments.

In carrying on foreign policy, government administrators must face the problem of how much to tell Congress and how far to go in soliciting advice. The Constitution requires the President to secure the advice and consent of the Senate so far as treaties are concerned, but in other areas, where neither the law nor the Constitution is specific, the administrators may themselves determine the extent to which they think Congress should be consulted. In fulfilling the treaty requirements, a prolonged debate has centered around the question of whether advice may precede the consent or whether advice and consent are given at the same time. On the legal side, there is little doubt that the constitutional requirements are met by a single procedural action. However, the requirement of advice may be considered to have some substantive meaning beyond the legal requirement that a vote be taken, and in many cases it may be politically desirable, as opposed to being legally necessary, to consult the Senate in advance—and the House as well.

Information on administrative activities given in congressional hearings may be supplemented by letters, telephone calls, and informal conversations. Committees may develop confidential and unwritten understandings with departments on how specific policy is to be carried out, what additional consultations with the committee are expected, and the nature of the decisions that will be made. Such close supervision may bring congressional committees very close to the actual administration of law. However, the organization of the committees is not designed for administering a program of any complexity. The participation by committees in administrative decisions is essentially selective and not extensive, and it is limited by the interest of the members and the available time of the committees.

The mandate of the standing committees to review the operations of the departments is included in the Reorganization Act of 1946, the pertinent provision thereof directing the committees to exercise "continuous watchfulness of the execution by the administrative agencies of any laws, the subject matter of which is within the jurisdiction of such committee." The implementation of the phrase "continuous watchfulness" ranges from relative indifference to periodic consultations on policy. How "watchful" must the committees be? Are they to comment and suggest, or merely to observe and appraise? When a new policy is being developed, such as the control of atomic energy, or when a contentious policy is being administered, the committees may demand a periodic review of policy, with frequent consultations. Professors Dahl and Brown have written that the Atomic Energy Commission reports every policy decision to the Joint Committee on Atomic Energy. Whereas in most cases decisions are reported after they have been taken, "it also appears that many important policy questions are carefully explored with the Joint Committee *before* a decision is made, and in some casees the initiative may come from the committee." [3] This intensive type of supervision may be desirable in developing such a product as atomic energy, where legislative and administrative experience is sparse and where the ordinary types of public control are absent, but it is a type of supervision which calls for more time and study than most committees are prepared to spend.

Review may also include the informal appeal of administrative decision to members of Congress or to congressional committees. If, as an instance, a government department makes an unpopular decision, an informal appeal may be taken to Congress by the group affected adversely, or even surreptitiously by an employee in the department who questions the wisdom of the decision. Congressional authority is so fluid, with so many channels of access available, that it is a relatively simple matter to call such cases to the attention of some sympathetic member of Congress.

The most spectacular method of congressional review is the investigating committee, the requirements for which are an intrepid sponsor, at least a rumor of dissatisfaction, adequate financing, the authority to subpoena witnesses and papers, proper publicity, and a diligent staff. Government agencies may be investigated for a variety of mo-

[3] Robert A. Dahl and Ralph S. Brown, Jr., *Domestic Control of Atomic Energy,* 1951, p. 14.

tives and purposes; the finding may reveal certain administration inadequacies or they may reveal nothing more than a political grudge on the part of the investigators. Investigators may even be called on to adjust policy disputes between government agencies, as the Truman Committee did on several occasions when it found war agencies quarreling publicly over the priority of various programs. Investigating committees have certain limitations as reviewers of policy, even though they succeeed in uncovering administrative shortcomings. Their most pronounced weakness is that they operate after the fact, that whereas they may expose they do not necessarily prevent. Moreover, the investigations may be conducted to prove a point, not to supply facts objectively, and in all they may be considered to be a substitute for a more effective continuous type of control exercised currently.

DEBATE

The consideration of government policy in congressional debate may be an indication to the departments that all is not well and that, if nothing is done, discontent may spread. All departments are alert to congressional criticism, and the *Congressional Record* is culled regularly for pertinent comments on their behavior. The effectiveness of congressional debate as a form of review is perhaps more limited than it need be. The department concerned cannot make an immediate reply, the allegation is left suspended in air, as it were, and the debate is one-sided and inconclusive. Although some partisan supporter of the Administration may attempt to make an explanation, he may not have the required facts on hand and his answer will be clothed in partisan rhetoric. For some years Senator Estes Kefauver (D., Tenn.) has attempted to persuade his colleagues to establish a question period, where members of Congress could ask questions directly on the floor of the House or the Senate, but the proposal has not been received with any enthusiasm.

Debate may also be used to control foreign policy, although a general debate, unfocused on a particular subject, is likely to ramble on inconclusively, with no agreement reached. Some risks are involved in debating foreign policy, for the debate may have repercussions more extensive than intended. Foreign nations—as well as domestic government agencies—must attempt to interpret the meaning of congressional debate. The fear of congressional indiscretions may also tend to enforce the cautiousness of officials in revealing information to Congress, so that, in its great desire to learn more, Congress might actually learn less.

Public debate of government policy raises acutely the subject of secrecy, for there are categories of facts whose incautious revelation might jeopardize the usefulness of some types of policy and be helpful to a potential enemy. However, in an attempt to make its control effective, Congress may wish to have access to facts which cannot be revealed. It is the irony of secrecy that it tends to feed on itself; nations which rely heavily on secrecy to protect their autonomous position may force other nations also to sever the lines of free communication and broaden the categories of proscribed information. Here is the dilemma. The legislature relies on the free flow of information in making and reviewing policy, yet some types of policy cannot be reviewed publicly without jeopardizing their success.

In the present state of interrelationships between countries, some aspects of policy cannot be debated in public (such as, for example, the location of storage depots for H-bombs). However, even in this hypothetical case, some telltale clew might slip out inadvertently through reference to an appropriation item for the maintenance of such a depot, or the establishment of a special base to protect the bombs, or the existence of a peculiar table of organization for military personnel, or the assignment to certain areas of military personnel with special qualifications. It might be possible under some conditions to develop legislative practices for secret debate of policy, but the trend and the ideology are in the other direction. Public access to legislative or constitutional sessions has not always been required, however. The proceedings of the Constitutional Convention of 1787 went unpublished for more than 40 years, the justification being that the interest of the public was properly limited to the decisions reached, not in the accompanying controversy of reaching them. The sessions of the Senate were secret until 1793, at which time the doors were thrown open for the debate on the claims of Albert Gallatin to a seat in the chamber. Treaties are supposedly secret until made public by the Senate, but the open nature of the treaty-making process tends to nullify the force of this requirement. Executive sessions may be held in secret, but they are infrequently used in modern times, and the single attempt of the Senate to hold a secret session during the Second World War merely turned the legislature into a whispering gallery.

Although opposing secrecy as a principle of government or of diplomacy, Congress, in fact, attempts to accommodate its behavior to the existing situation by establishing whatever controls it can over certain areas of secrecy. Departments with secret operations are encouraged to establish close liaison with the appropriate committees, and the committees, in turn, provide the necessary political support for the policy. The armed services have been sedulous in developing confidential relations with congressional committees, and so, too, has the Atomic Energy Commission (it is directed to do so by law). The State Department has had periods in which its confidential relationship with congressional committees has been excellent, but the relationships have not always been happy.

In the summer of 1953, a proposal of Senator Joseph McCarthy (R., Wis.) to investigate the Central Intelligence Agency raised anew the question of the kind of control Congress expected to exercise over this agency. The legislation creating the CIA included special provisions to preserve the confidential character of the agency by exempting it from the ordinary requirements of having to reveal the internal organization of the agency or the names, official titles, salaries, and number of personnel employed. The testimony of requests for funds is not made available to all members of Congress, and the funds are not clearly identified in the appropriation bills. The agency objected to the proposed investigation on the ground that such an inquiry would make public the sources of information, special assignments, and other information not intended for enemy eyes or ears.

As a substitute for the investigation, Senator Mike Mansfield (D., Mont.) proposed that Congress create a joint committee on central intelligence which would make "continuing studies" of the activities of the Central Intelligence Agency and the latter, in turn, would keep the joint committee "fully and currently informed with respect to its activities." [4] In the end, a different course was followed: A joint committee was not created, the McCarthy investigation did not materialize, but investigations were made by groups appointed by and accountable only to the President.

SUMMARY

In controlling the actions of government agencies, it is necessary for Congress to give directions and provide for some type of review. In the ordinary course of affairs, directions are given in the form of law, but the interest of Congress does not stop here. Of course, if laws were obeyed automatically, without imposed sanctions; if they were clear and obvious and did not need to be developed further; if there were no general problem of recruiting personnel for administering the laws and if all personnel had the same competence; and if the laws required no money in order to be effective, the interest of Congress would need to go no further than exacting sound legislation. The fact is, however, that Congress is continually interested in how laws are being administered. It wants to know, specifically, whether there has been adequate compliance with its expectations. In the ordinary expression of the day, these expectations are often stated in terms of "the will of Congress" which, it may be charged, has or has not been followed.

Certain standards of performance are regularly expected (such as fiscal regularity) for which there are well-established systems to determine whether there has been compliance. In some cases, however, standards may be difficult to express clearly, so that conflict may develop between the interpretation or administration of the law by administrators and the expectations of some vocal elements within Congress. The process of integration continues after the passage of legislation, and attempts are continually made to modify policy in accordance with changed demands or conditions. In addition, Con-

[4] *Congressional Record,* July 20, 1953, p. 9185.

gress will wish to know how policy is being developed in order that the required support of the government may be forthcoming. The whole process of government places great reliance on the validity of procedures and the good will of those who exercise authority, and the justification of this reliance requires a continued flow of information indicating that everything is in order. Routine controls may lack the dramatic impact of clashes of judgment on performance but they are surely necessary and become the standard types of control for which the others are a temporary substitute. It follows that areas of secrecy make effective control difficult and that procedures must be developed to create reliance not based on the free flow of information.

In applying specific reviews, Congress often acts less as a corporate body in making decisions and more as a forum where diverse criticism can be expressed. However, if Congress is sufficiently dissatisfied with a particular cause of action it can (on a theoretical level) set things right with the enactment of new legislation.

CHAPTER 8

Controls over Personnel

THE PURPOSE OF CONTROL

THE CONTROL EXERCISED BY CONGRESS OVER PERSON-
nel is a special case of the generalized treatment of controls found in
the last chapter. Congress is confronted with special problems in considering personnel, for it is organized primarily to make general rules,
not to select individuals for official positions, and any rule applicable
to one person alone might run afoul of the prohibition in the Constitution against enacting bills of attainder. Inasmuch as the appointing
power rests in the President (or elsewhere), but surely not in Congress, the control exercised by Congress over personnel is ordinarily
of an indirect variety. Nevertheless, within the limits imposed by the
organization of a legislation and the restrictions of the Constitution,
Congress as a whole may exercise considerable influence over personnel policy, and, in the case of individual members, over specific
types of appointments.

One may properly raise the question of what legitimate interest
Congress has in the personnel who carry out the law. Does not the
legislation itself provide sufficient control, without having Congress
extend the sphere of its concern to the particular personnel who
actually administer the law? It may be true that legislative standards

tend to reduce the opportunities for personal caprice and arbitrary action, but it is also true that the manner in which a law is administered is closely related to the abilities and attitudes of those who administer it.

Within the realm of its legal competence, Congress is responsible for giving general directions for the personnel policy to be followed by the government. It has the authority to prescribe how employees are to be recruited as well as to make provisions for personnel classification, salary scales, and retirement provisions. Important though these functions may be, Congress may not be satisfied with laying down the general rules to be followed. It may also wish to have some influence in selecting key personnel, rather than permit important selections to be made by someone not immediately subject to congressional controls.

Although the general contours of personnel policy can be enunciated in law, certain aspects of such policy, such as standards of competence, subjective preferences, personal rectitude, and devotion to duty fall into categories not readily encompassed within the framework of legal standards. Expectations develop within Congress concerning the kind of behavior which is anticipated and acceptable for the various types of bureaucrats. The hierarchy of the military establishment contains well-established roles for commissioned officers, infractions thereof being punishable under the Ninety-Fifth Article of War—"Any officer or cadet who is convicted of conduct unbecoming an officer and a gentleman shall be dismissed from the service." Similarly, the phrase, "sober as a judge," indicates a stereotype for expected judicial behavior. Definable and anticipated behavior of bureaucrats is less well developed and specific, although, as a negative standard, the bureaucrats are not permitted to behave as partisans and are directed to eschew active partisan participation or blatant partisan identification.

In developing reliable personnel it is not necessary for Congress to rely exclusively on controls imposed by law or even by institutions inasmuch as standards developed elsewhere may also be effective.

One such standard, inherent in the culture, is found in the concept of the responsible individual—the morally integrated person who can be trusted because of the totality of his ideas, beliefs, training, and indoctrination. Many situations exist in government where concrete controls are not practicable or are ineffective because they come into operation too long after the event, and here one relies on the individual himself being responsible, acting as one would hope and expect him to act. Numerous institutions in society support the values of the responsible individual, such as the church, the profession, the family, the lodge, and other types of associations. In addition to all this, values and ideas are held in common by members of the society to which the individual in authority belongs. One assumes that the individual in authority will share widely held attitudes regarding, say, violence as a method of resolving political conflict, cruelty to animals, democratic procedures, and respect for women, without special tests being established to see that these attitudes are in fact held.

Several factors enter the equation when Congress goes beyond the practice of developing standards by attempting itself to select or to influence the selection of personnel. Some might argue that the participation of Congress in the process of personnel selection might help in building a bridge of confidence between the people, the legislature, and the government, as well as in developing administrators better able to knit together the manifold strands of action affected by modern government. On the other hand, there is a possibility that congressional influence, unwisely used, might lower the standards by breaking down the integrity of the system of personnel selection. The factor of competence might be secondary to the relationship between the prospective appointee and the successful political party.

The interest of Congress in selecting personnel may be classified under the general headings of competence, integration, and support. Competence here means the technical ability to meet the requirements of the job. Basic technical qualifications for some types of jobs are fairly obvious, as in the case, for example, of a judge, an admiral, or a chemist, but in other cases it might be difficult to lay down specific requirements. A cabinet appointee, for instance, might not have any special technical experience, but here political qualifications including the ability to secure public support would be considered important. In organizing the British government after the last war, the Labor party named Ernest Bevin as Foreign Secretary, although Bevin's background was considerably removed from international politics. In this country, it is not considered necessary for the Secretary of Defense to have had any special experience with the armed forces—and, indeed, he must not belong professionally to one of the services. And so it goes. In such appointments, other qualifications are considered more important than technical competence, but the lack of technical competence should not be permitted to jeopardize the functioning of the agency involved. On these grounds, one might criticize the propensity of Presidents to select justices of the Supreme Court from sources other than the bench. A few justices with a broad political background might help leaven the loaf, but too many without substantial judicial competence would impair the functioning of the Supreme Court.

The category of integration mentioned above relates to the special traits or qualifications that will assist the appointee in reconciling—or at least in not accentuating—possible conflicting purposes. What is said here is the obvious content of personnel maxims. The appointee should be able to inspire confidence, to work with others, and to possess qualities that will cause him to be judicious, circumspect, and broad-gauged. But for Congress integration has a special meaning—it means the assurance that the appointee is not precluded by previous commitments from fulfilling his function adequately as a result of such things as an obvious conflict of interest between his associations or the sources of his income and the nature of the job.

Integration also means that the appointee must be generally acceptable to those groups and institutions with whom he must work. A Secretary of Defense must not be an obvious partisan of any one of the services—the Army, the Navy, or the Air Force—and a Secretary of Labor must not be identified with the position of any faction within the labor movement. Regional and occupational integration is also important as, specifically, in nominations to the Interstate Commerce Commission and, in general, in Civil Service regulations.

The third category, that of support, relates to the ability of the appointee to contribute to, or at least not to undermine, the confidence in the government held by various organized groups and by the public in general. The first aspect of support relates to the basic political loyalties where one would want to know whether the attachment to existing political institutions is sufficiently obvious that the appointee can be trusted. An example of the significance of political loyalties can be found in the early days of the Republic, when President Washington insisted on adherence to the new Constitution as a requirement for holding public office. It is found also in cases where individuals supposedly loyal to governmental processes are bribed or otherwise tempted by foreign countries to make untrustworthy decisions.

Support is frequently more fleeting and more particular than that of basic political loyalties, which is ordinarily assumed. In the more particular case, support may pertain to the relations of the appointee to some particular political group or to wings or factions of a political party. Partisan identification may be required in some cases (as for the cabinet), or it might be considered both unwise and unnecessary in other cases (as for promotions in the armed service). In general, however, the leading partisans of the victorious party will expect preferment at the hands of their friends (and at the expense of the government). The party controlling the presidency will be absorbed in making personnel appointments which increase its internal cohesion and external support. Appointments of cabinet rank are simultaneously designed to win favor with the party as well as with the public, for the party establishes its control over the government through its ability to man the key posts. In supporting appointments for such offices as those of federal marshal and federal postmaster, congressional partisans may be more concerned with the effect of such appointments on the various claimants within the party than the degree to which such appointments affect the support given the government by the public.

THE CONSTITUTION AND THE LAW

Although the structure of bureaucracy creates the general frame for personnel activities, Congress has considerable authority in determining the rules for selecting personnel. One may give some indication of the breadth of choice facing Congress by citing two extreme positions which might be taken. One would be that of no congressional control—no directions would be given, no statement of expected standards would be announced, no review of basic policy would be undertaken, and no criticism would be expressed of individual shortcomings. The President would be permitted to hire whomever he wanted for as long as he wanted, paying them what he wished and removing them for whatever reason that appealed to him. This would be folly. The other extreme would be mandatory congressional clearance for political reasons, the advice and consent of the Senate being required for all positions of whatever nature, and appointments limited to four years duration. This would be chaos. What, then is the type of control required? What directions should be given? What review exercised? Too much interference could easily upset the structure of bureaucratic authority; too little concern could result in oppressive, unjust, and even seditious acts going unchecked.

The authority of Congress over personnel is greater in appointing than in removing, greater in laying down principles for action than in making sure that the action is followed, and it may be summarized briefly as follows: The Senate must confirm certain nominations and may confirm an indeterminate number; Congress as a whole is empowered to enact laws regarding personnel policy, and it can also appropriate funds; congressional committees and individual members can exert influence on selections, assignments, preferments, and removals. Congress has no general authority to remove personnel, but it may impeach officials for treason, bribery, or other high crimes and misdemeanors.

Congress has considerable discretion in determining how government officials will be selected as a result of the four alternative methods of appointment enumerated in the Constitution—nomination by the President followed by the advice and consent of the Senate, or direct appointment by the President, by the heads of the departments, or by the courts of law. Nominations requiring the advice and consent of the Senate have an especial appeal to Congress because they provide a method by which it can learn what a nominee thinks about public policy before he assumes office. Men will have different attitudes on public issues—conservation, defense, federalism, transportation, and all the rest—which may affect the manner in which the law is administered. No set of laws, no requirements of the bureaucratic hierarchy, no standards of the service are so all-embracing that they exclude the relevance of individual judgments, preferences, and propensities.

The use of senatorial confirmation as a method of appointment is, of course, optional with Congress, with the exception that it must include ambassadors, consuls, Supreme Court justices, and presumably departmental heads. Its use may give the Senate very extensive authority over the personnel selected, for the number and category of officials falling within the advice-and-consent category is as broad as Congress wishes. Some are specifically included but none is excluded. In practice, Congress requires the advice and consent of the Senate for almost all categories of superior officers and a good many others besides. The number of nominations which the President sends to the Senate every year averages more than 10,000, and it has exceeded 50,000.

In addition to requiring the advice and consent of the Senate for some types of appointments, Congress also attempts to control personnel policy by prescribing general rules in permanent law. For the most part personnel are recruited by the Civil Service Commission, although some personnel are recruited directly by the agency concerned—such as the Foreign Service, the Tennessee Valley Authority, or the Armed Services. The emphasis in recruiting is on competence, the standard method of recruitment being competitive examinations, although some allowance is made for veterans' preference. In creating the Civil Service Commission, political and even administrative control was to be minimized by the legal provision that no more than two of the three Civil Service Commissioners "shall be adherents of the same party." The commissioners are appointed by the President with the advice and consent of the Senate and can, presumably, be removed by the President alone, but it was not intended that the Commission should be under the direction of the President. It can be argued that the principles undergirding civil service legislation are faulty, that bipartisan representation is not necessarily the best method for removing politics from personnel recruitment or of selecting the most able administrators, and that the Chief Executive should, in fact, have some larger part in selecting the personnel whom he directs. Whatever merits these arguments may have, the persuasive factor for Congress was the desirability of excluding both the President and the political parties from the process of selecting government personnel.

Congress also attempts to integrate the selection of personnel with the federal system by providing for the apportionment of appointments among the several states and territories upon a population basis. It can be argued here also that the most competent personnel are not necessarily distributed geographically in proportion to the total population, but the purpose of Congress was less to secure the best men than to advance the successful operation of the government by giving all areas an equal claim on the bureaucracy. The bureaucracy was not to be the exclusive preserve of any class or region.

Appointments to the various service academies—army, navy, air, marine—are also partly on an area basis in that the members of Congress themselves can make a limited number of nominations. Initially viewed, this procedure might seem to inject political partisanship into the service academies, but such was not its purpose and it does not appear to have happened. High qualifications bolstered by strict entrance examinations prevent the final selection of unpromising or unqualified candidates and limit the possibilities of friendship and obligation outweighing merit. The procedure can be defended as a method of integrating more closely the military establishment with the society which it defends. Military officers have some incentive for establishing friendly and continuing associations with Congress and Congressmen, and the belief that military officers do, in fact, come from all regions of the country may be a factor in establishing sympathetic relationships between civil and military authority.

The process of permitting members of Congress to nominate some of the appointments to the various service academies has worked sufficiently well and commanded enough support for proposals to have been made that the system of selection be extended to the Foreign Service. Unlike the regular Civil Service, the Foreign Service has no geographic quotas, and there have been complaints on this score by Senator William Langer of North Dakota. "Time and time again on the floor of the Senate," he said in one speech, "I have called the attention of the Senate and of the Administration to the fact that no citizen of North Dakota has been named to head any important office. Year after year has gone by without any citizen of North Dakota being nominated to any such office. At the present time no citizen of North Dakota is serving as ambassador or consul, and you all know that there is no better group of people anywhere than North Dakota people. . . . The next time the Senate is called on to confirm anyone to head any office I propose to oppose the confirmation. I shall do all in my power to see to it that the people of North Dakota finally get the recognition to which they have been entitled ever since the State was admitted to the Union in 1889." [1]

Congress attempts by law to exclude partisanship as a factor in selecting personnel. The bureaucracy should be neutral, having no political preference, according to this theory, and it should loyally serve whichever party is in office. Government personnel, save those who determine policy in "national-wide administration of federal laws" or "in relations of the United States with foreign powers," are prohibited from taking an active part in political campaigns or using their official authority to influence the election or nomination of any candidate. The federal law attempts to restrain the political activities of state or local agencies receiving grants or loans from the United States. The law also attempts to minimize congressional influence in appointments by providing that recommendations from members of

[1] *Congressional Record,* December 8, 1950, p. 16314.

Congress are not to be received or considered "except as to the character or residence of the applicant."

Despite the relatively strict legislation preventing political influence in selecting personnel, there is a curious ambivalence in Congress toward the degree of political preference which is thought desirable. In the past, many agencies have been permitted to recruit personnel outside of the Civil Service laws, with the President having authority to place these positions under Civil Service regulations if it were "necessary to the more efficient operation of government." All Congressmen are forced by their constituents to take some interest in personnel selection, and a good share of the time of a Congressman's clerical staff is spent in writing job letters, making appointments, discovering job vacancies, and in other ways helping worthy constituents, or former constituents, or friends of constituents, first get a position in the bureaucracy and subsequently work up in the hierarchy of office.

Congress has its own personnel problem to consider also, and one may distinguish four types of employment within Congress itself: the career-patronage; the temporary-patronage; the member's office staff; and the committee staff. Within the welter of spoils and patronage associated with political parties, a career system has in fact developed within Congress which provides a cadre of faithful, competent, and experienced personnel. The pattern of appointment varies, but in the case of more important positions it may be made by the party caucus. Tenure is possible inasmuch as both major parties are given appointments to fill. One may find within the Office of the Secretary of the Senate, the Clerk of the House, the Sergeants at Arms of the Senate and the House, and other congressional enclaves a number of careerist appointees who have what amounts to permanent positions, although the precise title of their job may change with the shift in fortunes of the party with whom they are identified. These careerist appointees contribute considerably to the stability of Congress, to the easy transition in party control, and even to the indoctrination of new members to the customs and manners of Congress.

The temporary patronage jobs encompass such positions as elevator operators, capitol guards, telephone operators, and the like; these jobs are assigned on the recommendation of members of Congress (and ordinarily of the majority party, although some appointments may be considered to "belong" to individual members of the party). The employment of office personnel is the prerogative of the Congressman concerned; each member has a quota which can be filled in whatever fashion suits him. There is no centralized system of recruiting personnel for the staffs of congressional offices.

The policy regarding personnel for committee staffs varies considerably, for there is no common agreement on the function of a staff, on whether the staff should be neutral, professional, and permanent, or whether it should be obviously political, serving the interests of the majority or of the minority and subject to dismissal or replacement for political reasons. Some staffs are temporary, being appointed primarily for political reasons (although they may also be competent) and subject to replacement where a new party or a new chairman assumes command. Other staffs—such as, for example, those of the appropriations committees, the foreign affairs or foreign relations committees, the Joint Committee on Internal Revenue Taxation, and the Legislative Drafting Service—are relatively permanent and provide the committees with a personnel career system.

NOMINATIONS: ADVICE AND CONSENT

The fact that senatorial confirmation is required for so many nominations suggests the question: With what type of nomination is the Senate concerned? What criteria does the Senate use before giving its approval? In general, the Senate is interested in appointments to positions which permit considerable discretion in the exercise of authority, where the basic political attitudes of the officials are relevant to the type of job being performed, where precedents are not well developed, and where directions cannot readily be given in the form of law. Although the Senate has identical authority over all presidential nominations submitted for advice and consent, it does not give all nominations the same sedulous attention. Its interest in some nominations is limited to routine questions relating to competence and the absence of favoritism, although it may also wish to check on possible oversights and irregularities in the selection process. It is not necessary or desirable, for instance, that Senators know personally the officers appointed or promoted in the armed services, but it is essential that they have confidence in the integrity and efficiency of the selection process. Here a case can be made for sympathetic supervision of the recruitment and promotion system by some group outside the administrative hierarchy.

For other types of nominations, the interest of the Senate is extended to factors directly related to the integration of policy and the acquisition of political support. In some appointments it might be desirable to give specific representation to certain types of associations (as in boards and commissions) but in general there should be a firm understanding of the degree and nature of influence exerted by external associations. It may wish to check on economic or political associations which might influence attitudes or decisions or reveal a conflict of interests. It may also wish to check the relevant attitudes, beliefs, and propensities of the nominee toward the prospective job. The Senate may limit its interest to the partisan overtones of the appointment, ignoring the presence or absence of other qualifications. In emphasizing the requirements of political and partisan support, the Senate may use its authority for the direct benefit of the personal political requirements of various Senators. There is the presumption in some quarters that individual members of the Senate, in their own capacity, "control" certain public jobs and that their nominees for such positions must perforce be approved.

The Senate's authority over nominations may act as a check on the President, forcing him to secure the consent of the Senate on all important appointments and, at times, compelling him to name the man designated by an influential Senator. But if the requirement of senatorial confirmation serves as a check on the President, it may also serve as a device by which the President gains senatorial support. The President has at his disposal many jobs which Senators covet for their loyal constituents, and the proper disposition of these jobs may indeed win for the President the gratitude of the Senators concerned.

Few of the thousands of nominations sent to the Senate annually are controversial, and these come from a relatively small list—heads of departments and agencies, appointments on boards and commissions, delegations to the United Nations, and ambassadorial and ministerial positions. Infrequently, there will be a controversy over the nomination of a general or an admiral. The control exercised by the Senate over noncontroversial and nonpolitical appointments is more in the nature of providing additional procedural safeguards than in exercising influence by demanding to be consulted before giving consent. The merit-type appointments are handled routinely: The nominations are referred to the appropriate committeee, which then notifies the Senators from the home state of the nominee, and if no objections are raised, the committee reports the nomination favorably. The Senate then confirms the nomination with little or no debate, and sometimes *en bloc,* perhaps consuming no more than a few seconds in the legal process of giving advice and consent. These merit-type nominations include, in peacetime, all appointments and permanent promotions for officers of the Army, Navy, Marine Corps, and Air Force. From 5000 to 50,000 nominations in this category are sent to the Senate annually. The list also includes all appointments and promotions in the Foreign Service below the rank of minister (ambassadors and ministers are in the "policy" category, and in a limited number of cases are controversial). The number of foreign service nominations submitted annually to the Senate varies from several hundred to slightly less than a thousand. Public Health Service nominations are also included, the number of which may approach a thousand a year. The laws regulating appointments in the Public Health Service have been inherited from an earlier day when terminology was less standardized and when the Senate had more time for supervising the administration of the Service through the control of personnel. The advice and consent of the Senate is required for the appointment of all officers of the Service, which includes the Surgeon General, Assistant Surgeons General, senior surgeons, surgeons, passed assistant surgeons, and assistant surgeons, and it extends to such other ranks as scientist, senior assistant pharmacist, and assistant nurse officer. The number of Coast Guard nominations submitted to the Senate fluctuates annually from less than a hundred to more than a thousand. These include all appointments and promotions of officers, who have the name and rank of naval officers, and extends to such categories as chief boatswain, chief pay clerk, and chief machinist. The number of nominations submitted annually from the Coast and Geodetic Survey is small—ordinarily less than a hundred. The grades and ranks of the officers correspond with those of the Navy.

As the government has grown, the number of appointments requiring senatorial confirmation has also grown. The Senate, it has been seen, plays a relatively small role in determining personnel appointments and promotions in the merit-type category, and one can raise the question of whether this control is necessary, whether, indeed, it hinders the Senate from doing other things which it might do better, or, if it takes so little time, whether it is worth while.

If the Senate were to conduct an inquiry into ways and means of eliminating redundant work, it would surely consider the possibilities of reducing the number of nominations that it must consider. The Senate as a body can know very little about the thousands of nominations to which it gives its advice and consent, and the process is a burden on individual Senators even though it may consume little time of the Senate itself. On the other hand, even though most nominations are noncontroversial, the requirement of senatorial confirmation does permit a public review if questions of fitness, aptitude or unfair administrative preferences are raised. The fact that senatorial confirmation may lead to a public review and require a public defense may cause the appointing boards to choose wisely when they appoint or promote. There is a real possibility, also, that senatorial confirmation adds dignity to the job and perhaps also inspires a greater sense of responsibility in the appointee. A case might be made for senatorial confirmation on the ground that the job carries with it a responsibility involving the prestige of the United States.

INTEGRATION OF POLICY

The Senate is also interested in the manner in which an appointment will blend with other commitments, and this, of course, extends to the question of policy and the political attitudes of the nominee. In 1943, the Senate spent several hours in debating the promotion of General Ben Lear to the permanent rank of lieutenant general, and although Lear was eventually confirmed with no negative votes being cast, his promotion was used as a vehicle to indicate dissatisfaction with the relationship between the Regular Army and the National Guard. This question of policy could be less easily attacked directly than indirectly through the promotion of General Lear, whose command included National Guard units.

In 1949 the Senate rejected the nomination of Mr. Carl A. Ilgenfritz to be Chairman of the Munitions Board, even though Ilgenfritz was considered competent and the factor of partisan politics did not enter. However, Ilgenfritz's association with United States Steel raised the question of a possible conflict of interest. The vote of 40–28 was not divided along party lines, for Ilgenfritz was opposed by an almost equal percentage of Republicans and Democrats. In the same year, the nomination of Mr. Leland Olds for a third term as a member of the Federal Power Commission was rejected by a vote of 53–15. Here the issue was the acceptability of Olds's decisions as a member of the FPC, and concerted campaigns were waged against Olds and also in his behalf.

There is occasionally a close relationship between controversial foreign policy and the nomination of particular individuals. When General George C. Marshall was nominated to be Secretary of Defense, his controversial career as Secretary of State was debated in the Senate before he was confirmed by a roll call of 57–11. Another instance relates to the nomination of Mr. Charles E. Bohlen to be Ambassador to the U.S.S.R., which revived the controversy over the Yalta agreement and the extent to which Mr. Bohlen himself shared responsibility for it. Senator Bourke Hickenlooper (R., Iowa) claimed that Bohlen had "defended almost in terms of a brilliant diplomatic victory what I consider to be a diplomatic disaster, and he has criticized severely those who have criticized what was done at Yalta." [2] Charges were also made that Bohlen's security file contained derogatory information, but the charges, being of a confidential and classified nature, could not be placed in the public record. A solution whereby the Senate could be assured of the nature of the charges without spreading the information broadside was provided by permitting Senator Robert A. Taft, a Republican, and Senator John J. Sparkman, a Democrat, to read a summary of the files of the Federal Bureau of Investigation. Senator Taft reported that the derogatory information consisted for the most part of statements of persons who disagreed with Mr. Bohlen on foreign policy. "There was no one who did not end up by saying that although he disagreed politically, he had full confidence in the character, the morality, and the general standing and reputation of Mr. Bohlen." [3] The nomination was debated off and on in the Senate for a month before Bohlen was finally confirmed by a roll call vote of 74–13.

PARTISAN SUPPORT: THE PRESIDENT, THE PARTY, AND SENATORIAL COURTESY

A President is ordinarily given a free hand in appointing the members of his cabinet and the entourage of his staff. Confirmation by the Senate is not always required, but when it is, the nominations are often considered routinely, with no objections being raised. Occasionally, however, a cabinet appointment is forcefully challenged and even rejected. President Calvin Coolidge, for instance, was thwarted in his attempt to appoint Mr. Charles Beecher Warren to the post of Attorney General. Many Democrats and some Western Republicans (the Sons of the Wild Jackass, as Senator Moses, of New Hampshire, once called them) attacked Warren because they feared that his past associations with large corporations would dampen his enthusiasm for enforcing the antitrust laws. A Democrat from South Carolina, Senator Lee S. Overman, supported Warren, however, under the

[2] *Congressional Record,* March 27, 1953, p. 2388.
[3] *Congressional Record,* March 25, 1953, p. 2278.

theory that the President "should be allowed to appoint his own official family without hindrance." [4] Neither the President's request nor Overton's support was sufficient to convince the Senate, and the nomination lost in the tie vote of 40–40.

The rejection of the Warren nomination is remembered not only because of the incident itself but also because the Vice-President, Charles G. Dawes, missed the chance to break the tie vote. During the consideration of the nomination, the Vice-President was taking a nap in his suite in the Willard Hotel, more than a mile from the Capitol building. Mr. Dawes was roused and sped on toward the Hill, but he failed to reach the Senate floor until the voting was over. The Dawes ride to the Capitol amused Senator George Norris of Nebraska, an opponent of Warren, who for the benefit of the occasion composed a parody of the poem, "Sheridan's Ride," and inserted it in the *Congressional Record*.[5]

President Franklin D. Roosevelt had difficulty in persuading the Senate to approve the nomination of Mr. Henry A. Wallace as Secretary of Commerce, a difficulty enhanced because of the unusual conditions surrounding the nomination. Mr. Wallace, who had been succeeded as Vice-President by Senator Truman, was in the embarrassing position of having no public office. In order to put Mr. Wallace in the cabinet, as President Roosevelt proposed to do, it was first necessary to find or create a vacancy. Mr. Jesse Jones, who was Secretary of Commerce at the time, was selected as the victim, and the fact that Mr. Jones and Mr. Wallace had quarreled embarrassingly during the war made the incident part of a long, spiteful feud. President Roosevelt wrote to Mr. Jones, asking him "to relinquish this present post for Henry," who during the preceding campaign had "displayed the utmost devotion to our cause, traveling almost incessantly and working for the success of the ticket in a great many parts of the country." [6] It was clearly implied that Mr. Jones had not been equally diligent.

[4] *Congressional Record.* March 10, 1925, p. 101.
[5] *Congressional Record,* March 12, 1925, p. 150.
[6] *Congressional Record,* January 22, 1945, p. 416.

The Senate received the Wallace nomination with some chilliness and proceeded to enact legislation removing the lending agencies from the jurisdiction of Commerce. This legislation was variously interpreted as a slap at Wallace and as a measure most certainly required if Wallace were to be confirmed. After this legislation was safely passed, Mr. Wallace was confirmed, 56–32, with the support of 90 percent of the Democrats and 29 percent of the Republicans.

President Eisenhower encountered opposition among Republicans to his nomination of Mr. Martin P. Durkin as Secretary of Labor. Mr. Durkin, a labor leader, was President of the United Association of Journeymen and Apprentices of the Plumbing and Pipe Fitting Industry of the United States and Canada. Although the Republicans were anxious to extend their relations with organized labor, the fact that Mr. Durkin was not only a Democrat but had also supported Governor Stevenson in the 1952 election made some Republicans believe that the President had gone too far. Senator Taft protested publicly, calling the nomination incredible, and a group of Republican Senators received assurances from President Eisenhower that they would be consulted on future appointments.

Partisan appointments of the President are frequently criticized in the Senate and may be debated at length. The nomination in 1943 of Mr. Edward J. Flynn as Minister to Australia falls into the partisan category. Flynn, the chairman of the Democratic National Committee and "boss" of the Bronx, had been one of the leaders in the movement for a third term for President Roosevelt. Whatever qualifications Mr. Flynn may have had for the post of minister in the diplomatic service, the nomination was considered from a strictly political point of view, and opposition developed to the extent that Mr. Flynn eventually asked that his name be withdrawn from further consideration.

Partisanship of a more gracious variety entered into the nomination of Mrs. Perle Mesta to be Minister to the Grand Duchy of Luxemburg. Mrs. Mesta was without diplomatic experience and was a pronounced partisan supporter of President Truman, but she was also a hostess who had entertained well. Senator Charles Tobey, a

New Hampshire Republican, defended the nomination in these words:

> Mrs. Mesta's life has been full of acts of hospitality and generosity, and she has been hostess at many banquets from which Senators have come very full of the good products of the fields and vineyards and of mirth and merriment. . . . She has not come before the committee, but the Senators have come before Perle Mesta, many and many a time, in these great feasts of the intellect and the palate, and many Senators have had ample opportunity to learn first hand of her qualities of mind and heart and her understanding of men and issues. And so I hope her nomination will be confirmed.[7]

She was confirmed.

Senators from the majority party may wish to control the appointments, or at least be consulted, on the politically critical jobs—those whose legal jurisdiction falls solely within the territory of a state. Any Senator would be interested, for instance, in the nomination of a federal judge to the District Court lying within his state, but he would have less claim to be consulted on nominations of judges to the Circuit Court of Appeals, which encompasses the territories of several states, or of justices to the Supreme Court. Any Senator would also be interested in the nomination of United States Attorneys, Marshals, Collectors of Customs, and the heads of various field offices. Postmasters should occasionally be included, although the prerogative of "approving" the candidate is frequently exercised by the Representative from the area involved. The desire of Senators to be consulted on patronage nominations is, of course, historic and traditional and is considered to be one of the prerogatives of the members of the majority party. The Senate is ordinarily willing to support the Senator (from the majority party) who objects to an appointment on the ground that his own choice was not given due consideration—the practice known as senatorial courtesy.

The control of the Senate over patronage nominations has been abetted by four-year appointments, an innovation introduced by the Tenure of Office Act of 1820. Under this plan, some appointments

[7] *Congressional Record,* July 5, 1949, p. 8830.

expire automatically after each presidential election. Senators are interested in controlling such appointments in order to meet the political
competition of rival politicians who may want their seat. Comparatively speaking, the Senators control little patronage, far less than
that of the President, who might award favors to the political enemies
of the Senators, and far less than that of a state organization, which
might attempt to defeat the incumbent. The lack in quantity of jobs
available is partly balanced by the quality of appointments controlled
by the Senate. Many of these appointments, such as judgeships, carry
considerable prestige, and the prudent disposal of these prestige positions will help Senators in building support for their own careers.

The Senate has shown considerable reluctance in extending the
control of the President over patronage appointments, the fear being
that the President would increase his now considerable political influence at the expense of the Senate. Most patronage nominations are
arranged, if we may use that term, between the Administration and
the Senators concerned before being sent to the Senate, and the
subsequent proceedings may then be quite perfunctory. If arrangements have not been made, however, rumblings of discontent may
develop, and offended Senators may even request that the nominee be
rejected.

Such was the case in 1939 when President Roosevelt and the two
Senators from Virginia, Glass and Byrd, quarreled over the appointment of a judge to a new judicial district in western Virginia. The
President nominated Mr. Floyd H. Roberts, a state judge of experience
and abilty, who had the support of the Governor of Virginia, James H.
Price, and the Representative from the western part of Virginia, John
W. Flanagan. In the meantime, the Department of Justice had asked
the two Virginia Senators to make nominations for the position, and
two names were submitted. A story also appeared in the Virginia
press that the President would take advice on nominations from Governor Price, who supported the Administration, rather than from
Senators Glass and Byrd, who did not.

When Judge Roberts' name was placed before the Senate Judiciary
Committee, the two Virginia Senators opposed the nomination, and

they were annoyed that their suggestions, which had been invited by the Department of Justice, had been ignored. Senator Byrd stated in the committee hearings that the nomination was "personally obnoxious" to him as well as to Senator Glass. These were the magic words which united the Senate in defense of its prerogatives. Senator William H. King (D., Utah), a member of the Judiciary Committee, stated that "under no circumstances" would he vote for a nominee when the two Senators concerned declared the nominee to be personally obnoxious to them. "I do not care to hear any witnesses, . . ." he said. "When two Senators from a state say the nominee is personally offensive to them, I am willing to terminate the case and vote against the confirmation of the nominee." [8] The nomination was reported adversely, and, in a roll call vote, was rejected by a vote of 72–9.

When the question of extending the scope of senatorial confirmation is considered in Congress from time to time, the pivotal question often rests on patronage rather than on efficiency in the merit system or on increasing the effectiveness of the Senate's control over governmental policy. During the Second World War, Senator Kenneth McKellar (D., Tenn.), a staunch advocate of increasing the Senate's share of patronage, repeatedly proposed that all government jobs paying $4500 a year or more require confirmation by the Senate. The McKellar plan was not adopted as a permanent policy, although the provision was made temporarily applicable to some war agencies. The proposal was not universally popular on the Hill, however, for not everyone in Congress wanted to increase the control over federal jobs exercised by influential Senators of the majority party.

The conflict over the McKellar plan showed again that Congress does not always have a clear idea of the purposes of confirmation, whether it is to be used to control policy, to provide patronage, or to promote efficiency and justice in the merit system. While Congress was debating the McKellar plan to provide more patronage, some important officials were permitted to hold office without having been

[8] Senate Committee on the Judiciary; Hearings: "Nomination of Floyd H. Roberts," February 1, 1939, pp. 2–3.

confirmed by the Senate. Among those was the position of Economic Stabilizer and others of comparable rank, which were created on the basis of delegated authority. In addition, the President is permitted to appoint administrative assistants and even the Director of the Budget without the advice and consent of the Senate—and the latter office surely has considerable influence over the development of public policy.

REMOVAL FROM OFFICE

Congressional controls diminish perceptibly once an appointment has been made, inasmuch as there are few methods for reviewing the administrative behavior of personnel and virtually none for removing personnel from office. Congress can complain publicly about official action and to a degree it can limit the sphere of activity by retrenching on funds, but it cannot itself remove officials. The decision to remove is made by the executive branch, the role of Congress being that of influencing and persuading, not of making the authoritative decision, yet here, too, Congress has a legitimate concern. The official in question may not meet the expected standards if, say, he is confronted with problems unanticipated when he took the office, or he may have failed to exercise proper judgment and foresight in meeting a crisis. In such a situation, the official should be expected to defend his judgment and foresight before some group which he himself does not control. Here the heart of responsible government is found in the continual explanation of and justification for official action. Initially the explanation and justification may be routinely considered, but the event may become of interest to an ever-widening number of people until, at some point, the official must defend his position before the attentive audience of the legislature and the public.

In the administrative development of law, a particular policy may be identified with certain personnel and, short of repealing the law, a modification of policy may be sought by advocating a change in personnel. Although Congress cannot remove officials save by impeachment proceedings (limited to cases of treason, bribery, or other high crimes and misdemeanors), it may nevertheless attempt to force the offending official from his job or compel him to change his policy. What with an accumulation of discontents, the erosion of confidence, and the possibility of a diminution in appropriations, the President may even be persuaded to remove the official rather than risk irritating Congress further. The President must decide at what point to drop unpopular officials because of congressional criticism, and he is continually replacing his principal administrators who, for whatever reason, appear to have lost the confidence of Congress. While he may heartily wish to protect his friends, the harsh demands of politics may force him to ask for the resignation of those who have otherwise been faithful to him.

The supervision exercised by Congress may place top administrators in a perpetual dilemma. They may believe that their first and primary loyalty is to the President, who appointed them to office and can surely remove them at will, but they must also develop some political support of their own, either in Congress or among influential political groups, which in turn will add to the political strength of the Administration. However, if the path of independence is followed too far, the administrator may conclude that he can be independent of the President in policy and in politics, and again he may be in danger of being removed from office. Secretary of Commerce Jesse Jones and Secretary of Defense James V. Forrestal are cases in point. Each of them had exceptionally good relations with Congress; each followed a somewhat independent political road; and each was removed from office for failing to take an active part in presidential campaigns— Mr. Jones in the campaign of 1944 and Mr. Forrestal in the campaign of 1948.

The prolonged controversy between Congress and the President over the authority to remove officials seems to have been largely won by the President. The attempt to restrict the President through the Tenure of Office Act failed when the Supreme Court decided in the case of *Myers v. United States* (1926) (272 US 52) that the law was unconstitutional. The case arose after President Wilson removed a postmaster without securing the advice and consent of the Senate. Legality aside, Congress has a considerable interest in creating procedures for appointments and removals, and the dissenting opinion of Mr. Justice Holmes in the *Myers* case seems more closely attuned with political requirements than the somewhat legalistic opinion of the court majority. Mr. Justice Holmes argued that "Congress alone confers on the President the power to appoint and at any time may transfer the power to other hands. With such power over its own creation, I have no more trouble in believing that Congress has power to prescribe a term of life for it free from any interference than I have in accepting the undoubted power of Congress to decree its end. I have equally little trouble in accepting its power to prolong the tenure of an incumbent until Congress or the Senate shall have assented to his removal."

The President's authority to remove officials is in some cases still restricted by law. The Comptroller General, for instance, can be removed only by a joint resolution of Congress, after notice and hearing, and for specific causes—"and for no other cause and in no other manner except by impeachment." This provision, placing the authority for removing the Comptroller General exclusively in the hands of Congress, caused President Wilson to veto the initial Budget and Accounting Act. Although several Comptrollers General have been out of official favor since the above provision was enacted in 1921, no President has challenged the constitutionality of the provision or provoked Congress by attempting to remove a Comptroller General from office.

Granted that the initiative for removal ordinarily rests with the President, it is fair to ask whether Congress can take any action to facilitate the removal process. The petition is seldom used, but on one historic instance it brought quick results. The incident occurred in 1924 during the controversies over leasing naval oil reserves to private companies at Teapot Dome and other locations. Many Senators believed that the Secretary of Navy, Mr. Edwin Denby, was incompetent to hold his job because of the poor judgment he had shown in his appointments and decisions. These views led to the introduction of a resolution stating that it was "the sense of the Senate that the President of the United States immediately request the resignation" of Mr. Denby, which was passed by a vote of 51–25. Denby resigned within a month.

Attempts of Congress to remove officials through the passage of legislation have met with less success, as in 1943 when, after a prolonged congressional controversy, the following provision was included in an appropriation bill:

No part of any appropriation . . . which is now, or which is hereafter made, available . . . shall be used, after November 15, 1943, to pay any part of the salary, or other compensation for the personal services of Goodwin B. Watson, William E. Dodd, Junior, and Robert Morss Lovett, unless prior to such date such person has been appointed by the President, by and with the advice and consent of the Senate. . . ." [9]

To remove individuals in such a fashion, the Supreme Court said, violated the constitutional prohibition against bills of attainder. "Legislative acts that apply either to named individuals or to easily ascertainable members of a group in such a way as to inflict punishment on them without a judicial trial are bills of attainder prohibited by the Constitution." [10]

Another method of removal sometimes used by Congress is the creation of personnel standards which the current officeholders are unable to meet. This device might also fail to meet the test of constitutionality, but no successful challenge has yet been made. In the controversy over price control in the Second World War, there was some dissatisfaction in Congress with officials who had little practical experience to supplement their academic training. To remove such individuals from office without actually naming names, Congress added a provision that none of the funds appropriated to the Office of Price Administration could be used to pay the salary of "any person who directs the formulation of any price policy . . . unless, in the judgment of the Administrator, such person shall be qualified by experience in business, industry, or commerce." [11]

A similar effort to remove by indirection occurred in 1948 when

[9] 57 Stat. 431, at p. 450, July 12, 1943.
[10] *United States v. Lovett,* 328 US 303, 1946.
[11] 57 Stat. 494, at p. 526, July 12, 1943.

Congress provided that no salaries could be paid to the Commissioner of the Bureau of Reclamation, the Assistant Commissioner, or the Regional Director if such person was "not a qualified engineer with at least five years' engineering and administrative experience." The purpose of the rider, Senator Joseph C. O'Mahoney (D., Wyo.) said, "though it is couched in terms designed to fix qualifications of persons who fill these three categories of positions by requiring that they shall be engineers, was in fact designed to remove two officials who have been appointed according to law, namely Mr. Michael Straus, the Commissioner of Reclamation, and Mr. Richard Boke, who was the Regional Director for District No. 2 in California." [12] Senator O'Mahoney said that he would not move to eliminate the provision, because the Senator in charge of the bill "has the votes" and the measure was adopted in both Houses. Messrs. Straus and Boke were thus deprived of their pay but not of their jobs, for they continued to hold their positions regardless of the congressional rebuke. When the Democrats regained control of Congress, appropriations were enacted giving the two officials their back pay.

On another occasion Congress attempted to remove certain individuals from the payroll of the National Labor Relations Board, the chief target being Mr. David Saposs, the head of the Division of Economic Research. The House Committee on Appropriations, finding that "no need exists for the Division of Economic Research," said that it expected "that this section will be entirely eliminated." [13] The unit was abolished, all right, but in its place a new unit known as the Division of Technical Assistance was created, which Congress found was employing almost the same personnel and doing substantially the same work as the previous unit. This attempt to circumvent Congress by means of a technicality irritated a number of Congressmen, and further hearings were held. The circumvention ended when Congress attached another legislative rider to an appropriation bill,

[12] *Congressional Record,* June 14, 1948, pp. 8098–99.

[13] Subcommittee of the House Committee on Appropriations, Supplemental Hearings, Department of Labor-Federal Security Agency Appropriation Bill for 1941, August, 1940, p. 1.

stating that "none of the appropriation . . . shall be obligated for the Division of Economic Research or for the Division of Technical Assistance." [14]

SUMMARY

Congressional control over personnel is a specialized type of control which Congress exercises over the government in general. Special types of problems are raised in establishing controls over personnel inasmuch as a general rule, such as a rule on recruitment policy, may not go as far as Congress wishes in checking the policy as developed by some chief administrator. On the other hand, a special rule for or the senatorial confirmation of each appointment will either exaggerate the significance of patronage or run counter to the constitutional prohibition against the passage of bills of attainder. In this country, governments do not fall because they fail to secure the support of Congress, but the personnel in official positions are nevertheless significant factors in how congressional policy is actually carried out. In establishing controls over personnel, Congress is interested in giving general directions for recruitment and creating standards of competence; it is also interested in having assurances that there has been compliance with the expected standards, that the various ends of policy are in fact integrated, and that the personnel selected assist in obtaining public (and sometimes partisan) support of the government.

The variety of purposes to be served by control clearly requires some differentiation on the part of Congress in formulating procedures for considering various categories of personnel. Although this must be done within the constitutional framework, the Constitution provides broad alternatives for Congress in selecting the method by which appointments shall be made: The President may be permitted to make nominations by and with the advice and consent of the Senate, or the appointing authority can be given to the President alone, to the heads of departments, or to the courts of law. Congress

[14] 54 Stat. 1031, at p. 1037, October 9, 1940.

is also empowered to lay down basic personnel policy in the form of law, but it has no specific authority to remove officials on its own account.

The number of nominations now requiring the advice and consent of the Senate runs into the thousands but, as would be expected, differential treatment is given by the Senate to the various categories. The first category encompasses those nominations which are routinely considered, the primary purpose of the Senate being to make sure that the selection system operates fairly and that opportunity is provided for complaints to be made. The second category encompasses nominations where there is a question of how policy identified with the nominee will be integrated with other types of policy. There may be considerable controversy over nominations of this type. The third category, while sometimes including the content of the second category, encompasses nominations of primary political significance, where the crucial question relates to the effect of the nomination on partisan competition. It is here that the custom known as senatorial courtesy is exercised—the practice in which the Senate defers to a member who states that a nomination is "personally obnoxious" to him.

There is no definite method by which Congress can remove officials from office, but in practice it may exercise considerable influence. It may attempt through various legislative devices to encourage officials to resign, and it also has available the authority, seldom used, to impeach officials for high crimes and misdemeanors. No President, of course, can afford to allow his relations with Congress to deteriorate too far, and from time to time he will permit officials to resign who are closely identified with a controversial policy.

CHAPTER 9

Controls over Federal Finance

THE BUDGET SYSTEM

THE FACT THAT THE GOVERNMENT OPERATES ON AN annual budget has considerable significance for Congress in controlling public policy, for decisions are made every year on whether to continue policy which has already been legally authorized and the total undertakings of the federal government are reëxamined, with past policies reappraised and appropriations revised accordingly. This means, in effect, that an opportunity exists every year for modifying past commitments through appropriations. The annual budget affects practically every form of governmental activity, making the control over appropriations one of the most important of all the techniques used by Congress in exercising authority. Indeed, control of or through the purse may in some cases supersede such other forms of control as that of law and personnel, for if governmental activities can be stopped or started by the simple means of withholding or appropriating funds, other controls may become less meaningful. The political equilibrium is especially sensitive to controls over money, for the possibility of securing desired ends through federal funds—

or of losing them when funds are denied—provides the spark for politicians and pressure groups in seeking federal funds.

Although fiscal control has developed into a technique of great sweep and influence, it is nevertheless not the type of procedure which is easily operated through ordinary legislative procedures. The whole budget system, with its controls reaching into every facet of governmental activity and encompassing personnel and management as well as policy, is essentially a device constructed for administrative supervision. Both the preparation and execution of the budget require considerable centralization of authority in the President and his staff agency, the Bureau of the Budget. Although Congress participates in the system of budget making, questions are not always raised in a manner which permits Congress to determine policy or to make a deliberative decision, based on full evidence, nor are the provisions for continuing review as well developed as they might be. Nevertheless, the whole tempo of government is now geared to the expectations of annual supply and review, and Congress must accommodate its procedures accordingly if it is to establish effective command over this powerful instrumentality. In fact, however, there are certain inadequacies in the method by which and the degree to which Congress makes policy through appropriations or uses fiscal control to review administrative performance. Review over spending should provide Congress with sharp insights into the adequacy of existing policy or the extent to which administrators have complied with instructions.

From a legal point of view, Congress has an amplitude of authority over appropriations, for the Constitution provides that no money can be drawn from the Treasury "but in consequence of appropriations made by law." However, the Constitution leaves unsettled the question of how Congress is to proceed in appropriating funds by law, nor is the control to be exercised by Congress over federal funds otherwise clearly defined in theory or practice. As a method of providing annual supply, the budgetary device should enable Congress to consider fiscal policy from a broad point of view, including its effect on the economy, and a minimum requirement would appear to be the ability of Congress to make decisions on total amounts spent, including the possibility of balancing income and outgo. However, present procedures make it difficult for Congress to make an independent decision on total spending, although several procedural changes have been proposed to make this feasible. It is not that Congress is uninterested in balancing the budget, or in reducing the debt, or in maintaining a stable monetary policy, but the lack of procedures for considering the budget as an entity makes it difficult for Congress to make decisions with such purposes in mind.

THE PROCESS

In enacting the annual budget, Congress makes a basic decision on how some 60 billion dollars are to be allocated among competing claimants. The final budget is the product of many decisions made over a period of time by the executive branch and by Congress alike. The underlying principles of the federal budget system were developed in the Budget and Accounting Act of 1921 and supplemented by procedural and organizational changes in Congress itself. These principles recognize the institutional requirements imposed by the Separation of Powers, and they involve four distinct procedural steps, two performed by the President and two by Congress. But whereas the control of the President was greatly increased, the part to be played by Congress was never fully developed or the impact of the budget on legislative control fully comprehended.

In step one, the President—with the assistance of the departments and agencies concerned and of course the Bureau of the Budget— must prepare annually a unified budget encompassing the total fiscal requirements of the government, and he submits these estimates to Congress in January, accompanied by a budget message. In step two, Congress reviews the budget estimates and authorizes funds in the form of appropriation bills. In step three, the government spends the money, with the Treasury Department and the Bureau of the Budget having some centralized control over the rate and the purposes of expenditures. In step four, the General Accounting Office audits the accounts and submits its reports to Congress, to whom it is accountable and in whose name it acts. The circle is then completed, with

Congress being supplied with additional information on past spending performance which will assist it in making future decisions.

The Bureau of the Budget is in general charge of developing the budget estimates from the numerous requests although the President reviews the amounts, and the instrument becomes "his" budget. The law provides that the budget should contain estimates of expenditures and appropriations which the President believes necessary for the support of the government for the ensuing fiscal year; estimates of receipts during the ensuing fiscal year; expenditures and receipts during the last fiscal year; the amount available for expenditure; the condition of the Treasury at the end of the fiscal year in progress and at the end of the ensuing fiscal year if the financial proposals contained in the Budget are adopted; and recommendations for meeting any estimated deficiencies.

Congress makes a procedural distinction between authorizations for grants and the actual appropriations, so that under ordinary circumstances the passing of a law precedes the granting of funds. The authorization contained in statute law must be implemented by appropriations. The separation is based on the interpretation of the constitutional provision that no money shall be drawn from the Treasury "but in consequence of appropriations made by law." Appropriations not being considered to be law, it follows that the enactment of a law must precede the granting of funds.

This bifurcated method of making policy results in some conflict between the legislative committees and the appropriation committees and some duplication of their activities. A legislative committee develops a plan, let us say, for the development of hydroelectric power or for foreign aid, and the legislation will include an "authorization" for spending the millions or billions required by the program. However, the legislative committee is not empowered to include appropriations along with the authorization, so no specific funds for the programs are included in the bill. Before funds are granted they will ordinarily be requested by the Bureau of the Budget, but in any event they must be reported by the Appropriations Committees and agreed to by Congress in the usual way. The Appropriations Committees sometimes report a sum considerably less than that authorized by law. This may annoy a conscientious legislative committee and even lead to charges that the Appropriations Committees are usurping power by making policy on legislative matters. On the other hand, some groups will be grateful for whatever funds the Appropriations Committees are willing to report. Legislation authorizing the appropriation of funds is frequently proposed in such a fashion that a decision on ultimate costs will not be definitive. It will be said, for instance, that the proposed legislation is "merely an authorization," that, of course "the appropriations will have to come later." Once the law authorizing funds has been passed, the interested groups can then argue that funds should be appropriated because Congress has already authorized the money to be spent. The process of appropriating funds may lead to a duplication of activity, with the same issues debated before different groups. The most notable example of this in recent years has no doubt been the program of foreign aid, which called for debate, votes, and enactment of the legislation, followed by debate, votes, and enactment of the appropriations.

There is considerable interest in fiscal policy when the President's budget message is sent to Congress, but this interest is not sustained during the long tedious process of enacting the appropriation bills. Rather than considering the budget as a whole and at one time, Congress enacts some ten or more regular appropriation bills each session in addition to numerous special, supplemental, and deficiency bills. The total amount appropriated is determined by adding the sum of the regular appropriations to the sum of supplemental appropriation bills enacted the following year. An attempt is made to enact all regular appropriation bills by July 1, the beginning of the fiscal year, but this goal is not always reached and sometimes bills do not get to the President's desk until September or October.

The procedure for considering appropriation bills is similar to that for considering legislative bills, except that by custom appropriations always originate in the House of Representatives. Hearings in committee are followed by debate in the chamber and similar action in the Senate. A conference committee resolves differences between the two Houses, after which the bill is sent to the President. Approval is axiomatic; the President seldom vetoes appropriation bills, and he has no authority to veto items of appropriations.

The Appropriations Committees of each House have considerable influence over appropriations. Although these committees are overruled from time to time by the parent body, their knowledge of and command over the budget are considerable, and the members of the committees ordinarily enjoy the high respect of their colleagues. The committees rank high in prestige; the demand for membership on the committees exceeds the positions available; and the committees are able to retain their membership. Subcommittees have primary jurisdiction over specific appropriation bills, subject to review and approval by the full committee, but inasmuch as the effective operation of the committee depends on comity and coöperation, the review is exercised with restraint.

The hearings on appropriation bills are critical techniques used by Congress in giving directions on policy and in reviewing past performance. The administrators are continually under pressure to defend past action and explain new proposals. Conflicting attitudes may be expressed, with committee members, interested in protecting the taxpayers' money, acting suspiciously hard to convince when additional funds are requested, and the bureaucrats, anxious to expand their sphere of action, seeking to justify their estimates persuasively and convincingly. If there were no conflicting attitudes and the bureaucrats and the committee members saw eye to eye, legislative review would be less meaningful; hearings proceed on the assumption that the administrator must make a convincing case to a doubting legislator.

Some of the questions are sharp, penetrating, and to the mark; some seem to be superficial and irrelevant. Control may be achieved, however, not only as the result of the particular questions which are actually asked but also because of the questions which might be asked. The fact that administrators must be prepared to defend themselves on all scores and to answer, or attempt to answer, all questions raised at the hearings is in itself a kind of supervision which forces the administrator to put his agency in good order. The hearings are conducted in private in an atmosphere which encourages the development of facts and the discussion of issues.

Some types of questions have become standardized as a result of the committees' long experience in seeking to prevent the misappropriation of funds. The questions reveal the model bureaucrat idealized by Congress to have Spartan-like qualities who places the public interest ahead of his own comfort. The bureaucrat can presumably be trusted in larger affairs if he acts prudently in smaller affairs affecting him personally. Self-control and self-sacrifice precede control over others. How much money is to be spent for cars? How much for personnel? How much for books and periodicals? How much for printing? How much for public relations? How much for travel allowances? Congressmen may be interested in some of these relatively trivial items because they are tangible, they are understandable from their own experience, and they are easily subject to directions in law. It may be easier to decide the number of new cars an agency may purchase than the number of jet planes for which contracts should be authorized.

The staff of the Appropriations Committees is not large, ordinarily one major clerk being assigned to each appropriation bill. Such a small staff often invites unfavorable comparisons with the expanded size of the bureaucracy, and the suggestion is frequently made that Congress employ a considerably larger staff to control the bureaucracy more effectively. However, this proposal is based on a mistaken conception of the function of Congress and the ability or usefulness of a large congressional staff. It is not necessary that the staff be large in order to establish effective controls—the important question concerns the issues which are decided and the best procedure for raising these issues. The proposal assumes, in the first place, that misuse of funds could be detected by anyone, whereas, in fact, appropriations involve standards of judgment, questions of ends, and essentially political decisions on how scarce resources are to be allocated. The goal to be reached, it seems to me, is to establish procedures so that Congress can decide the significant questions on spending funds.

The budget should be organized so that these questions could be posed, and Congress should be provided with an audit that would systematically supply it with information essential for making these decisions.

In addition to reviewing expenditures on its own account, the Senate committee becomes, in effect, a revisionary body for the decisions made on appropriations in the House. Departments which have received less than they wanted from the House may ask that cuts be restored, and dissatisfied interest groups have a chance to plead their case. The Bureau of the Budget may also have submitted supplemental estimates which the Senate committee will consider.

Legislative debate on appropriation bills is uneven and varies considerably in quality. The greatest interest is perhaps expressed in the bill for the Interior Department, which carries appropriations for such politically sensitive items as flood relief, dams, reclamation projects, and hydroelectric development. Appropriations for the armed services are on the opposite end of the spectrum of congressional interest. These bills may be passed relatively quickly with debate lasting less than an hour, but even within this limited period extraneous interests may be introduced in the debate.

In the normal procedure of debate, a committee member opens the discussion with a general informative statement on the content of the bill and the subjects at issue; this is followed by a statement from a minority member of the committee. The subsequent debate may be informative, with the House (or the Senate) making tentative decisions on how much money a department may be granted for specific purposes. One of the discomforting elements about the deliberations, however, is the difficulty in learning how a particular issue is finally resolved. The debate and subsequent vote may lead one to believe that an unpopular program has been terminated and that an administrator has been rebuked. However, it may later develop that the great contest has been a mock affair, with the decision reversed in the other chamber, or by the conferees, or later in the year when supplemental appropriations are made, or seemingly to have no appreciable effect on the operation of the policy in dispute. This is one of the results of bicameralism, where there are dual debates and dual decisions, and the process of making a final and conclusive decision may be prolonged. When applied to controls over appropriations, however, bicameralism may have a reverse twist by increasing the difficulty for Congress in establishing its controls over a policy already in operation. There are many ways in which the full effect of a congressional decision can be averted.

One of the techniques by which Congress attempts to control policy is that of itemizing appropriation bills, a practice inaugurated by Jeffersonian Democrats at the turn of the nineteenth century as a reaction against the former practice of granting unspecified sums to the Federalists. Under present practice, there are between 600 and 800 appropriation items, which in 1953 ranged from a low of $500 to a high of more than $12 billion. These two extremes were as follows:

Legislative Branch, For an additional amount for "Stationery (revolving fund)," first session of the Eighty-second Congress, $500, to remain available until expended: $500.

Department of the Air Force, For construction, procurement, and modification of aircraft and equipment, armor and armament, spare parts and accessories therefor; specialized equipment; expansion of public and private plants, Government-owned equipment and installation thereof in such plants, erection of structures and acquisition of land without regard to section 1136 Revised Statutes, as amended, for the foregoing and other purposes, and such land, and interests therein, may be acquired and construction prosecuted thereon prior to the approval of title by the Attorney General as required by section 355, Revised Statutes, as amended; industrial mobilization, including maintenance of reserve plants and equipment and procurement planning; and other expenses necessary for the foregoing purposes, including rents and transportation of things; to remain available until expended: $12,685,055,000.[1]

To a degree, Congress attempts to control policy by specifying the limitations and conditions under which funds can be spent. The textual matter of appropriation bills contains restrictions and specifica-

[1] *Appropriations, Budget Estimates, Etc.*, 1952, pp. 6, 82.

tions on how the funds are to be spent, including limitations on travel, the purchase of new automobiles, the spending of money "for publicity or propaganda purposes designed to support or defeat legislation pending before the Congress," construction of dams, and the like. The Secretary of Defense was told in 1952 that "in so far as practicable" he should "assist American small business to participate equitably in the furnishing of commodities and services financed with funds appropriated to under this Act." The Mutual Security Agency could not purchase commodities from the Commodity Credit Corporation "at less than the support price" except when the commodity had "substantially deteriorated in quality" or was in "danger of loss or waste through deterioration or spoilage." The State Department could not spend funds "for the promotion, direct or indirect, of the principle or doctrine of one world government or one world citizenship."

The rules of Congress ordinarily prohibit legislative riders, except those whose net effect will be to reduce expenditures (the Holman rule), but legislation may be included by suspending the rules through an extraordinary majority. The following restriction, appearing in the Interior Department Appropriation Act for 1952, expressed policy as well as limited the expenditure of money:

Provided further, That no part of this or prior appropriations shall be used for construction, nor for further commitments to construction of Moorhead Dam and Reservoir, Montana, or any feature thereof until a definite plan report thereon has been completed, reviewed by the States of Montana and Wyoming, and approved by the Congress.[2]

Congress is sometimes charged with misusing its appropriation function by adding legislative riders which contain subject matter extraneous to the appropriations being considered. The riders make it more difficult to make an independent decision on the legislative issue, but its main purpose may be to circumvent a presidential veto— and in this it is quite successful. In 1938, for instance, Congress added a rider on resale price maintenance to the appropriations bill for the District of Columbia. The President complained to Congress about

[2] Bureau of Reclamation appropriation, Public Law 136.

this indirect method of legislation, but inasmuch as he did not wish to veto the appropriation bill, the legislative provisions became law despite his strong objections.

Congressional frustration in controlling spending is reflected in proposals that the departments be directed to cut spending by some definite percentage. This approach rests on the assumption that all appropriation objects are of equal value and that a program could be kept in balance if all items were reduced equally. Following the same line of argument, it is also proposed that "the way to balance the budget is to direct the President to bring in a balanced budget." There is little doubt that the President could balance the budget if he did so independently of all other considerations. However, an effective balancing of income and outgo requires that the demands of various claimants be adjusted so that the total amount to be spent comes within the total amount of funds available. The President might meet the requirement that the budget be balanced by deleting items which Congress under no circumstances would want excluded, such as funds for defense, the postal service, or the judiciary. Congress would then have the unpleasant task of unbalancing the President's balanced budget. Balancing the budget requires the adjustment of conflicting demands, and this is properly a function for Congress to perform.

An additional factor that makes it difficult to control total spending is that there is little choice in making appropriations for some types of accounts, such as interest on the public debt, veterans' pensions and services, refundable internal revenue collections, federal old-age and survivors' funds, unemployment funds, and others. In the fiscal year 1953 appropriations in this category totaled more than $19 billion. In addition, some grants-in-aid are, in effect, moral commitments to assist the states—such as the Federal Aid Highway Act of 1952— and cannot readily be revised by Congress in making appropriations. In addition to all this, Congress frequently permits contracts to be authorized, although funds are not specifically granted at the time, and contract authorizations also create commitments which must be fulfilled.

In considering the budget, the amount of revenue anticipated may be known in general terms, but decisions on the amount to be taxed and the amount to be spent are made by two different procedures and are under the jurisdiction of different types of committees. The present law requires the President to suggest how additional revenue might be raised if the budget estimates exceed the anticipated income, and members of the tax committees have participated in attempts to place a ceiling on appropriations. In practice, however, neither of these two methods has been effective in bringing spending and taxing into balance. The failure of Congress to consider revenue and appropriations as coördinate parts of fiscal policy is partly explained by our political history, and the development of separate taxing committees and spending committees is a case in point. In the early nineteenth century, a single committee in each House had jurisdiction over both functions. The major source of revenue was the tariff, and when the tariff became increasingly a partisan issue, the question of the rates of the tariff became dissociated from revenue needs. The consideration of appropriations was removed from the revenue-raising committees at the time of the Civil War, and since then the appropriations committees have had their independent existence.

One factor which should facilitate the consideration of the budget as a whole is the practice of having a single fiscal fund for the federal government, rather than having a number of pockets for specific purposes. In general, revenue derived from specific sources is not earmarked for specific purposes, a practice followed by many states. For instance, the income from gasoline taxes does not have to be applied to the construction of roads nor the income from the issuance of passports to the support, for example, of the lighthouse keepers. Theoretically, having but one central fund should make it easier for Congress to make unencumbered decisions on policy, without having to consider relationships extraneous to the issue.

There are exceptions to the use of a single fund. Many government corporations such as the Commodity Credit Corporation have independent revolving funds which do not come under ordinary budgetary estimates and are not subject to annual appropriation supervision.

(However, they ordinarily receive their administrative expenses from congressional appropriations.) Trust funds are also an exception. From time to time, proposals are made in Congress that additional funds be established, or at least that a legal relationship be established between funds received from certain sources and certain objects of expenditure. The provision that a percentage of income from tariff revenue be applied to the problem of disposing of surplus agricultural properties, for instance, provided the legal basis for the initial school lunch program. During the controversy over the offshore oil reserves, proposals were made that a percentage of anticipated oil revenue be used for public schools, and in the debate it was made to appear that if the federal government lost jurisdiction over the area, schools would be deprived of funds which were rightfully theirs. On the whole, the most flexible budgeting is provided by a common fund, so that the merits, for instance, of a free lunch program need not be directly associated with farm tariffs or federal aid to education or with disputes over the jurisdiction of offshore oil reserves.

The budget may also be used to determine the extent of funds to be used to support particular public policies, and, by so doing, to determine what policies are to be followed. This fact has significant implications as to the ability of Congress to determine public policies. In theory, policy is determined by law, and of course law underlies appropriations. However, funds are required for the execution of policy, so that, to a degree, policy can be determined and directed by the control of supply. If the supply is reduced or terminated, the policy is changed or ended. To a degree, then, the annual consideration of the budget gives Congress an opportunity to review all policy, based on law, which requires money. The possibility of reviewing all policy through appropriating money sometimes leads to a dispute between the legislative committees and the appropriations committees on the proper function of each. Although Congress is continually making decisions on policy by increasing or decreasing funds, the method of considering appropriation bills does not always permit it to select alternatives or to determine priorities in spending. Within any particular bill, choices might be made, as on the size of a dam or the number of dams to be built, but there is less opportunity to debate the merits of spending money on dams as opposed to highways.

Some types of policy cannot readily be controlled through appropriations, and notably in areas of foreign policy. It is an ironic fact that the types of policy least adaptable to control by law are also least adaptable to control by appropriations. Personnel policy may also be influenced through appropriations, but as has been shown, Congress has little control over personnel once an appointment has been made. However, Congress may influence personnel policy indirectly by the manner in which it responds to requests for funds, and administrators who have for whatever reason displeased Congress may find that funds for their agency have been cut.

The fact that all government agencies must rely on annual appropriations raises the further question of the degree to which they can rely on their supply of funds being continued regularly. Every agency goes through a watchful period when it is uncertain what decision Congress will make, but it is difficult to generalize on the degree to which this uncertainty affects future plans or current programs. Sometimes Congress resolves the uncertainty by abolishing the agency completely, as it did during the war, by failing to provide funds for the National Resources Planning Board, the Fair Employment Practices Committee, and the National Youth Administration. On the broader question of the continuity of supply for the government as a whole, Congress attempts to provide supply on an annual basis (although if bills are not enacted by the end of the fiscal year, temporary legislation permits spending to be continued at the existing rate). However, Congress makes no attempt to use the budget as a political bludgeon, by which decisions or resignations can be forced, through the threat of withholding all governmental funds.

The system of considering appropriation bills separately has its defenders, but this emphasis on individual bills and items within bills demands a price. It is argued that individual items can be given greater attention than would be the case in a single-budget bill, and that a single bill would be too bulky for Congress to consider properly.

There is no doubt that a single-budget bill, composed of existing appropriation bills, would be quite bulky, but the bills as they now exist could be slimmed down considerably. The present method of considering the budget estimates makes it difficult to cut appropriations effectively over a period of time, although this generalization might be challenged by agencies which have felt the sharp slice of the economizer's knife. There is not one set of purse strings but many, and the fact that a large number of bills are considered means that economies which are effected in one bill may be offset by increases in another bill. During the process of making appropriations, the aggrieved agency has several opportunities for requesting Congress to restore budget cuts, and it can also ask its own "public" to petition Congress; if the cut is not restored at the time, supplementary appropriations may be requested during the fiscal year.

An attempt in the Congressional Reorganization Act of 1946 to reform the budgetary procedure proved to be so cumbersome and unworkable that it has been dropped in practice although it still exists in law. The essence of the plan was that Congress should place a ceiling on spending before it proceeded to consider appropriations bills. A joint committee was set up composed of all members of the two appropriations committees and the two revenue committees. This joint committee was to determine maximum spending amount, and a resolution embodying its recommendations was to be submitted to each House. The decision made by Congress in this resolution would be binding on all future action. This was an extravagant proposal, and it is difficult to see how the drafters of the bill could have expected the plan to work. The idea of placing a ceiling on appropriations without reference to individual amounts or without providing new procedures for considering the various appropriation bills was unrealistic enough, but it was even more unrealistic to think that this type of heterogeneous group, having no traditions in common and no background of behaving as a corporate group, could meet temporarily and develop a fiscal policy within a few weeks. The proposal was a great failure.

Another approach was the use of a single-budget bill, which was used in 1950. This procedure received a good deal of favorable comment, but it was not popular in all quarters and has not been attempted since. It was argued that a single bill would provide a better method for Congress to consider the totalities of the budget; a decision could be made on the total amount to be spent, and comparative priorities could be made on types of spending which were to be permitted. Attempts to increase amounts for favorite projects could be measured by the yardstick of fiscal policy, not by the merits of the particular policy and by the support that could be gathered for one particular vote.

Unfortunately, personalities entered into the dispute over the adequacy of the single-budget bill, and the proponents of the procedure were perhaps guilty of pushing their plan too fast, without having the prior approval of others also interested. There was no general agreement in Congress that the single-budget bill should be substituted for the numerous appropriation bills with which Congress was familiar. There was considerable support for a single-budget bill in both chambers and among both parties, and resolutions were introduced proposing the change. However, the House Committee on Appropriations, under the leadership of Representative Clarence Cannon (D., Mo.), did not think that further authorization was necessary, and it proceeding to report a single omnibus bill, rather than a dozen bills. Senator Kenneth McKellar (D., Tenn.), the chairman of the Senate Committee on Appropriations, was openly hostile to the new method.

The single-budget bill also ran into procedural difficulties. It was reported to the House on March 21, which allowed ample time for the bill to be considered by the House and the Senate. However, the House did not complete its consideration until May 10. The end of the fiscal year arrived, and the bill had not yet been reported from the Senate Committee. At length, on July 8, the Senate Committee reported the bill, and the Senate passed it on August 4. Conferences followed. It was finally signed by the President on September 6.

The single-budget bill had the further disadvantage of being considered during the period of the outbreak of fighting in Korea, which considerably upset budget estimates. Despite the fact that the single-

budget bill contained appropriations of over $30 billion, it was neces-
sary for a supplemental bill of more than $17 billion to be enacted
in September, and a second supplemental bill to be enacted in December. These requests made precise budgeting difficult.

CONTROL AFTER SPENDING

The Budget and Accounting Act provides for the systematic accounting and review of expenditures. The agency principally responsible for performing this function is the General Accounting Office
which, according to the basic Act, is to be "independent of the executive departments and under the control and direction of the Comptroller General of the United States." The Comptroller General has
power to settle the accounts of budget officers by determining whether
funds have been spent legally and to carry on investigations for the
benefit of Congress or of congressional committees. He also has power
to prescribe "the forms, systems, and procedure for administrative
appropriation and fund accounting," to investigate all matters relating to "the receipt, disbursement, and application of public funds,"
and to settle and adjust all claims, demands, and accounts concerning the government. In his reports to Congress, the Comptroller General is directed to make recommendations "looking to greater economy
or efficiency in public expenditures." He must also report "every
expenditure of contract made by any department or establishment in
any year in violation of law." He is furthermore directed to make
"such investigations and reports as shall be ordered by either House
of Congress or by any committee of either House having jurisdiction
over revenue, appropriations, or expenditures."

In theory, the General Accounting Office is an agency of Congress,
but in fact, the relationship is not especially close. The theory that the
General Accounting Office is an "arm of Congress" is continually
stressed in the literature of the agency. Comptroller General Lindsay
C. Warren has written that the General Accounting Office, "as a
representative of Congress," is an "important part of our system of
checks and balances." The accounting provisions of the Budget and
Accounting Act, he says, "marked a return to the basic concept of

legislative control of public moneys in its full sense." In the passage of the Act, "congressional control over financial matters was greatly strengthened, and for the first time the Congress had its own non-partisan and nonpolitical agent to assure the furnishing of necessary information concerning the financial transactions of the Government and to enforce the congressional intent as to expenditures." [3] Within Congress, the Comptroller General has enjoyed the highest prestige and the greatest confidence, and Congress has resisted several attempts to modify the present audit arrangements.

As part of the budget reform within Congress, a committee structure was created to parallel the creation of the General Accounting Office. At the time of the passage of the Act, there were some dozen Committees on Expenditures in each House, which more or less paralleled the departmental structure; these committees were combined into one committee in each House as part of the movement for fiscal reform. The new theory of congressional control of funds provided for unified and consolidated Appropriations Committees (one for each House) which would consider the budget estimates and unified and consolidated Expenditures Committees (one for each House) which would consider the reports of the Comptroller General.

The Expenditure Committees failed to develop into useful committees for controlling funds. They rarely met during the first quarter century of their history, and they did not develop the type of fiscal control anticipated when the Budget and Accounting Act was passed. In 1946 the committees were reconstituted and their jurisdiction was expanded by the Congressional Reorganization Act (the name of the Senate committee was later changed to the Committee on Government Organization). In this last reorganization, the committees were given jurisdiction over plans for reorganizing the government, and this phase of their activities has provided them with a long agenda of business. The House committee has the following five subcommittees: Executive and Legislative Reorganization; Federal Relations with International Organizations; Government Operations; Intergovernmental Relations; and Public Accounts—the only subcommittee directly con-

[3] *Annual Report,* 1950, p. 1.

cerned with fiscal control. The subcommittees of the Senate committee are Reorganization, Investigation, and Wild Life Conservation—none is directly concerned with fiscal control.

One might well ask why Congress has failed to develop a public accounts committee which is a functioning part of the system of fiscal control. One reason may be that neither the Comptroller General nor the committees of Congress has had a clear vision of the part Congress should play, or might play, in reviewing spending after appropriations have been made. No committee or committee chairman within Congress has insisted on having the type of information necessary for this purpose, nor has the Comptroller General provided such information. Despite the avowals of the Comptroller General that he is an "arm of Congress," the most that can be said is that he acts for Congress but not with Congress. In short, the Comptroller General has not provided Congress with very much information on how funds have been spent. One need not describe here the extensive quarreling which existed, until recently, between the various governmental agencies and the Comptroller General over the authority of the latter to settle accounts and to prescribe the forms, systems, and procedures for departmental accounting. In settling accounts, the Comptroller General is sometimes said to determine what the law is and whether appropriations have been spent legally. This keeps the departments within the bounds of the law as determined by the Comptroller General; their protests on some of the interpretations convince many in Congress that the Comptroller General has hit the mark.

It is also claimed that the Comptroller General in effect audits his own accounts and, therefore, is not in a position to send Congress any information on how money might be better spent. His emphasis is on legality, not on wisdom or on results, and the assurance that funds have been spent legally does not necessarily mean that a penny has been saved or that Congress has any further information on how much money should be appropriated.

One type of information sent to Congress by the Comptroller General concerns the expenditures made "in violation of law" and disallowed by him. The list may total in the neighborhood of ten million dollars. However, this type of information does not give Congress much assistance in appropriating money; it may merely indicate those items whose legality was disputed by the departments and the Comptroller General. In one sense of the word, this money may be considered to have been "saved"; in another sense, it is not actually saved for it can be spent for other objects approved by the Comptroller General.

The Comptroller General also submits a large number of reports to Congress and its committees, which, in one year recently, amounted to 64 reports to Congress and 621 reports to committees. The number of reports is more impressive than their content. Some concern legislation pending before committees—a report on the bill, "Relief of Former Army Officer from Liability to Refund Overpayments of Retired Pay," is an example. Some contain interpretations of law, such as the question of the legality of paying the salary and travel expenses of a county committeeman (agriculture) to attend certain types of meetings. Some contain evaluations of the expenditure of funds for certain objects, such as the development of Chatham Field and the Logan International Airport. The Comptroller General does not provide a general overall audit for Congress which indicates how money is spent and the purpose for which it is spent. It does not use the technique of auditing to reveal useful information to Congress in a regularized manner. It acts more as a trouble shooter, giving Congress specific information on request. It may be, indeed, that a false distinction has been made between the functions of reviewing spending and of appropriating funds. It is probably unnecessary to have separate committees perform these functions, and an argument can be made for consolidating this work in the Appropriations Committees.

BUDGETARY REFORM

Proposals for budgetary reform spring up like mushrooms; some have considerable merit, while others are worthless and mischievous. The more popular reform proposals include the following: that a superbudget committee be created to determine fiscal policy; that a vastly enlarged staff be employed "responsible only to Congress"; that all appropriation accounts be consolidated into a single-budget bill; that the President be given an item veto; that a better system of accounting be developed; that a system of congressional liaison be established in making up the budget; that the President be compelled by law to balance the budget; and that appropriations be made bi-annually.

The annual budget represents a change from an earlier day in the method of making policy decisions; it is, indeed, an enormous undertaking which, in its totality, provides funds for carrying out almost all government policy. Congress is accustomed to dealing with limited policy by small committee groups, and the budget may seem to be vast and unwieldy, leaving Congressmen with a feeling of awe, frustration, and helplessness. What can an individual Congressman do about a 60-billion-dollar budget?

There are three major purposes to be accomplished by budgetary reform. The first is to strengthen congressional control over the totality of spending; the second, to strengthen congressional control over policy decisions; and the third, to give Congress further information on past spending. These purposes are so interrelated that excessive emphasis on one may diminish the emphasis on the others. In examining the reform proposals, one should bear in mind the three-fold objectives.

An annual budget makes it possible for Congress to decide the total amount of money to be appropriated, but Congress lets this decision go by default. If Congress is not interested in making decisions on totals, it might well consider returning to the former system of permanent appropriations. There have been many proposals for permitting Congress to act on the budget as a whole, including the ill-starred proposal in the Reorganization Act that Congress determine the total amount of spending before it proceeds to consider the individual appropriation bills. The procedure of allowing one group to set the ceiling on spending and another group to make thousands of decisions on amounts, the total of which would be within those ceilings, seems to me to be an unrealistic way of proceeding.

On the whole, the single-budget bill offers the best vehicle for Congress to assert its control over total amounts of spending. This procedure provides a method by which Congress can consider the budget as an entity and debate fiscal policy in the round. More than this, in considering individual items, an opportunity is presented to compare the merits of individual programs and establish some system of priorities in spending. This is always done, to a degree, but a single-budget bill would make it possible to make comparative judgments on all demands for appropriations. As for the budget instrument itself, there is great need for simplification on the one hand and further explanations on the other hand. It would seem possible to devise a budget bill that would permit Congress to make major decisions on policy, with accompanying statements that would clarify purpose and achievement. The present profusion of budgetary documents is better designed for informing the expert and the technician than for imparting information to lay members of Congress.

Many questions of policy must, perforce, be decided in the allocation of funds, and the consideration of the single-budget bill should assist in developing and clarifying policy decisions. There are other ways in which policy can be expressed. It would seem desirable that congressional leaders be asked to assume some responsibility in developing the budget initially, and that the President confer with the leaders on budgetary questions in the same fashion that he consults with them on questions of legislative policy and personnel policy. In the literature of budget making, the dogma has been developed that the President should not deal with troublesome politicians in framing a budget, but a preferable theory would consider budget making as a political decision in which Congress has a considerable interest.

Policy decisions may take the form of stipulations in appropriation bills on how money is to be spent. This function comes properly within the jurisdiction of Congress, and the major criticism would be that the instructions are often of a petty nature. It seems essential that Congress retain the authority to specify how funds are to be spent, and for this reason the proposal that the President have the power to veto items seems to be an unnecessary relinquishment by

Congress of its authority. The present bifurcation between legislative committees and appropriation committees in formulating policy has its effect on budget making. The device of a centralized budgetary system has given budgetary staff agencies considerable authority over agencies of the line—those which actually carry out policy. The adoption of a budgetary system by the national government has resulted in a similar centralization of authority in the appropriations committees, with conflict developing between legislative committees primarily concerned with functions and appropriations committees primarily concerned with spending. The fact remains, of course, that the actions of legislative committees in authorizing funds have important consequences on budgetary commitments. Inasmuch as authorizations for spending become commitments carrying obligation of fulfillment, Congress might well consider establishing further internal controls over legislative authorizations for the spending of money. There is now no centralized control over this whatever, and there is no procedural method for making Congress aware of the total figures involved.

On the subject of controlling past spending, Congress might place greater reliance on improved audit procedure and less on an enlarged staff. In reality, Congress has at its disposal an immense accounting system which is in close touch with government spending all over the globe. This vast bureaucracy of accounts has never been mobilized effectively for purposes of congressional control, and, except in special cases, Congress is given little information, based on performance audits, on how effectively money has been spent for particular projects. Performance audits of the General Accounting Office should be available to the Appropriations Committees in making decisions. The Expenditures Committees have not proved useful for auditing accounts, and their jurisdiction over affairs of the General Accounting Office could well be transferred to the Committees on Appropriations.

CHAPTER 10

Controls Through Investigations

THE CONTROL EXERCISED BY INVESTIGATING COMMIT-
tees is often dramatically expressed, especially when it results in open
conflict between a committee and some witness who, perhaps ob-
stinately, refuses to answer questions put to him or to produce the
documents requested. The large number of cases involving investigating committees which have been decided by the courts in recent years
give some indication of the controversial character of investigations.
Emotions may color any attempt to evaluate their work objectively.
The ability of investigating committees to evoke such strong feelings
of approbation or disapprobation is to some a measure of their
competence, to others, a measure of their excesses. Some of the latter,
surely, would like to tighten the procedures of investigating committees while the former would claim that procedural changes might in-
fringe on the free-rolling character of the committees and tend to sap
their effectiveness.

Some investigating committees are little different from ordinary
legislative committees in that they are procedurally correct, their bark
isn't loud, and they have no bite. Everyone is polite to everybody
else. On the other hand, the actions of some committees reach the

headlines, if not the courts, and the committees may be able to add to the discomfiture of witnesses by asking embarrassing questions, publishing confidential or possibly indiscreet correspondence never meant for the public eye, and setting uncoöperative witnesses on their way to jail. Government agencies may also be apprehensive, and the possibility of investigating committees descending on them unannounced and with an axe to grind may make officials regret their choice of career.

In the preceding chapters, the point was developed that congressional control is concerned with giving directions and reviewing actions. The whole investigating controversy can be placed in perspective by considering it as part of a broader question of determining the purpose and method of congressional controls—of how best to mobilize, process, organize, and utilize essential information. The failure to develop a workable theory on the nature of congressional controls has often distorted the controversy over investigations by raising the wrong questions. Legal answers go only part way in providing an acceptable solution. The issue frequently raised by investigations may be stated simply: How in marginal cases can Congress force reluctant witnesses to disgorge information? This relatively narrow issue of compulsion is really part of a broader question, which might be stated as follows: What pertinent information does Congress need to establish effective controls over policy? Although the first question needs to be answered, its answer should be relevant to the broader problem of control.

One might say initially that there is perhaps no thoroughly satisfactory boundary for limiting Congress in compelling desired information to be produced. If the proposal that no limits should be imposed is coupled with the intention to organize congressional authority around this proposal, the way is opened for a new type of Congress which indeed might destroy the autonomy of other institutions, make meaningless the whole concept of confidentiality, and replace the rule of law by haphazard instructions, threats, and demands. On the other hand, any considerable restriction on the investigative power would deprive Congress of an unparalleled weapon necessary for its own survival, which enables it to search out and expose wrongdoing. Clearly neither alternative is appealing, and to remove ourselves from the horns of this dilemma it is necessary to consider the function of investigating committees not only from a legal but also from a political and institutional point of view.

In giving authoritative directions it is customary for Congress to enact a law of general applicability which in turn is administered by a politically neutral government agency. Laws which punish a named person with no opportunity given for a judicial trial fall within the category of bills of attainder and as such are prohibited. In the realm of investigations, however, Congress skirts the edge of this treacherous ground of personal legislation by giving to specific individuals directions which are not otherwise of general applicability and whose content is not found in law. However, the exercise of such authority is different in kind and degree from that required in making law—there is a difference in formulating the issue, a difference in applying the rule, and a difference in results.

RAISING THE ISSUE

Investigations find their justification in the basic requirement that Congress have access to pertinent facts, and it was stated earlier that a legislature such as Congress can exist only under conditions where there is a free flow of information. An indication of the importance of reliable information for a legislature is found in the fact that the postwar constitutions of Japan and Germany were amended to include authority for legislatures to create investigating committees and to interrogate administrators.

Although the Constitution makes no reference to congressional investigations as such, the necessary authority is deduced from the provision that "all legislative powers" rest in Congress. It is evident that Congress requires facts to make law, and from this premise it can be argued that if the necessary information is not otherwise forthcoming, Congress may compel witnesses to testify and to produce papers on matters relevant to the legislative proposal. Congress may also require information for other purposes not directly related to legislation; it may need facts in impeachment proceedings, in election cases, and in controlling government agencies. The Senate may additionally require further information in considering treaties and nominations submitted by the President.

In carrying on investigations, two types of issues are raised. One relates to choice—to the political question of allocating such scarce legislative commodities as time, money, authority, and energy. All this falls under the general category of political competition discussed earlier. The second issue, concerning the relationship between the committee and the witness, arises from the fact that, in its investigative activities, Congress does not have full command over all pertinent data and over all participants in the process. Nonmembers must perforce participate in congressional investigations, and the subject of discussion may relate to information especially vital to other systems of action and to attitudes, expressions of opinions, and the behavior of individuals in their private capacity. The issue of giving orders to individuals and of making public certain types of information which have hitherto been private raises questions of purpose, of procedure, and of permissible secrecy (public or private)—all placed against a background where neither law nor political thought has established well-worn paths.

The exercise of investigative powers antedates the Constitution, and there are precedents of a sort where American colonial legislatures asserted authority to punish witnesses adjudged in contempt. There are British precedents also, including an instance where a committee of the House of Commons sent a man to the Tower of London for lying before the committee. However, these historical examples are sparse, and they did not occur often enough to be thought of as part of the operating folklore of a legislative body. They were something added to ordinary procedure when the normal process was inadequate.

Congressional investigation as such extends as far back as 1791 when Congress created a committee with extraordinary powers for investigating the St. Clair expedition against the Indians, which had met with unexpected misfortunes. Investigations were continued on into the nineteenth century, when a large number were held on the conduct of various government officials. Although the records of these investigations have been poorly preserved, the available sources indicate that the committees were often embarrassingly active and that investigations did not originate with Senator McCarthy, with Representative Dies or—for those with longer memories—with Senator Nye, Senator Black, or Senator Walsh.

The fact that investigations may be concerned with the adequacy of existing policy, or the need for new policy, or the failure to enforce policy may lead investigators to subjects far afield from the ordinary legislative routine. They may very shortly be involved in the procedures of various kinds of institutions, governmental and nongovernmental. The exposure of facts may, as a general principle, be in the public interest, yet the fact that the selective exposure of certain institutions or certain types of action may affect policy or reputations makes the conduct of any investigation an issue having considerable political consequences.

The procedures followed by congressional investigations are so similar to those of an ordinary committee hearing that it is not always possible to draw a sharp line between routine hearings and hearings which are commonly known as congressional investigations. So long as individuals are willing to talk freely and to pay their own expenses, any committee can hold hearings and carry on investigations indefinitely. On the other hand, some committees are given special authority and special funds to investigate particular activities. In addition to the investigations of committees, facts may also be found by commissions, often having a membership chosen from the executive branch and the public as well as from Congress; by the Legislative Reference Division of the Library of Congress; and by the staffs of congressional committees.

In cases where facts are not forthcoming through ordinary procedures or where hearings are believed inadequate, special action may be taken to authorize an investigation. This may involve the appropriations of funds and the granting of special authority to compel the attendance of witnesses or the production of papers. It was the expectation of those who sponsored the Congressional Reorganization Act of 1946 that investigations would henceforth be carried on exclusively by the regular standing committees, but this has not happened. Special inquiries may still be authorized, so that in fact investigations may be undertaken either by a committee specially created for the purpose or by a regular standing committee. Approximately 50 investigations are carried on every year, many of which receive little publicity and fail to impress themselves on the public consciousness, and in addition continued requests for investigations are made but never authorized.

The number of investigations authorized annually, compared with the number which are proposed, shows not only that some control is exercised over investigations but also that the majority does not stamp out indiscriminately all proposals to investigate. The so-called majority does not always act as a unit, of course, and in many cases only a few defections from the majority would be needed to enable the minority to create an investigation. But more than this: It may also be to the advantage of the majority to carry on investigations where needed so as to be assured that the policy they support can be defended with honesty.

In examining the legality of investigations, the courts have in general upheld the use Congress has made of its investigative power, although some issues have been contentious. They have upheld the authority of Congress to investigate such diverse topics as old age pensions, interstate crime, the sale of surplus property, campaign expenditures, and the unauthorized publication of treaties. The single case where the courts denied Congress the authority to investigate is that of *Kilbourn v. Thompson* (1881) (103 US 168), which arose from Congress' attempt to investigate the bankruptcy of a real estate pool operating in the District of Columbia. The court found the inquiry to be invalid because it related to "a matter wherein relief or redress could be had only by a judicial proceeding." Neither the Senate nor the House had "a general power for making inquiry into the private affairs of the citizen." The authority to investigate was limited to matters in which the two Houses had "jurisdiction," which did not include proceedings in bankruptcy.

The Supreme Court has stated that neither House is invested with " 'general' power to inquire into private affairs and compel disclosures" but only with a limited power of inquiry. However, the limits are not closely defined, and the Supreme Court has also said that "the two Houses of Congress, in their separate relations, possess not only such powers as are expressly granted to them by the Constitution, but such auxiliary powers as are necessary and appropriate to make the express powers effective." In other words, the authority of Congress to investigate is as extensive as its authority to legislate, and the court has argued further that the former is necessary to the latter. "We are of opinion," the Supreme Court said in *McGrain v. Daugherty,* that "the power of inquiry—with process to enforce it— is an essenital and appropriate auxiliary to the legislative function," and it argued that a legislative body could not legislate wisely without recourse to information. Inasmuch as requests for information are often unavailing and volunteered information is not always accurate or complete, "some means of compulsion are essential to obtain what is needed." [1] In a later case concerning the contempt of Dr. Francis Townsend, the leader of an old age pension movement, the appelate court went further and said that an investigation need not result in legislation in order to make it valid. The authority of a committee "to conduct a hearing for legislative purpose is not to be measured by recommendations for legislation or their absence." [2]

In view of the fact that investigations (like other activities of Congress) should have a purpose and that authority (of whatever nature) should be controlled, it would seem desirable that Congress be as punctilious in authorizing investigations as it is (or should be) in authorizing government action through law. In other words investigations should have a clearly worded mandate lasting for a specific period of time; they should have definite although limited authority; and they should be held to prudent accountability for the expenditure of funds and the activities of the staff. All these control techniques are now utilized by Congress, although not always to the same degree.

[1] *McGrain v. Daugherty* (1926) 273 US 135, 174, 175.
[2] *Townsend v. United States* (1938) 95 F 2d 352, 355.

In recent years, moreover, there has been a propensity to give permanent investigative authority to certain committees or subcommittees, a policy which prevents Congress from assessing the results of investigations before extending the grant of authority.

DELIBERATION

The deliberations of investigating committees are in many respects similar to the deliberations of committee hearings—that is, through questions and answers. However, the fact that some testimony may lead to criminal prosecutions makes investigations somewhat analogous to the procedures of grand juries. This parallel has led to proposed reforms, based primarily on judicial lines, which include such innovations as the cross-examination of witnesses. It might be ill-advised to press reforms so far along this line that investigating committees would be transformed from their amateur status as fact-finding bodies into professionalized judicial bodies. If district attorneys and grand juries are not doing their work properly, the reform should come at that point—not by changing the nature and function of congressional investigating committees. Reform might better be pressed in two other directions. One reform would place greater emphasis on the committee's developing an impressive final product (and less on some of the more controversial aspects of acquiring information). Another would be the creation of a more adequate and efficient system of congressional controls which would make it less necessary to employ the device of special investigations.

In view of the fact that investigating committees have special authority over witnesses, the courts have been willing to examine the committees from the point of view of the legality of their organizational structure. Two points are especially pertinent—the controversy over the quorum and the validity of one-man investigating committees. The subcommittee-of-one becomes controversial because there are no immediate operating controls; the single person in charge of the committee has authority to issue subpoenas and to hear testimony without the safeguards or the restraints provided by other members of the committee, including those from the minority. The witness is cut off from his relations with the outside world, except in so far as the subcommittee-of-one chooses to permit. Although the legality of such one-man committees has been upheld, the question of fairness and equity cannot be excluded from a situation where the witness has little protection from a questioner who might attempt to bully him into making a contemptuous remark.

The use of the one-man subcommittee has increased since the ruling of the Supreme Court in the Christoffel case (1948) (338 US 84), in which it was said that the committee must have a quorum "actually and physically present" if it is to be "the instrument of criminal conviction." The court's decision was contrary to congressional usage, although the court did discover a case, long forgotten, where the House had once refused to consider a bill because a committee lacked a quorum when it reported the bill to the House. The dissent of Mr. Justice Jackson, which is more in keeping with judicial and congressional precedents and the requirements of parliamentary behavior, said that the court was "denying to the records of the Congress and its committees the credit and effect to which they are entitled, quite contrary to all recognized parliamentary rules, our previous decisions, and the Constitution itself." The court should not devise a new rule "to extend aid to one who did not raise his objection when it could be met and who has been prejudiced by absence of a quorum only if we assume that, although he told a falsehood to eleven congressmen, he would have been honest if two more had been present." In no event, Mr. Justice Jackson said, should the court "put out a doctrine by which every congressional Act or committee action, and perhaps every judgment here, can be overturned on oral testimony of interested parties." Whatever defects the one-man subcommittee may have, it does have the merit of assuring the presence of a quorum at all times.

The questions raised by broadcasting investigations over radio and television are, of course, part of the broader question of broadcasting legislative proceedings and court proceedings. There will be no analysis of the problem here—only a comment or two, with an indication of possible prejudice. Granting that there may be some "educational" value in broadcasting official proceedings, the more vital question relates to the possible effect on the institutions involved of such educational exercises. One would want to know the effect, say, on deliberation of being watched by a million pairs of eyes. Would a different emphasis be placed on some aspects of the process, and other aspects ignored? In short, would the broadcasting of proceedings tend to have a disintegrating effect on the process itself? One has a certain sympathy for the opinion of the judge in the case of *United States v. Kleinman* (1952) (107 F Supp 407), where it was held that the obligation of a witness to coöperate with a committee does not extend to testifying before television cameras. The purpose of putting a witness on the stand "is to get a thoughtful, calm, considered and, it is to be hoped, truthful disclosure of facts," the court said, and the atmosphere of the hearings should be directed toward that end. The court found that witness Kleinman, when refusing to testify before the Kefauver Committee, had been confronted with "television cameras, newsreel cameras, news photographers with their concomitant flashbulbs, radio microphones, a large and crowded hearing room with spectators along the walls," and other such distractions. It believed that the "obdurate stand" of the witness should be viewed "in the context of all of these conditions."

OBSTRUCTIONS TO DELIBERATION

Deliberations do not always run smoothly, and especially if witnesses resort to obstructive tactics by failing to appear, to answer questions, and to produce papers. The general rule is that a witness must appear if he is subpoenaed, whatever may be his reluctance to testify or whatever doubts he may have about the legality of the proceedings. The legal questions can be raised later.

The authority of Congress to compel the attendance of government witnesses is less clear inasmuch as members of the executive branch are in a strong constitutional position to resist subpoenas. There are some hazards in determining the precise extent of congressional or executive authority in these relationships, and no controversy has been permitted to reach a crisis where supremacy was established. Whatever the extent of legal authority may be, it would not be desirable for one branch to be able to command or to refuse unconditionally, a situation which would change the nature of the government by giving virtual supremacy to one branch. As it is, a relatively harmonious pattern of relations has developed between Congress, its committees, and the executive departments, in which the question of ultimate authority seldom arises.

In a number of specific cases, Presidents have refused to comply with requests for testimony made by Congress, courts, and grand juries. For instance, President Jefferson rejected a subpoena to appear as a witness in the trial of Aaron Burr; President Buchanan refused to be cross-examined "either personally or by a substitute" by the so-called Covode committee; after leaving office, President Truman refused to honor a subpoena issued by the House Committee on Un-American Activities. The President's ability to issue pardons enables him, in effect, to prevent the legal punishment of executive witnesses who fail to comply with subpoenas, and on numerous occasions officials have refused to testify until presidential approval has been given.

In addition to appearing before a congressional committee, there is a further presumption that the witness should testify when asked, not that he may have good grounds for refusing. One of the most tantalizing cases of refusal to testify occurred when Henry W. Grunewald sat mute before a subcommittee of the House Committee on Ways and Means, even refusing to tell his name. The following excerpt shows the difficulty faced by the committee in establishing elementary communications with the witness:

Chairman King: Have you made any effort, Mr. Grunewald, to secure counsel other than Mr. Maloney?

(No answer from the witness.)

Chairman King: Have you or have you not made any effort since the recess of this committee to secure counsel?

(No answer from the witness.)

Chairman King: All right, the photographers will stand in recess.

Mr. Curtis: Mr. Grunewald, why don't you tell us whether or not
                     you have made any attempt to get counsel?

(No answer from the witness.)

Mr. Curtis: Don't you have any desire to be coöperative in this
                     hearing at all?

(No answer from the witness.)

Mr. Curtis: Are you able to hear what is being said, Mr. Grune-
                     wald?

(No answer from the witness.)

Mr. Curtis: I say, are you able to hear what is being said to you?

(No answer from the witness.) [3]

In sentencing Grunewald, Judge Holtzoff of the District Court cited as
"mitigating circumstances" the bad advice Grunewald had received
from his attorney. "The fact that a defendant is advised by counsel
to commit a criminal act is no defense," the judge said, "but in determining sentence it may be mitigating. The average client feels he
has a lawyer who knows what he is doing." [4]

The Supreme Court has said that the rule laid down by Dean
Wigmore concerning testimony before courts of law has applicability
also for congressional investigations. Dean Wigmore wrote as follows:

For more than three centuries it has now been recognized as a fundamental maxim that the public . . . has a right to every man's evidence.
When we come to examine the various claims of exemption, we start with
the primary assumption that there is a general duty to give what testimony
one is capable of giving, and that any exemptions which may exist are
distinctly exceptional, being so many derogations from a positive rule.[5]

It follows from these precepts that a witness must attempt to
coöperate with the committee and not act independently and capri-
ciously. Several years ago a House Committee was questioning Dr.
Francis Townsend about his old age pension scheme, and in particular
about the background of his organizers. Irritated at the turn of the
questioning, Dr. Townsend told the committee that because of the

[3] *Congressional Record,* April 9, 1952, p. 3905, H. Rept. 1748, 82d Cong.
[4] S. Doc. 99, February 9, 1954, pp. 14–15.
[5] Wigmore's *Evidence,* 3d ed., §2192. See *United States v. Bryan* (1949)
339 US 323, 331.

unfriendly atmosphere he would answer no more questions and was "retiring from this sort of an inquisition." With that, he left the room. Dr. Townsend was convicted of contempt, but he was pardoned by the President.[6]

The question is frequently raised: What kind of questions must be answered? The rule laid down by the courts is that a witness may be cited for contempt only if the question is pertinent, although it does not follow that all questions need to be pertinent. During the investigations of the Kefauver Committee, a witness refused to answer a series of questions relating to his personal background, including the question of the business in which he was engaged in Chicago in 1927, whether the witness knew a named individual, and where the witness had acquired money for purchasing an interest in a restaurant in Florida in 1942. The court admitted that it might be "ultimately helpful" for the congressional committee to ask a series of background questions which it could not demonstrate to be pertinent, but pertinency must be established if an attempt is made to convict a witness for refusing to answer a question. It would never be necessary to show pertinency, the court said, if it accepted the government's contention that the questions were preliminary only.[7]

Personal feuds may enter the questioning, and an incident which occurred during an investigation of the Jackson Administration shows that strong language and even physical threats have not been unknown. Representative Balie Peynton, a Tennessee Whig and a member of the special committee, was angered by the answer of a witness, one Reuben M. Whitney. Approaching Whitney as if he were about to draw a weapon, Peynton said: "I want you to understand, sir, that I claim no protection from the Constitution; and if you insult me, you damned dog! I will take your life." Whitney was arrested for contempt of the committee for not answering the question, but he was eventually discharged, the House believing that Whitney had reason to fear bodily damage in Peynton's presence.[8]

[6] *Townsend v. United States* (1938) 95 F 2d 352.
[7] *Bowers v. United States* (1953) 202 F 2d 447.
[8] See House Journal, February 16, 1837, p. 420; 3 *Hinds' Precedents* §1666.

During the extensive investigations carried on by Congress since the war, some witnesses have claimed immunity under the Fifth Amendment, saying that they should be excused from testifying because their testimony would tend to incriminate them in a criminal trial. Congress has not pressed contempt charges against such witnesses nor have perjury suits been instituted where the privilege has been falsely claimed. However, the legal ability of a witness to refuse to testify before a congressional committee on such grounds is not clear, although it is clear that both the law and the Constitution protect a witness from the consequences of testifying against himself in a criminal case. The law provides that no testimony given by a witness before a committee of either House "shall be used as evidence in any criminal proceeding against him in any court, except in a prosecution for perjury committed in giving such testimony" (18 USC §3486); the Constitution, in the Fifth Amendment, provides that "no person . . . shall be compelled in any criminal case to be a witness against himself." The prohibitions, it will be seen, are against the use of the testimony in a criminal prosecution, not against the giving of testimony before a congressional committee. This distinction has led to legislation which, in effect, attempts to strike a bargain by which a witness can be compelled to testify in return for guaranteed immunity from prosecution, authorized by the courts.

The flexibility in practice of committees in requesting papers makes it difficult to state a general rule which is ordinarily followed. Despite the claims of the government for the need to classify documents and restrict their circulation, under a combination of congressional pressure and public interest the government may choose to reveal a good deal. Such was the case in the investigation in 1951 of the dismissal of General MacArthur and in the investigation in 1945–1946 of the Pearl Harbor disaster. As for private individuals, the courts have said that the papers requested by a committee must be pertinent, and the refusal to produce papers must be willful. As a matter of fact, however, documents of a personal, confidential, and nonpertinent nature may be found in the files of material which is otherwise pertinent. When private groups open their files for the convenience of committee investigators, a vast amount of material may be seen, and perhaps made public, which may hitherto have been personal and confidential.

The point at which a request for papers will be considered an unreasonable search and seizure has not been clarified by the courts. In a case concerning the Federal Trade Commission, the court said that it was "contrary to the first principles of justice to allow a search through all the respondent's records, relevant or irrelevant, in the hope that something will turn up." [9] This injunction was repeated in a later case, which arose out of the activities of a committee headed by Senator Hugo Black (D., Ala.) investigating the lobbying carried on in connection with the Holding Company bill in 1935. The Federal Communications Commission assisted Senator Black's committee in securing copies of Western Union telegrams containing editorial instructions for the Hearst press. The court said that it could not interfere once the telegrams were in the possession of the committee, but it could have provided a remedy had it been called on sooner. If the Senate committee were "to attempt to force a telegraph company to produce telegrams not pertinent to the matters the committee was created to investigate, the committee could be restrained at the instance of the sender of the telegrams." [10]

There have been many controversies between Congress and the executive branch over the production of papers, with the latter being in a strong legal position to resist congressional demands. In fact, however, the executive branch may go a long way in coöperating with Congress and supplying the papers requested. An early precedent for resisting congressional demands occurred during Washington's administration, when the House asked the President to produce certain papers relating to the negotiation of a treaty with Great Britain. The President refused to comply, saying that it was essential to preserve "the boundaries fixed by the Constitution between the different departments." The House of Representatives was also rebuffed by President Tyler in 1842 when it asked for a list of the names of mem-

[9] *Federal Trade Commission v. American Tobacco Co.* (1923) 264 US 298.
[10] *Hearst v. Black* (1936) 87 F 2d 68.

bers of Congress who had been applicants for public office during the preceding four years. Tyler refused, saying that the appointing power was solely in the hands of the Executive, and he could not accept the position that all papers which come into the hands of the President or the departments must necessarily be subject to the call of Congress merely because they relate to a subject within the sphere of legitimate congressional power. He stressed the applicability of the maxim that "the rights of one person or body are to be exercised so as not to impair those of others." [11]

During the Civil War, the Joint Committee on the Conduct of the War was authorized to send for persons and papers in carrying on its inquiry. This grant of authority was broadly used. In the period since the Second World War, the President has tightened his personal control over the production of executive papers, the most stringent directive being that of March 13, 1946, which prevents the release of the confidential reports of the FBI and other investigative agencies except with the express authority of the President.

The House of Representatives was prepared to challenge the President's order of March 13, but in the end it was caught in the embarrassing position of first shaking a fist and then a finger. The issue arose over the attempt of the House Committee on Un-American Activities to secure a letter written by Mr. J. Edgar Hoover, the Director of the FBI, concerning the activities and associations of Dr. Edward U. Condon, the Director of the National Bureau of Standards. The committee had in some fashion come into possession of at least part of the letter, from which a phrase derogatory to Dr. Condon had been extracted and publicized. The committee first attempted to secure the full letter by a subpoena directed to the Secretary of Commerce, the recipient of the FBI letter, but the Secretary declined to coöperate, saying that "as a matter of law" the executive branch was not required to furnish information of this kind to a congressional committee and that he had reached the conclusion that the release of the document would be "prejudicial to the public interest." Then the House stepped

[11] Quoted in *Congressional Record*, February 25, 1926, p. 4548.

in. By a vote of 302–29, it passed a resolution "directing" the Secretary of Commerce to transmit the letter. Nothing happened. The Secretary of Commerce did not produce the letter. The House did not arrest the Secretary, bringing him before the bar of the House, and it did not cite him for contempt, with the case referred to a United States District Attorney.[12]

Although Congress may itself punish acts of contempt, it has been found inconvenient to bring witnesses before the bar of the House or Senate and to keep them in custody until the contempt is absolved— but for a period no longer than the session of Congress. Since 1857, the courts have been empowered to punish specific contemptuous actions, but it is probable that Congress still retains the authority to punish these same actions.

The question whether the authority of the President to pardon extends to actions of contempt punished by Congress has never been answered, but pardons of this nature would appear to lie beyond the President's competence. As has been mentioned, the President pardoned Dr. Francis E. Townsend, who had been found guilty by the courts of contempt of Congress, and presumably the President could also pardon any executive officer who had been found guilty by the courts of contempt for refusing to answer questions or produce papers.

The decision whether to cite a witness for contempt rests initially with the committee, and there are numerous cases where witnesses who were patently contemptuous have not been cited. Under prevailing practice, a committee will present a report to the parent chamber in which the offending action is described; pertinent quotations from the testimony and copies of warrants and other official papers may also be included in the report. Following the debate, a vote is taken, and if in the affirmative the case is certified to the district attorney. The committees are ordinarily upheld by the parent chamber, although the Senate did reject certain proposals for contempt citations made by the Kefauver Committee. If the violation occurs when the parent chamber is not in session, the complaint can be certified by the Speaker of the House or the President of the Senate.

[12] See *Congressional Record*, April 22, 1948.

DECISION

We may finally ask: What types of decisions are made by investigating committees? What is the final product of their long deliberations? It should again be emphasized that however influential the investigation committees may be, they have no authority to formulate policy themselves. The report or the findings may be informative, but additional action is needed in order to transform suggestions into policy.

After a period of well-publicized hearing, the report itself may come as an anticlimax, something to be filed and forgotten rather than a document which synthesizes the findings, with a clear exposition of the direction future policy might take. In some cases, as in the special investigation of the removal from command of General MacArthur, a committee report may not even be submitted.

The government agencies need not take the advice given by investigating committees, for they are under no legal obligation to do so. The difficulty of following congressional advice is surely compounded if different committees give different signals—and this happened during the Second World War on issues of price control, production, and reconversion. In the case of the War Production Board, however, such an intimate relationship was developed with the Truman Committee that the latter was able to exert considerable influence over policy.

The jurisdiction of congressional committees is such that the specially created legislative committees cannot themselves report out legislation for the consideration of the House or Senate. Legislation must first be submitted to the standing committees and await their additional approval before being considered on the floor. Granted that the requirement of this additional step may serve as a kind of leash on investigating committees, it may also serve to isolate the investigating committees from the main stream of policy formation. The jealousy between committees being what it is, there may indeed be a propensity on the part of legislative committees to ignore the recommendations of their impetuous rivals, the investigating committees. What has happened, for instance, to the recommendations of the Kefauver Committee after the revelation of the pervasive influence of organized crime?

Another kind of recommendation is that submitted to a federal district attorney for further legal action and perhaps prosecution. The case of obdurate witnesses has already been mentioned. The committee may, however, go further and suggest that special legal action be taken on the basis of the findings unearthed during the investigations. This procedure was followed in the case of the irregularities in the Teapot Dome oil leases uncovered by the Senate Committee on Public Lands. It was followed also in the perjury trial of Harold Christoffel, where evidence at variance with Christoffel's sworn testimony was produced by diligent committee members. The evidence of criminal and conspiratorial activity uncovered by investigation committees raises questions of political controls which go far beyond the topic of this discussion. What kind of national and authoritative counterpoise is needed when organized violence intimidates or otherwise assumes control of the instrumentalities for making policy and enforcing law in the states, cities, and local communities?

SUMMARY

Investigating committees are yet another technique by which Congress exercises oversight over policy. They are in truth a particular method of finding facts which may become controversial because Congress itself does not control all the participants in the process. Congress may find it necessary to give direction to individuals—it may even choose to punish disobedience—and in so doing it makes specific rules applicable to known individuals rather than, as is customarily the case, making general rules applicable to categories of people. It is difficult, however, to make a convincing case for restricting the legal authority of investigation committees, for situations come readily to mind where it seems desirable to compel the witness to give testimony and produce evidence. However, caution and restraint are needed, for investigations may present to individual members the opportunity to advance personal ambitions or even to engage in vilifying practices. To place the case in as extreme a form as possible, one might envision a Congress where every member was chairman of a one-man subcommittee, with legal competence to issue subpoenas, interrogate witnesses, compel the production of papers and the giving of testimony, and hasten the stubborn on to jail. Although such decentralized legislative authority might be legal, one might well question whether it would be necessary or wise or would fulfill the functions of a legislature.

The fact that investigations also deal in the allocation of scarce political commodities—in the selection of issues for investigation, the appointment of members, the securing of funds—means that the activities of investigations are also an item of value in political competition. Deliberations ordinarily take place through questions and answers, but in establishing oversight over policy the use of methods other than investigating committees should not be overlooked. Investigations might well be restricted to those areas where regular methods of establishing controls are clearly unsatisfactory, for the broad purpose of review is to make certain that ordinary procedures are working well and that essential information is flowing freely. Nor should the controversy over securing information be permitted to overshadow the significance of the ultimate findings. Although investigating committees may in themselves have no authority to make official policy, they may nevertheless influence the action of the government, or of other committees, or of the law-enforcing agencies.

A reëxamination of the functions ordinarily carried on by Congress may clarify the relationship between investigations and other activities. In making policy, Congress is interested in establishing general rules; in reviewing policy, it is interested in the successful execution of the policy. Except in a few cases which are politically significant, Congress ordinarily has little reason to be concerned with individual aberrations, either in the public at large or in the governmental structure. Its procedures are designed to give it easy and continuous relationships with those with whom it must deal officially, and it would have little time for carrying on essential duties if it were caught up in the snarl of individual delinquencies. An investigation may be necessary if ordinary procedures break down, or in the absence of a general rule framed as a law, but investigations are at best a supplement to, and not a replacement for, ordinary procedures. For instance, while it may be necessary on some occasions for Congress to investigate a financial scandal, the long-time goal would not be achieved by having copies of all current documents sent to the committee but by establishing procedures where financial irregularities would be less likely to recur.

CHAPTER 11

Conclusions

IN THIS CONCLUDING CHAPTER, IT MAY BE WORTH
while to identify more clearly the major contours of the congressional edifice and to look further into the nature of the interrelationships between Congress and other institutions. Having discussed in
some detail how Congress operates, we can now make a few generali-
zations on the adequacy of Congress as an instrument of government.
Adequacy, however, requires an understanding of what Congress is
up to, a knowledge of what it does as measured by a standard of
what it is supposed to do.

It was said earlier that the objects of congressional interest are
polarized, being directed toward the people, on the one hand, and
the governmental structure, on the other hand. In one case it provides
representation in making policy and exercises accountability on behalf
of the larger group. In the other case it formulates policy to be followed and sets up a network of controls over its operation. This
legislative link between the people and the government is not inert,
acting merely as a conduit of communications without taking any
action of its own. Indeed, so many things happen at this juncture—
ideas are expressed, opinions are mobilized, decisions are made—

that it would not be incorrect to think of Congress also as a transformer.

A satisfactory theory of the function of Congress must go beyond the issue of representation by considering also the nature of the organization through which representation operates. This organizational form is not obvious and cannot be taken for granted. If representation were the only factor of importance, the framework for its expression would need be no more complex than that required, say, for a plebiscite. It is not argued here that representation is unimportant, that elections have no effect, or that changes in the type of representation or the method of selection would not influence the behavior and perhaps even modify the internal organization of Congress. It is argued, rather, that a theory of Congress which goes no further than analyzing the nature of its representation is insufficient.

A satisfactory theory of Congress also requires something more than a consideration of the needs of the governmental bureaucracy inasmuch as such theories frequently give scant and inhospitable attention to the significance of legislative functions. In holding this view one need not belittle or ignore the significant part played by the bureaucracy in carrying out public policy. It is argued, rather, that a need exists for an integrated theory of the functions of Congress, a theory not derived from writings primarily interested in representation or in administration but which, at the same time, is broad enough to encompass the relations of the latter facets to the legislature. Congress is something more than an agglomerate of representatives pressing hard for their own special interests; it is something less than a permanent administrative unit which carries out policy. In short, our theory of representation through political parties or of administration through bureaucracies is better developed than our theory of the function of the legislature. And to top it all, we seem to be developing a theory of the presidency which combines the authority of a sovereign with that of an elected plebiscitary leader, all centralized in one person.

In acting in the intermediary position between the government and the people, Congress must behave in a certain fashion under certain prescribed conditions. Foremost, it must maintain an autonomous system of action which will permit it to be master of its own house; it must develop the competence and ability of its own members; and finally it must determine the adequacy of policy and policy standards.

THE NECESSITY FOR AUTONOMY

Let us consider briefly the need for making Congress autonomous —for creating an internal system of authority which cannot be overturned by every gust of wind from the outside. The position of autonomy is necessary in order that Congress can act in an authoritative capacity, adjusting conflict between groups and developing an ordered pattern of action under which various parts of society can interact productively and harmoniously. Autonomy helps provide the environment in which contentious types of conflict can be discussed calmly and determined rationally. Externally groups, solicitious of what Congress does, may attempt to promote their interests through organized persuasion, but such activity must not be permitted to challenge the autonomous position of Congress, whose function, as has been said, goes beyond the consideration of the interests of these groups or taking the part exclusively of any one of them.

In the whole business of prescribing and restraining, of making policy and establishing controls over it, Congress must be aloof to a degree. It can't be everybody's friend, all the time. If a legislature is subjected to such rigorous external pressures that it cannot maintain its own identity, if rules having the sanction of government are in effect made by private groups, society may shortly find itself deprived of the benefit of a stable and effective political authority. Government would be up for grabs, with individuals and groups appropriating indiscriminately the symbols of government for their own purposes. It may at times be especially difficult to maintain legislative autonomy in a democracy, what with petitioners having easy access to positions of authority and with those who make difficult decisions being subject to electoral reprisals. Yet if Congress is to function adequately, or even to function at all, it must at all cost protect the integrity of its own internal organization for making policy.

Congress is sedulous in maintaining some conditions necessary for autonomy, and particularly in restricting access to the floor of the chambers or of executive sessions of committees. But legislative autonomy is not always achieved. The fact that committees and subcommittees may take action in the name of Congress and that, for some types of policy, there is little insistence on the necessity for corporate action lessens the autonomous position of Congress as a whole. Nor is autonomy always maintained in deciding the agenda. Pressure groups are occasionally strong enough to upset timetables and legislative plans by forcing the House or Senate to consider some favored proposal. The past success of some groups in dictating the agenda of Congress—bonuses for veterans, Townsend pension plans, Ruml tax plans, state regulation of insurance companies—is an ominous warning that internal controls over the legislative process can slip away. It would be calamitous for the legislature if the controls slipped too frequently on too many subjects into the hands of those basically unsympathetic with the legislative process.

The autonomy of Congress is also affected by the attitudes held by members of their proper function. The existence of a legislature carries with it the assumption that the members thereof should be confronted with all issues concerning which the legislature itself is confronted, and the legislature itself is organized internally so that it can consider the merits of all relevant interests, not merely those which are strong, vocal, and influential in elections. If the legislature is to be a legislature in fact as well as in name, it must consider the effect of its decisions on all groups, not only those whose interests are apparent.

Although the proliferation of interest groups may be considered to be a corollary of the increased interrelations between the economic and political systems, this proliferation should not be permitted to affect the integrity of the legislative process itself. The necessity for adjusting conflict still remains, and order is not established by destroying the autonomy of the legislature through the clamor of private groups. Some groups would be well advised to impose a degree of self-discipline when tempted to bring persistent and vigorous pressure on Congress. High-powered methods of persuasion may occasionally secure special advantage, but their long-run effect might be the disintegration of legislative authority. Who would then have authority? And on what terms?

MEMBERSHIP COMPETENCE: SKILLS, KNOWLEDGE, BEHAVIOR

If members of Congress are to be more than agents who plead for particular interests and attempt to win the support of their constituencies (however necessary these activities may be), they must develop special legislative competence and assume certain attitudes toward themselves as legislators. In the transition from the electoral to the legislative process, politicians successful at the polls are transformed into legislators who must now perform a set of functions somewhat different from those required for election. This may involve certain ambiguities. Successful candidates are not always effective legislators; similarly, members who are effective legislators, including those who may have been initially appointed to office, may have difficulty in winning elections. We may inquire, then, what is involved in transforming civilians into officials with certain authority and capable of participating in making laws and influencing policy in a manifold variety of ways.

Legislative competence requires the acquisition of some of the skills enumerated earlier—of proposing and opposing, of negotiating, of deliberating, of persuading, and of deciding. Although all members may not have such skills in equal degree, so far as the legislature as a whole is concerned it is necessary that at least some of the members possess such skills. If the process is not to be an empty charade, the skills must be supplemented by substantial knowledge. Congress is often criticized for its parochialism, and in the early stages of their careers new members are likely to know more about the political requirements of their own regions than of other parts of the country. This is natural enough. In a larger sense, however, members from whatever region must be trained to think as legislators in broader terms—that is, to consider the interrelationship of one proposed course of action with another, whether it occurs in the region, state, nation, or world. Much of this knowledge must be gained from experience alone, for the legislator is confronted with a magnitude and variety of problems of national and international significance which he would not be likely to encounter in other varieties of experience. The legislator must, perforce, develop a conception of national need and national policy and the interrelations between the nation and other areas of the world. His development is abetted by being forced to consider certain types of issues as a member of a legislative chamber and the committees thereof. This learning process, served by debates, hearings, investigations, and reports, is occasionally supplemented by inspection on the spot, including at times travel to foreign lands. It is not necessary at this point to describe in detail how Congressmen might increase their vision or their knowledge or their competence; it may be sufficient to emphasize the significance of these acquisitions as hallmarks of an effective Congress and of effective Congressmen.

The consideration of the standards of behavior expected of an individual legislator raises difficult questions, partly because of the dearth of adequate theory to guide our beliefs. The concept of a republican form of government—meaning here nonmonarchial—eschews controls through titles, hereditary office, and the aristocratic belief that a repository of ideals and standards is developed in a class structure. The assumption of legal equality, equal voting rights, and other accoutrements of republicanism do not provide an obvious substitute for such standards. It has been shown, however, that political institutions of whatever nature—including legislatures—permit some selected individuals to have authority and exercise influence over others. But what standards are those in authority to use? Does the mere fact of election give the member, or the institution, full power to do whatever he, or it, pleases? No, indeed! We can suggest, instead, that the republican office and the republican institution must also create obligations on the part of its members and restraints over those in authority. The development of a system of restraints and compunctions provides in effect a set of standards by which legislative behavior can be judged and to which it might reasonably be expected to conform.

The ideal type of legislator is assumed to be a free, moral person capable of objective, rational, and impartial judgment. As one who makes law regulating human action, the legislator must be concerned with moral ends as well as with the procedures and methods for achieving them. The supposition that a representative, once selected, owes no obligation other than to his constituents is at best a mistaken idea which misinterprets the nature and competence of the representative base. The constituent-district may be considered an entity for the purpose of choosing someone to participate in a broader association and to represent its interests therein, but this selection does not encompass the total obligations placed on the behavior of this member.

The rule for judging the permissible extent of external influences—the receiving of gifts, campaign contributions, and the like—should be developed against some standard broader than that of constituent interest and should bear some relationship to the ability of members to make independent judgments. A possible standard would prevent members from assuming the type of obligations to external groups or individuals which would make it impossible to form such a judgment. In this difficult area where rules of conduct are not yet well developed, prevailing practices may blunt the significance of this assertion. Some legislators may indeed be embarrassed by the extent or nature of their external commitments but inexorable requirements of elections and electoral procedures may give members no broad alternative of action. In regulating the nature of external influence, an attempt should be made to protect the legislator from having to mortgage his conscience to secure office or from using his office, once acquired, to advance his own economic ends. Lawmaking is a subtle operation which becomes possible in part because of the confidence of the public in the judgment of the members and in the process by which they make decisions. Thus, the behavior—the moral integrity— of the legislator and the belief of the public in the efficacy of the final product cannot be completely separated. The type of loose-living or crass behavior associated with, say, gambling or boozing, may have no obvious effect on the ability of legislators to make perspicacious decisions, but because such behavior may decrease confidence in the legislature, it becomes undesirable.

Many of the injunctions given above may seem to emphasize the negative and be considered apart from their essential purpose. Their purpose is to provide the conditions under which legislators might acquire wisdom and judgment, to create a forum where lucid and intelligent discussions can take place and where the legislators will have the courage to say that which is pertinent and the good taste to suppress that which is personally offensive.

POLICY AND POLICY STANDARDS

In turning to the question of the formation of policy by Congress, our concern now is less with matters of organization than with the purpose to be achieved through such organization. We are not here especially concerned with the structural intricacies of the committees or of the parties, in whether there should be ten, twenty, or a hundred committees, or none at all, in whether the Speaker may sometimes behave like an autocrat or the seniority system should be retained, abolished, or modified. Other questions should first be answered in order to place such topics in their proper context. In evaluating the adequacy of the internal organization of Congress, we are interested rather in the kind of functions which are fulfilled and the type of activity which is encouraged.

It was said earlier that a legislature requires something more than representation to become an effective body, and we may add here that it also requires something more than procedures. The "something more" is a repository of beliefs and practices which, in the case of Congress, make it in effect the political conscience of the nation. The law which governs the relations between men is more than an edict; it must also express justice and wisdom, compassion and understanding, solicitude for those who are aggrieved and protection for those who are threatened. In making such law, in acting rightly and discreetly, Congress requires what amounts to a continuing memory. It needs a repository for the standards placed over its own members and over the agencies and individuals with whom it is directly concerned. In the legal sense, the repository of standards is embodied in the United States Code, which contains all law currently in effect, but in making policy the legislature needs something more than a legal repository to jog its memory. It requires also an accumulation of facts and judgments pertinent to the various areas of public policy, as, for example, transportation, monopolies, flood control, importation of goods, international commerce, the development of areas of strength in the world, and the like. In making policy, in other words, the legislature needs to have some continuity of thought, some durable attitudes toward policies, some continuing standards of judgment which are applicable. Such standards are, of course, not static and can be modified, but they do not grow spontaneously and must be developed procedurally and thoughtfully over long periods of time.

The legislature traditionally attempts to express standards of policy in the form of law, but in addition it is desirable for some of the members, at least, to have some knowledge of the background of policy so as to provide an element of continuity in legislative understanding. Hence, the rate of turnover of committee membership and membership in the House and Senate is directly related to the continuity of congressional interest and knowledge in specific policy.

In developing policy through law, Congress has traditionally thought it desirable to spell out in some detail the elements of policy, and it is not ordinarily content to lay down policy exclusively in general terms. Through its mastery of relevant detail, Congress develops policy which becomes more meaningful because it is better understood. The failure to develop policy in some detail might readily reduce the legislative process to an ephemeral proceeding in which intentions are vaguely stated in resolutions. The consideration of some degree of detail is necessary if the legislature is to retain its mastery of policy formation and be more than an echo chamber. Attention to detail is also necessary in reviewing policy, for the execution of a law may falter if full attention is paid to broad principles while the details are permitted to drift. The committee structure of Congress has its greatest utility in giving detailed consideration to public policy, for in general the committees have the talent, the staffs, and the energy to consider the minutiae of proposals. Their ability to acquire competent testimony from skilled experts gives Congress potential access to the facts necessary for making informed decisions.

In giving attention to detail, Congress might consider going somewhat further than it now does. In enacting legislation or otherwise formulating policy, for instance, it might be more solicitous in making certain that congressional requirements are fully met. A committee might be given the responsibility for seeing to it that congressional interests were protected in formulating policy by asking the following questions: What type of legislative controls are included in the legislation? Is the delegation of authority as specific and as unambiguous as possible? In the event it is necessary to delegate authority extensively because of the difficulty in predicting precise requirements, are provisions included for Congress to reconsider the legislation and to make the grant more specific? Is authority delegated within the framework of existing administrative organization, and if not, why not? Have authorizations for spending funds been coördinated with other aspects of fiscal policy?

The emphasis placed on detail, however, should not preclude Congress from developing a corporate opinion within the two chambers. Some of the value of the legislative process will be lost if policy making becomes so decentralized that the function of the two chambers is restricted to ratifying decisions made elsewhere. It would be advisable, I should think, for Congress to develop further a sense of corporateness for determining policy, so that the Senate and the House—rather than their committees—are in fact the heart of the process of enunciating policy.

Without some central theory of the proper function of committees, it is possible for the committees to get out of hand by fissioning off or multiplying or allocating authority in a haphazard fashion. It is difficult, of course, to regulate the precise number of committees which are to be permitted, such as was done by the Reorganization

Act of 1946, for within this rigid framework of permissible committees the subcommittees have grown in tropical profusion. The
possibility of every member becoming chairman of his own subcommittee is an absurd projection of present trends.

The issues with which Congress is concerned are conditioned by
the provisions of the Constitution, the needs of the bureaucracy, the
nature of its internal organization, the interests of its members, and
the requirements of society. The reach of Congress sometimes exceeds
its grasp when it attempts to perform functions for which its organization is not well suited. In general, the organization of Congress is
well designed for enacting legislation but less well designed for exercising controls over governmental action and, of course, poorly designed for administering policy itself.

The organization of Congress is better suited for operating within
areas of freedom in the world than in areas characterized by totalitarian systems, strict ideologies, party lines, propaganda, controlled
thought, centralization, and crude political machinations. Within the
United States, the organization of Congress is better adapted to providing systems of order applicable to parts of society rather than to
exercising strict controls over all of society. In other words, it is
more competent in readjusting the equilibrium where normal relations have broken down than in developing or controlling policy in
which government is the sole entrepreneur or regulator.

Even with the best of intentions, the modern legislature cannot
regulate everything. There are limits to its span of control, to use a
bureaucratic term, and it is not well suited for operating in a nation-
state which is administered exclusively, as it were, from the center.
However, Congress can function well on a less grandiose scale of
endeavor where a wide variety of choices and alternatives enable
it to be selective in the kind of order it provides and maintains.
And Congress can make decisions which have due regard for the
people most affected as well as for the necessary techniques of
administration. It is no small achievement for Congress to mobilize
specialized opinion, to mold this opinion to the requirements of a
disturbed and troubled area of policy, to provide a new pattern of

order, and finally to make a decision which ordinarily is accepted and acceptable.

EXTERNAL RELATIONSHIPS

Let us now turn to the second phase of the summary, the relation of the operation of Congress to other governmental institutions. This discussion assumes the continuation of the present constitutional allocation of authority, including an independent and partially autonomous President, the civilian and military bureaucracy, the federal system of state and national government, the judicial system, and the bicameral structure within Congress. It might appear at first blush that the course of an institution as old and established as Congress is as fixed as the stars and that it has specific, continuing relationship with other political institutions. In truth, however, the relationship may change and is frequently unstable. The legal authority of Congress as described in the Constitution does not clearly indicate the nature of the relationship between Congress and other political institutions. The law forms a general framework in which action occurs, but the nature of the interrelationships may be influenced by a variety of factors, such as the personalities involved (as in conflicts between the President and Congress), crises which require authority to be concentrated in the hand of central administrators, or (not inconceivably in the event of a major disaster) the decentralization of authority to local communities.

The preservation of the equilibrium position of Congress within the total governmental structure is not simply a legal or constitutional problem, although it is that too. Congress can lose its influence not only through the delegation of authority or encroachments on its autonomy but also by shifts in the fulcrum of authority. The government is not a single, monolithic unit but rather an aggregate of systems whose specific interests may be affected by the action of other governmental units. A constitutional government is concerned in part with maintaining the proper balance between the various component units. But the balance is not always easy to maintain inasmuch as each of the various units is associated with and partly dependent on the actions of the others, and the actual lines of influence may diverge from the legal and constitutional norms. For example, the President recently requested the Governor of a state to veto a certain bill, an incident which illustrates how lines of influence may not follow legal channels of authority.

It is the function of a constitutional system to keep the various units of government working together harmoniously, to resolve the conflicts within and between them, and to prevent any unit from establishing mastery over others and over private groups and individuals. This ideal is not always achieved, and there have been many historic instances of particular units of government attempting to gain mastery over their competitors. In other times and other places, leaders variously known as president, king, protector, governor, *Führer,* or secretary general of a party have attempted to dominate and control all instruments of government. Civil and military bureaucracies have also attempted to gain supremacy, and there is no dearth in these days of military juntas and dictatorships. Federal states have in times past attempted to dominate their weaker sister states, as with Prussia, or even the federal government, as with the states of the Confederacy.

In any struggle involving force, the courts are in a weak position, having no independent arms other than the bailiffs and no administrative system of organization. However, there may indeed be conflict over the authority exercised by courts (as in the controversy over judicial review), and other units may wish to control the courts or decrease their influence (as in the conflict in the 1930's over the proposal to increase the membership of the Supreme Court). The legislature, also, may attempt to dominate the scene, a possibility which troubled the Founding Fathers, but despite precautions taken in drafting the Constitution, a long, unseemly conflict between President Andrew Johnson and Congress occurred during the period between 1865 and 1868.

Even without any intention of securing domination, forces in society tend to augment the influence of Congress *vis-à-vis* other institutions. Many interest groups are willing to have Congress, rather than the states, regulate their affairs, and states may appeal to Congress for fiscal assistance and other types of aid. Decisions of the courts have expanded the authority of Congress, and the requirements of a national policy for waging wars are obvious. On the other hand, local interests may not yield to the centralization of political authority, an extreme form of this position being the contention of Senator John C. Calhoun that state authority is supreme and could, in fact, nullify an Act of Congress. The local factor is present in many deliberations of Congress.

The effective authority of Congress may also be decreased when major policy decisions are made by the President, the Secretary of State, the Joint Chiefs of Staff, or other units of the bureaucracy. The equilibrium of influence between Congress and other political units is constantly fluctuating, and over a period of time this changing equilibrium may augment or retard the relative influence of Congress.

However much individual Congressmen may be sympathetic toward preserving the autonomy of the states and other local authorities, Congress itself often acts as a centripetal force which increases the centralization of politics. Pressures on Congress demand national answers simply because Congress has abundant resources at its disposal for making policy; it is not only well organized, having the ability to make binding decisions on many issues, but it also has access to extensive funds. The requirements imposed by election make it likely that some members of Congress will give a sympathetic ear to the proponents of centralization. These pressures may arise from private interest groups as well as from government officials, and they may be concerned with activities of a local nature. One has only to stand on a street corner in a local community to see the pervasiveness of the federal government: federal funds for schools (including lunches) and for street and highway construction; insured loans of various categories; compulsory insurance for numerous disabilities; recruitment agencies for the armed services; the regulation of prices in the corner drugstore; the support of prices for the farmer; inspections, licenses, and on and on.

Pressures for centralization may also come from the members of

Congress. Although in the total legislative process it is possible to construct a statement of monetary accounts, the fact that a variety of independent decisions are made does not force any balancing of favors acquired against costs accrued. Congressmen, therefore, may be prone to request favors for districts or states or regions without regard to costs, the latter being someone else's concern. The present method of organizing Congress makes it easy, and the system of elections makes it attractive, for Congressmen to "do something" for their constituents. The advocates of central authority may win merely because of the relative ease in securing congressional consent to legislative proposals. It would also appear, however, that indiscriminate centralization of authority may distort the nature of the federal system and make it difficult to develop effective political accountability.

The existence of the presidency limits the nature of the problems which Congress might otherwise have to face and provides an institutional and legal framework within which congressional answers to these problems must be given. Whatever type of executive might exist—an independent President or a set of ministers selected by the legislature —the core of the problem would remain that of the type of relationship existing between the legislature and executive in formulating policy and in exercising controls. In short, Congress must operate within an institutional framework which gives the President an independent source of authority. The nature of the office and the method of selecting the President seem to me to preclude any operation of the legislature through a rigid party system, with sharp party divisions, votes of confidence, and other means to promote internal party unity and cohesion. Whatever may be said for strict party systems in other countries, it would not appear that the methods proposed to be followed are sufficiently clear or the results to be gained sufficiently attractive to make the pattern one which we need emulate. Indeed, if party unity were to mean that the President could, in effect, determine policy without any reciprocating control over the President on the part of Congress, the results for Congress as an independent legislative body would be disastrous.

The proper role for Congress, it seems to me, is to operate under the assumption that it should not attempt to gain complete mastery over the presidency and the bureaucracy nor should it permit them to establish mastery over it. This statement is more than a homiletic exhortation of the obvious. It means, rather, that Congress should concentrate on the functions of formulating and controlling policy and not be dissuaded from this by proposals to establish its own supremacy or claims that the President has inherent power or special perspicacity which places effective policy decisions beyond the competence of Congress.

Research Guide

THIS RESEARCH GUIDE HAS BEEN PREPARED TO AC-
quaint students with the availability and usefulness of legislative documents for carrying on research. The practice of Congress in printing
a full account of debates and public hearings and in requiring reports
on many types of activities has created a sizable reservoir of source
material useful for studies of the legislative process. Although some
legislative activity takes place behind closed doors, and remarks are
deleted or made off the record, the printed documents nevertheless
present a remarkably complete record of what has transpired and,
with interpretation, why it transpired.

The maximum use of this material for research purposes is often
neglected, even in those colleges and universities serving as government depositaries, and the documents may, to some, present such a
ponderous mass of material that they are not used with confidence.
An attempt is made in this Research Guide to select some paths
through this documentary maze, particularly by using selective case
material which will treat in a more detailed fashion some of the subjects covered in a more generalized way in the content of the book.
References are made to other legislative writings, chiefly from Amer-

ican sources, and in some cases to analytic writing which may provide helpful concepts and patterns for organizing the research.

The suggested cases are of the simple assignment variety, designed to give the student some awareness of the component aspects of the legislative process through an examination of original documentary sources. Although full answers to some of the questions would require a greater mobilization of resources and concentration of effort than could be supplied by short, frequent assignments, the thoughtful consideration of the questions might serve to encourage analytic thinking. It should be emphasized that the cases are suggestive only. The instructor may wish to refine the assignments by asking questions more precisely stated; or to expand the assignments with the use of supplementary source material; or to systematize the assignments with the use of various types of research techniques; or to construct more careful theory through conceptualization and precise analysis.

The documents cited can be found in any library acting as a government depositary, of which there are several hundred located in colleges, universities, and public libraries. None of the documentary material should be difficult to locate with the possible exception of congressional hearings, which are not included in the government serial set; it has been necessary for patient library staffs to collect the hearings independently and develop their own system for cataloguing this material. The following documents are relevant to the subsequent assignments:

The Serial Set. 1817 to date. Contains official reports and documents, including those produced by congressional committees.

Numerical Lists and Schedules of Volumes. 1933 to date. Contains cross-reference indices, showing number of serial set where reports, documents, and the like can be located. Earlier reference guides were known as the *Checklist* (1789–1909) and the *Index* (1895–1933).

Monthly Catalog, United States Public Documents. 1895 to date. Useful for looking up congressional hearings, for example; also contains references to other government publications.

Catalog of the Public Documents of Congress. 1893–1940. An excellent guide for the period covered. The issuance of this fine catalogue has regrettably been discontinued.

Congressional Record. 1873 to date. Pagination of temporary edition varies slightly from that of bound volume. Earlier records of congressional proceedings are to be found in the *Congressional Globe* (1833–1873); *Register of Debates in Congress* (1824–1837); *Debates and Proceedings* (1789–1824).

House Journal (located in Serial Set).

Senate Journal (located in Serial Set).

Rules and Manual, United States House of Representatives (located in Serial Set).

Congressional Hearings. Miscellaneously filed and distributed. See above-mentioned *Monthly Catalog* for thoroughly inadequate index of hearings. (Both the Senate Library and the House Library print indices of their own holdings, which are not distributed officially but are nevertheless reliable and almost definitive in their content.)

Statutes at Large of the United States. 1789 to date.

United States Code.

Congressional Directory.

The Budget of the United States Government.

Hinds' and Cannon's Precedents of the House of Representative (11 volumes).

Biographical Directory of the American Congress, 1774–1949.

Decisions, Court of Claims.

Decisions, Comptroller General.

Appropriations, Budget Estimates, Etc. (prepared by Appropriations Committees; located in Serial Set).

CHAPTER 1. THE REQUIREMENTS OF A LEGISLATURE

Many of the writings on Congress, or on parliamentary government in general, pay due attention to the representative nature of the legislative assembly as well as to its function in making law. Although we now know a good deal about electoral conflict and voting behavior, the theoretical statement of representative government has not gone very far beyond that by John Stuart Mill in *Considerations on Representative Government* (1861). Prosiness aside, and passing over Mill's infatuation with proportional representation, the study is for other reasons an inadequate statement of the theory of representation for modern times. Although the legislative structure for making law is, of course, most important, many of the writings on legislatures frequently stop short there and do not go on to analyze the intellectual and procedural requirements which are necessary in order that the legislature can in fact make law. A happy exception to this statement is the three-volume work by Josef Redlich (A. E. Steinthal, trans.), *The Procedure of the House of Commons* (1908). This work, too little known in this country, is a clear and on the whole successful attempt to relate parliamentary procedures to the total political and social system of the country. Jeremy Bentham's *The Theory of Legislation* (C. K. Ogden [ed.], 1931) is legalistic—and utilitarian. The work by the philosopher, Elijah Jordan, *Theory of Legislation* (1952) contains a number of arresting comments but it is difficult to read and its usefulness for legislative inquiry is marred by a special vocabulary which, in many cases, seems inappropriate.

A number of useful, general works have been written on Congress, some of which contain more detailed description on its operation than does the present volume. Among those which can be read with profit are the following: Ernest S. Griffith, *Congress, Its Contemporary Role* (2d rev., 1956); George B. Galloway, *The Legislative Process in Congress* (1953); Bertram M. Gross, *The Legislative Struggle: A Study in Social Combat* (1953); Stephen K. Bailey and Howard D. Samuel, *Congress at Work* (1952); Harvey Walker, *The Legislative Process: Lawmaking in the United States* (1948); Robert Luce, *Congress, an Explanation* (1926); and W. F. Willoughby, *Principles of Legislative Organization and Administration* (1934). There is also a short, earlier book of the author, *This Is Congress* (rev. ed., 1946).

Woodrow Wilson's *Congressional Government* (1885), recently published in a paperback edition, is a favorite of many, although its use of the British Parliamentary model restricts its value. An attempt at a systematic analysis of legislatures has been made by Robert Luce, a former Representative, in a four-volume series. Although the work abounds in illustrations, it does not coalesce satisfactorily and is less useful than would appear. See *Legislative Assemblies* (1924); *Legislative Principles* (1930); *Legislative Problems* (1935); and *Legislative Procedures* (1922).

CHAPTER 2. MEMBERSHIP SELECTION

A considerable quantity of literature has been produced on the topic, Who should be represented? much of which deals with particular electoral methods. One of the most comprehensive surveys of the different electoral systems is found in the report of the Royal Commission on Systems of Election, *Report of the Royal Commission Appointed to Enquire into Electoral Systems* (Cmd. 5163, HMSO, 1910, reprinted 1929). The volume by Alfred de Grazia, *Public and Republic* (1951) gives a historical description of the development of American representation, a theme also found in *Threshold to Freedom* (1949), by Harold F. Gosnell.

A field of research which is claiming some attention is the examination of the background of legislators (and administrators) as a means of identifying factors which might influence decisions. In their study of small groups, social psychologists have developed reference analysis as one method of approaching a similar problem, but the possible utility of this conceptual approach for legislative studies has not yet been tested. In studying legislative backgrounds, a clear idea of the usefulness of the investigation for legislative theory is necessary if the study is not to end in the production of an unassimilated mass of facts. In some cases, such as the acquisition of legislative skills, the background of a legislator might provide pertinent material, although the enumeration of categories of professions or occupations or the adumbrations of educational achievements may have no obvious significance unless specifically related to particular aspects of the legislative process. Nor is it necessarily rewarding to begin with the assumption that every interest or group or occupation or class should be represented equally or specifically. In the legislative process itself, erstwhile candidates are given new roles to perform, with responsibilities and functions often different from those previously encountered. If the element of environmental determinism in legislators is considerable or inflexible or antilegislature in content, the legislative process would not function satisfactorily and perhaps it would not function at all.

Donald R. Matthews has written a thoughtful analysis of the general topic in his volume, *The Social Background of Political Decision-Makers* (1954); this study contains a short bibliography on leadership and the effect on political selection of such factors as class, social change, personality, and revolution. A subsequent study by Mr. Matthews is entitled *United States Senators* (1955). The work of Harold Lasswell, *Psychopathology and Politics* (1930), attempts to find some basic psychological pattern among those who enter politics as a vocation. Biographies and autobiographies of legislators may be revealing not only for an account of the prelegislative background but also for precise vignettes of the legislative process. In addition to the official statements found in the *Biographical Directory of the American Congress, 1774–1949* and the *Congressional Directory,* the following books may be of occasional interest: L. W. Busbey, *Uncle Joe Cannon* (1927); W. A. Robinson, *Thomas B. Reed* (1930); H. Jerry Voorhis, *Confessions of a Congressman* (1948); James G. Blaine, *Twenty Years in Congress* (2 vols., 1884); James Willard Hurst, *The Growth of American Law: The Law Makers* (1950), Section II, "The Legislature"; J. E. Salter, ed., *Public men in and out of Office* (1946); G. F. Hoar, *Autobiography of Seventy Years* (2 vols., 1903); and James E. Watson, *As I Knew Them* (1936).

Some politically-minded mathematicians have been attracted to the problems presented by legislative apportionment, with different results flowing from different methods. One of the best general surveys of the various issues associated with apportionment is found in the special edition of *Law and Contemporary Problems,* entitled "Legislative Reapportionment," published in the spring of 1952. The works of the mathematician, Walter F. Willcox (the "Legislative Reapportionment" study contains numerous bibliographic references), and of Laurence F. Schemeckebier, *Congressional Apportionment* (1941), are standard. The recommendations of a committee on apportionment of the American Political Science Association is found in the *American Political Science Review,* March, 1951, pp. 153 ff., "The Reapportionment of Congress." The legal and political conflict over the issue of creating new congressional districts in Illinois is recounted by Franklin L. Burdette in "The Illinois Redistricting Case," *American Political Science Review,* October, 1946, pp. 958 ff. Numerous studies have been made of the difficulties encountered and of the tactics pursued by state legislatures in reconstituting legislative districts. See also E. C. Griffith, *The Rise and Development of the Gerrymander* (1907).

Statistics on voting for candidates for Congress (both Senators and Representatives) are found in the statistical section of the *Congressional Directory*; maps of congressional districts are also found in the rear of that volume. A study of contested elections has been made by V. M. Barnett, Jr., "Contested Elections in Recent Years," *Political Science Quarterly,* June, 1939, pp. 187 ff. Reports on campaigns and campaign expenditures are made indifferently, but that produced by Senator Green's committee for the 1944 election is especially thorough: see S. Rept. 101, March 15, 1945.

CASE: LEGISLATIVE CONSIDERATION OF APPORTIONMENT

Examine the debate on single member districts versus the general ticket, found in the *Congressional Globe,* 28th Congress, 1st session, 1843–1844; although the debate was inconclusive it does bring out some of the political and constitutional issues involved. Examine also the debate on the Automatic Apportionment Act of 1929; the best of the debate took place in the prior congressional session on H. R. 11725 (70th Cong.). See also H. Rept. 2010 and S. Rept. 312, same Congress. The "Message from the President on Congressional Redistricting," sent to Congress by President Truman, is found in H. Doc. 36 and *Congressional Record,* January 9, 1941, pp. 114 ff. Congress did not debate the proposed legislation.

What principles does Congress appear to favor in determining how seats shall be apportioned? What part does political expediency or advantage appear to play?

Does there appear to be general support in Congress for the single-member district?

Do the arguments convince you that either major fractions or equal proportions is inherently the fairer method of calculating apportionment?

What in your opinion were the moving factors in the "final" settlement of the apportionment problem in 1929?

Why is Congress loath to prescribe standards for districts? What standards might be desirable, other than those of equality of population, contiguity, and compactness?

CASE: GERRYMANDERING AND EXPENDITURES

Examine the population of each congressional district (as found in the *Congressional Directory*) and process the material in such a fashion so as to reveal the various distortions and the extent to which some districts vary from a given norm.

Examine a district which appears to have been obviously created by an attempt to gerrymander the area: What purpose did the gerrymanderers attempt to achieve by their particular creation? Note the electoral returns of that district over a period of time to determine whether the purpose of the gerrymanderers was ostensibly achieved.

Create several "model" legislative districts. What elements would you include in your model? How many models would you have? Show how your model would be applied in practice in some actual real-life situation. What would be the effect of the multiplicity or accumulation of these models into an electoral *system,* or on the party system?

CASE: CONTRIBUTIONS AND EXPENDITURES

There is considerable divergence in the procedures for controlling campaign expenditures, with no clear theory as to the need, method, or purpose for controlling funds. Research and analysis are needed in this area. The legal restrictions are found (for the federal government) in 2 USC §241–256 and 18 USC §208. What is the underlying purpose found in this legislation?

The records of campaign expenditures filed with the Secretary of the Senate and the Clerk of the House of Representatives "shall be open to public inspection" for at least two years, according to the law, but they have been incompletely analyzed.

In several cases, Congress has refused membership to candidates whose campaign expenditures were believed excessive. See, for example, the following cases:

Truman Newberry: Case put to Senate September 17, 1918, and debate continued intermittently through 1921. See also *Newberry v. United States*, 256, US 232 (1921); and S. Erwin, *Henry Ford v. Truman H. Newberry* (1935).

Frank L. Smith: Investigation authorized by S. Res. 195, 69th Cong., 1st sess., 1925. See S. Rept. 1197, 69th Cong., 2d sess., S. Rept. 92, 70th Cong. 1st sess., and S. Rept. 603, 70th Cong. 1st sess. See also C. H. Woody, *The Case of Frank L. Smith* (1931).

William S. Vare: See S. Res. 195, 69th Cong., 1st sess.; 1. Rept. 1197, 69th Cong., 2d sess.; S. Rept. 1858, 70th Cong., 2d sess.

What conclusion might one make, on the basis of this record, regarding the ability of Congress to set up standards for membership? Do any principles emerge regarding standards which must be observed? Is there any apparent reason for the differing decisions in the Newberry and in the Smith and Vare cases?

CHAPTER 3. THE INTERNAL SYSTEM OF AUTHORITY

Legislative organization and process may be viewed from the requirement imposed on the members: that of assuming certain legislative roles in carrying on the functions expected of Congress. Members of Congress must behave in a certain prescribed way; they must be "acculturated" to the legislative environment; they are given certain prerogatives, not held by ordinary men, which enable them to fulfill their functions; and they are subject to disciplinary action, often of a subtle nature, for failing to behave in the manner expected. Literature relating to acculturation and to role analysis is applicable in analyzing the internal structure of authority and influence. An example of the fruitful results of role analysis is found in the study of Ralph K. Huitt, "The Congressional Committee: A Case Study," *American Political Science Review,* June, 1954, pp. 340 ff.

For the development of special legislative privileges, see M. P. Clark, *Parliamentary Privilege in the Colonies* (1943). The leading case relating to the arrest of legislators for indictable offenses is *Williamson v. United States,* 207 US 425 (1907). For general studies of ethics and politics, see George Graham, *Morality in American Politics* (1952); Paul H. Douglas, *Ethics in Government* (1952), and H. Hubert Wilson, *Congress: Corruption and Compromise* (1950).

In studying the internal system of authority within Congress, the following points are especially pertinent: (1) the division of functions among the various units; (2) the selection of membership from these units; (3) the nature of influence exercised by these units over the legislative process; (4) the relationship of these units to each other so that there is, in fact, a legislative system.

In view of the fact that the basic process and function of the two chambers are remarkably similar, it is possible to make fruitful comparative studies of the actions of the Senate and the House at various stages of the legislative process. For a general historical study of bicameralism, see T. F. Moran, *The Rise and Development of the Bicameral System in America* (1895). Studies of individual chambers, such as that by G. H. Haynes, *The Senate of the United States,* 2 vols. (1938) or by William S. White, *The Citadel* (1957), encompass material pertinent to other sections of this outline.

One of the best general works on the committee system is that of L. G. McConachie, *Congressional Committees* (1898); although somewhat dated, it is nevertheless a storehouse of useful material. Several monographs have been written on individual committees, including that of E. E. Denison, *The Senate Foreign Relations Committee* (1942); A. C. F. Westphal, *The House Committee on Foreign Affairs* (1942); A. R. Ogden, *The Dies Committee* (1944); and A. C. McCown, *The Congressional Conference Committee* (1927).

Although there is a considerable amount of verbal lore concerning party organization in Congress, the fact that so surprisingly little has actually been written on the subject makes this area a rich field for further research. The following studies should be consulted: C. W. Chiu, *The Speaker of the House of Representatives Since 1896* (1928); P. D. Hasbrouck, *Party Government in the House of Representatives* (1927); C. R. Atkinson, *The Committee on Rules and the Overthrow of Speaker Cannon* (1911); George Rothwell Brown, *The Leadership of Congress* (1922); Hugh Bone, "The Senate Policy Committee," *American Political Science Review*, June, 1956. See also the biographies and autobiographies mentioned earlier.

Some of the research material in this area is elusive and can be developed only by more penetrating techniques than those ordinarily available in the classroom; nevertheless, considerable raw material suitable for further analyses is available from such official publications as the *Congressional Record*. Some insight into the public roles played by the various party officials can be gained by a sedulous examination of the *Record* for a single session, in which attention is focused on the part played in the political process by certain known party leaders: the Speaker; the Majority leaders of the House and Senate; the Vice-President; the chairmen of the steering committees, policy committees, and the like. Although a good deal of the political discussion may take place off the floor, some of it pours over into public debate, and in addition, the public actions of the political leaders mentioned may give some clew to the nature of the activities which occur off the floor. After making individual studies of the roles played by the various party leaders, a synthesis of the functions performed would give at least a rudimentary picture of the structure and operation of the party organization.

CASE: PARLIAMENTARY PRIVILEGES REGARDING TESTIMONY BEFORE GRAND JURIES

Examine the incident concerning Representative Hamilton Fish in which the House of Representatives waived the privilege of immunity to enable Representative Fish to testify before a grand jury. See *Congressional Record,* November 17, 1941, pp. 8933–58, *passim,* and H. Rept. 1415 (1941). To what extent do special legal privileges appear to be necessary for carrying out the legislative functions? What sanctions are available if these privileges are violated?

CASE: PERQUISITES AND PENSIONS

The problem remains: To what extent should legislators be given special compensation? On the one hand, it is necessary that they be rewarded in such a fashion that they can perform their functions adequately; on the other hand, the rewards must not be so considerable that the legislators have preferential treatment beyond the requirements of the job, or that they will wish to hold office at all costs, or that they will receive such an advantage that political rivals cannot compete effectively for office. Here is the area where muckrakers have been active in exposing cases of nepotism, favoritism, junkets, free haircuts, and other types of preferential treatment—the area of Senator Plunkett and "honest graft." What are the standards for "adequate compensation"? What should be the determining rule? Examine the incident where Congress first enacted, then repealed (and later reënacted) a law granting pensions for its members. See H. R. 3487, 77th Cong., 1st and 2d sess. (1941–1942): hearings; debate; passage; repeal. What conclusions can be reached concerning the principle of retirement benefits for elected officials? Why was the provision repealed? What are the arguments for and against such pension plans as applied to elected officials? What are the outer boundaries for compensating legislators?

CASE: SENATORIAL CENSURE

Congress attempts to protect its own internal organization from encroachment from without or from unacceptable behavior on the part of its own members. The roots of legislative autonomy may be emphasized by a review of historic developments, such as the incident when Charles I entered Parliament and seized John Pym and four other members. A list of the various cases of expulsion, exclusion, and censure which have occurred in congressional history is found in *Congressional Record,* April 8, 1952, pp. 3702 ff. Examine the following cases:

Censure of Senators Tillman and McLaurin, *Congressional Record,* February 22, 1902, pp. 2085 ff. and pp. 2203 ff.; censure of Senator Bingham, S. Res. 146, *Congressional Record,* November 4, 1929, pp. 5131 ff.; censure of Senator McCarthy, S. Res. 301, *Congressional Record,* November 8, 1954–December 2, 1954, resolution passed 67–22. December 2, 1954, p. 16392. What standards of behavior seem implicitly required in these three cases? Was the rule of acceptable behavior clear before the infraction occurred? What policy should Senator Bingham have followed? Was Senator McCarthy censured on trivial grounds, as some have contended (both friend and foe), or was the censure related directly to the ability of the Senate to function?

CASE: COMMITTEE ASSIGNMENTS

The problem facing a political party in organizing the House or the Senate (after a period of control by the opposition party) can be studied by examining the availability and allocation of committee seats. Select a year, such as 1955, 1953, 1949, or 1947, in which there was a reorganization of committees. What free choices did the party have in making assignments? How were these allocations made? What factors, does it appear, were influential in the final assignment of committee seats? Was any objection made to the assignments on the floor of the Senate or House, or were the assignments approved without comment? Do the restrictions on the size of committees, the number of committees, and the ratio of party membership-committee membership implicit in the rules of the Senate and the House appear to be overly restrictive? Additional information on committee allocation in individual cases may be gathered by direct correspondence with the legislator concerned.

CASE: TENURE OF MEMBERSHIP WITHIN COMMITTEES

Make a study showing the relative attractiveness of the various committees. To which committees are new members regularly assigned? In which committees does one find the highest median period of length of service on committees? of length of service in Congress? Is there any relationship between these data and the safe or contested electoral districts?

CASE: ELECTORAL TURNOVER IN HOUSE AND SENATE

From the statistical material obtained in the *Congressional Directory,* make a chart showing the percentage of membership turnover in the House and Senate over, say, the last 20 general elections. Does there seem to be a trend toward increased instability of membership in the Senate? If so, how might this be explained? What was the median tenure of members of the House and Senate during the period covered? Does this have any implications for the continuity of congressional policy? What other factors might be considered? What pattern would emerge if one plotted on a map the districts which, over the past 40 years, have provided members of the House who were among the highest 5 percent in accumulated seniority?

CHAPTER 4. THE EXTERNAL SYSTEM OF INFLUENCE

One may look at the influence exerted on Congress and the information provided for its use as a vast communications network through which the special interests of the outside world are brought to the attention of Congress. Many people attempt to influence Congress, but only some are successful. Who are they? Why are they successful? Similarly, various types of information are made accessible to the members of Congress, but only some of it receives attention. How well and by whom is this process of selection performed? In examining this inward flow of suggestions on how Congress should act, the following questions are pertinent for whatever categories of influence and information are being considered:

1. Who is exerting the influence? Is it someone in an official position; someone directly connected with legislation; someone in private life; or someone from an alien and competitive political system (a foreigner or foreign government)?

2. On whom is the influence exerted? Is it particularized, as to an individual member; or more general, as to a committee; or still more general, as to one or both chambers?

3. What is the substantive nature of the influence? Is it pertinent to the subject matter under consideration? Does it relate to preferences or attitudes of the influencer? Does it recommend that specific action be taken on legislation? Does it recommend that an attempt be made to influence the bureaucracy in a certain way? Does it relate to personnel?

4. What techniques of influence are used? Is the influence brought by word of mouth, or by special messenger, or by the printed word? Is it direct, or indirect and subtle? Are the techniques of such a nature that they tend to prevent Congress, or a committee, or a member, from acting autonomously?

5. What sanction does the bearer of influence possess which will enable him to be persuasive? Alternatively, what is the motivation for members of Congress in listening to or taking the advice? Is the sanction "legitimate"? Is it of such a nature that it might pervert the legislative process or the character of the members themselves? Might it raise the possibility of further conflict at some future time?

Various presidential and congressional biographies are replete with illustrative material concerning the relations between the President and Congress, and a historical account of this relationship is found in W. E. Binkley, *President and Congress* (1947). For more analytical treatments, consult E. S. Corwin, *The President: Office and Powers* (1940) and Pendleton Herring, *Presidential Leadership* (1940). The articles by Richard E. Neustadt, "Presidency and Legislation: The Growth of Central Clearance," and "Presidency and Legislation: Planning the President's Program," *American Political Science Review*, September, 1954, pp. 641 ff. and December, 1954, pp. 980 ff., are informative and raise provocative questions for further research. Not a great deal has been written on the influence of departments in legislative matters, although anyone familiar with Congress knows how sedulously the departments pay attention to legislative reactions and how they attempt to smooth the way for legislative approval of proposed action. The monograph by J. Leiper Freeman, *The Political Process: Executive Bureau-Legislative Committee Relations* (1955) gives an illuminating account of departmental-congressional relations; other treatments are found inferentially in such studies as that of Arthur Maass, *Muddy Waters: The Army Engineers and the Nation's Rivers* (1951); Charles M. Hardin, *The Politics of Agriculture* (1952); Stephen K. Bailey, *Congress Makes a Law* (1950); and Morgan Thomas, *Atomic Energy and Congress* (1956).

A number of studies have been made of various lobbies and their activities and there is in addition a vast quantity of material unearthed in congressional investigations, but a theory of what may be called "legitimate influence," geared to the requirements of the legislative process, remains to be developed. For bibliographic sources see the following: Pendleton Herring, *Group Representation Before Congress* (1929); David Truman, *The Governmental Process* (1951); Harwood Childs, *Labor and Capital in National Politics* (1930); E. E. Schattschneider, *Politics, Pressures and the Tariff* (1935); Peter Odegard, *Pressure Politics: the Story of the Anti-Saloon League* (1928); Earl Latham, *The Group Basis of Politics* (1952); Fred W. Riggs, *Pressures on Congress: A Study of the Repeal of Chinese Exclusion* (1950); United States Temporary National Economic Committee, *Economic Power and Political Pressure,* Monograph No. 26 (1941); Wesley McCune, *The Farm Bloc* (1943) and *Who's Behind Our Farm Policy?* (1956); Allan S. Everest, *Morgenthau, the New Deal, and Silver: A Story of Pressure Politics* (1950). The Annual Report of the National Convention, American Legion, which is printed as a government document and found in the serial set, is replete with information on legislative activities and interests of the Legion lobby.

The courts do not attempt to influence Congress directly (except in very special cases) but of course the courts and the Constitution itself provide guides to and restraints on congressional action. The literature on judicial review of legislative acts and of the interpretations placed on various phrases of the Constitution is, of course, extensive, and no attempt will be made here to do more than call attention to its significance in providing an ideological framework within which Congress operates. Some of the pertinent legal material on legislatures has been gathered together in casebooks: See especially Hutting and Elliott, *Cases and Materials on Legislation* (1950), Chap. 6, "Legislation and the Courts: Interpretation of Statutes," and Read and MacDonald, *Cases and Other Materials on Legislation* (1948), Chap. 7, "The Methods of Interpretation and Construction."

CASE: PRESIDENTIAL MESSAGES

Examine the messages sent to Congress by the President during a single session of Congress. Organize the messages in various categories and attempt, so far as you can, to learn the success of the President in securing legislative approval of his proposals. Was the State of the Union Message specific, providing a guide for legislative action, or did it deal in generalities, leaving the implementation of the program to subsequent legal instructions? Would it appear that Congress should extend the categories of information on which the President is obliged to report? Does it appear to you that the President should have additional means to secure acceptance, or at least the consideration, of his proposals? How might this be done? Is there any evidence that the content of the proposals was discussed with congressional leaders before the messages were sent to Congress?

CASE: DEPARTMENTAL REQUESTS

Examine the annual reports of departments or independent commissions to learn what legislative requests were made. Was a convincing argument made for the legislation? Examine the actions of the pertinent legislative committees during the subsequent session of Congress to see what may have happened to the requests.

CASE: REGISTRATION OF LOBBYISTS

The requirement for the registration of lobbyists is discussed by Belle Zeller, "The Federal Regulation of Lobbying Act," *American Politicial Science Review*, April, 1948. The quarterly reports on lobbying are published in the *Congressional Record,* such as (for later years):

> 1952, 1st quarter, May 21, 1952, pp. 5707 ff.
> 1952, 2d quarter, July 7, 1952, pp. 9763 ff.
> 1952, 3d quarter, January 3, 1953, pp. 73 ff.
> 1952, 4th quarter, April 7, 1953, pp. 2776 ff.
> 1953, 1st quarter, June 15, 1953, pp. 6571 ff.
> 1953, 2d quarter, August 3, 1953, pp. 11165 ff.
> 1953, 3d quarter, February 10, 1954, pp. 1609 ff.
> 1953, 4th quarter, April 2, 1954, pp. 4502 ff.
> 1954, 1st quarter, June 2, 1954, pp. 7554 ff.
> 1954, 2d quarter, August 20, 1954, pp. 15571 ff.

Investigate the registration of congressional lobbyists for one quarter, having in mind the following questions: Who is represented? Who are the lobbyists? Do the registrations indicate how influence is exerted? Does the amount of money spent seem to you to be alarming? Do you think this type of registration hovers on the brink of unconstitutionality? Where would you draw the line on compulsory registration? What type of information do legislators require about lobbyists in order to do their job? Is this information found in existing registrations? Does the extent of registration seem to indicate the need for more specific types of representation? What type of protection do legislators need from external influence? What political function is served by external pressures and influences?

CASE: ON ACTIVITIES OF LOBBIES

Congress has made periodic investigations of lobbies and their activities, including the following:

1929–1931, Senate Judiciary Committee (Carraway)
1935, House Rules Committee
1935–1938, Senate Special Committee to Investigate Lobbying Activities (Black)
1950, House Select Committee to Investigate Lobbying Activities (Buchanan)

Examine a volume selected from these hearings. What techniques were used by lobbyists to persuade legislators? Did the activities suggest any possible need for regulation? What is the relationship between lobbying activities and the constitutional provisions regarding free speech and the right of petition?

CASE: PRESSURE GROUPS AND POLICY MAKING

The source material for studying the impact of pressure groups in policy making may not be readily available in documentary form, but one will find an abundance of material if one goes beyond the ordinary sources and uses the fugitive material found in brochures, reports, and other media of communications and persuasion. One possible approach would be to trace the activities concerning a particular controversial issue over a period of time. Such an investigation would give at least a profile of the activities involved in the process of developing policy, of the groups which are active, and of the interrelation between the development of a favorable climate of opinion and the ultimate legislative activity. Such issues may concern, for instance, farm prices, public housing, communications, defense, civil liberties, and education.

CASE: AID TO EUROPE

Before the Marshall Plan went into effect, a number of special committees—some congressional, some executive—were appointed to investigate and make recommendations on the need for economic assistance to Europe. The relevant sources are cited in the publication, *The European Recovery Program: Basic Documents and Background Information,* S. Doc. 111 (1947). Examine the documents from the point of view of the composition of the membership of the various commissions and their possible influence in securing passage of the Marshall Plan; the efficacy of the committees in focusing public attention on the issue and pointing up the type of decision which had to be made; and the analysis of the substantive nature of the issue.

CASE: HOOVER COMMISSION

Recent attempts to reorganize the government and reassess its functions have been preceded by the studies by two commissions, both headed by former President Herbert Hoover. Examine the work of these commissions from the following points of view: (1) the membership of the commissions and their ability to influence legislators and the public favorably; (2) the function of the commissions in pointing up the issues to be resolved; (3) the substantive analysis of the commissions.

CHAPTER 5. THE PROCESS: ANALYZING THE PROBLEM AND RAISING THE ISSUE

In turning to the more dynamic aspects of Congress in which the total process of making policy is considered, the concept of system is important, for system connotes a series of interrelated functions performed over a period of time by different individuals and groups. The various groups or units which have hitherto been examined can now be considered as a part of a broader system to which their actions relate. In considering the question of how political issues are raised, inquiry may be directed outward toward the totality of groups and institutions involved in raising policy issues, as well as inward, toward the controls exercised within Congress in selecting the issues for consideration. For a generalized analysis of the institutional requirements for making decisions, see the study by Snyder, Bruck, and Sapin, *Decision-Making as an Approach to the Study of International Politics* (1954).

The broad question of who raises political issues and of how they are raised offers a fruitful area of inquiry. There are practitioners galore in this field, some of whom are employed by public relations firms, but there is little formalized knowledge or systematic studies of their activities. In many cases it is apparent that attempts are made to isolate the issue, to reach agreement among possible competitive groups, and to "sell" the solution before the issue is brought to the attention of the legislature: The issue is posed; the urgency dramatized; the interest groups alerted; the executive agencies persuaded—then a full-scale barrage of concentrated persuasion is brought to bear on the critical control points within Congress. It would be enlightening to have a series of well-designed case studies in this field of policy formation. The well-known volume by Stephen K. Bailey, *Congress Makes a Law* (1950), portrays the interaction of interest groups, government agencies, party leaders, and members of Congress in developing policy. The volume of cases edited by Harold Stein, *Public Administration and Public Policy* (1952) contains several pertinent cases, especially "The Foreign Service Act of 1946," pp. 661 ff. The volume by Lawrence H. Chamberlain, *The President, Congress and Legislation* (1946), is concerned with the relative impacts of Congress and the President in originating legislation. My own book, *Congressional Politics in the Second World War* (1956), shows the manner in which congressional policies were influenced under the strain of war conditions. In *Congress on Trial* (1949), James M. Burns considers the adequacy of congressional reaction in three major policy areas. See also Charles M. Hardin, *The Politics of Agriculture* (1952). Several of the volumes already mentioned are pertinent here also, including those of Arthur A. Maass, Fred W. Riggs, Bertram M. Gross, and Morgan Thomas.

In examining the controls exercised within the legislative process, we enter a field which is often considered to be technical and specialized but which performs the important function of transferring a perhaps inchoate proposal into concrete policy having a legal base. We are interested here in the manner by which the legislative system chooses and selects issues among competing alternatives; in the structural base for making these decisions; and in the crucial points in the system where external influence may be successfully exerted. There is a plethora of writing in this area, but inasmuch as some of it may be stated in technical, procedural terminology, it may appear to some to be excessively forbidding. The following studies are pertinent to this inquiry: F. M. Riddick, *The Congress of the United States* (1941), which contains a full account of legislative procedures; D. S. Alexander, *History and Procedure of the House of Representa-*

tives (1916); R. V. Harlow, *The History of Legislative Methods in the Period Before 1825* (1917); S. T. McCall, *The Business of Congress* (1911); John Q. Tilson, *Parliamentary Law and Procedure* (1935); and Jeremy Bentham, "An Essay on Political Tactics," in *Works.* The 11-volume compilation, *Hinds' and Cannon's Precedents of the House of Representatives,* is valuable for historical precedents.

CASE: INVENTORY OF THE BUSINESS OF CONGRESS

A good deal can be learned about Congress by making an intensive examination of the business conducted by Congress during a single session. Although gross figures may be misleading and less than inclusive, still they may be gathered in such a fashion that they provide considerable information about the extent of congressional activity. One approach would be to make an inventory of the totality of certain categories of congressional activity, which could include such items as the following: bills and resolutions introduced, reported out, and enacted; committee meetings and hearings, including number of witnesses testifying; investigations requested and carried out; nominations submitted and accepted, rejected, or deferred; treaties submitted and considered; hours consumed in debate and hearings; reports received; executive orders requiring further congressional action, and the like. An inventory of this nature would, at the very least, reveal the scope of congressional activity. It would also lay the basis for answering questions regarding the most effective way in which Congress can use the time at its disposal. What kind of activity might be curtailed (assuming Congress is now fully employed) if Congress were to consider additional types of policy questions, such as those relating to controls over departments or to foreign policy?

CASE: TIME FLOW OF CONGRESSIONAL OUTPUT

The activities of Congress are accomplished procedurally within a definite span of time and they encompass the three focal points of selection, consideration, and final action. The business of Congress as a whole develops a certain rhythm, with the agenda becoming increasingly crowded as the target date for adjournment is approached.

A useful research project would be the development of a time-flow chart, showing the various activities of the total legislative system during a session of Congress. The construction of such a chart would involve the processing of the relevant data in such a fashion that the interrelationship of the various activities could be correlated with the passage of time.

CASE: ACTIVITIES OF CONGRESSIONAL COMMITTEE

This assignment examines the function of congressional committees in selecting legislation for consideration by Congress. Select any committee for study. What was the work load of the committee so far as legislative activities were concerned? How many hearings were held? How many reports were filed? How many bills were reported back to Congress? Did the committee work through standing subcommittees and, if so, did the subcommittees appear to be semi-autonomous in considering and reporting legislation? What investigative activities were carried on? Examine some dozen reports made by the committee (or as many more as are necessary to make a fair sample) to ascertain the following information: (1) Did the committee appear to split along party lines, or were the reports unanimous and nonpartisan? (2) Did the reports include statements on legislation submitted by interested departments and the Bureau of the Budget? (3) Were the reports submitted by the chairman of the committee, or did other members also participate in submitting reports?

CASE: ACTIVITIES OF A MEMBER DURING A SESSION

The public record gives only a partial account of the activities of a member inasmuch as some part of every day is spent in caring for the needs of constituents rather than in duties which are strictly official. Nevertheless, some idea of the scope of the burden falling on an individual member—Representative or Senator—and of the particular interests of this member can be determined by analyzing his participation in committee work and legislative debate. Using the Index of the *Congressional Record* as a guide, determine the following information: What type of legislation did the legislator introduce (including private bills, resolutions, and amendments offered from the floor)? With what particular interests or with what type of political issue did the member seem especially concerned? How extensively and how frequently did the member participate in debate? Was he ever given the responsibility for handling the legislation on the floor? (Make a time-flow chart, showing the participation of the member in debate on various subjects through the session.)

CASE: COMPETITION BETWEEN COMMITTEES FOR JURISDICTION OF LEGISLATION

The jurisdiction of committees not always being clear, the presiding officer (of the House or Senate) may have some leeway in referring a bill. Examine a case where a controversy occurred over such referral and determine the factors which appeared to motivate the decision. Examples of conflict over committee jurisdiction may be found in the consideration of the War Labor Disputes Act in 1943; the Contract Settlement Act in 1944; and the Armed Forces Unification Act in 1946. Does the present method of referring bills appear to be satisfactory? Would it be desirable to have some centralized control over the activities of the various committees, or should they be free to explore whatever topic appears to them to be pertinent or in which they are interested?

CHAPTER 6. DELIBERATION AND FINAL DECISION

There is less material on deliberation than might be hoped for, and on the whole the topic has received less than its due attention. The function of deliberation in adjusting conflict in democratic societies is considered by W. Y. Elliott, *Pragmatic Revolt in Politics* (1928), but the analysis is not applied specifically to the legislative process. What type of argument do legislators make which they believe will be persuasive? They frequently talk at several levels: technically before experts; logically before their colleagues; broadly assertive before the constituents when appealing for support.

The topic of majority rule has been frequently discussed but not always in a legislative context. See, for instance, Edwin Mims, *The Majority of the People* (1941); Willmoore Kendall, "The Majority Principle and the Scientific Elite," *Southern Review,* Winter, 1939, pp. 463 ff., and "Prolegomena to Any Future Work on Majority Rule," *Journal of Politics,* November, 1950, pp. 694 ff.; and Herbert McCloskey, "The Fallacy of Absolute Majority Rule," *Journal of Politics,* November, 1949, pp. 637 ff. An interesting analysis of the relative voting weight of members of Congress and of the President is found in the article by L. S. Shapley and Martin Shubik, "A Method for Evaluating the Distribution of Power in a Committee System," *American Political Science Review,* September, 1954, pp. 787 ff. The establishment of strict controls over debate in the House of Commons as a means of countering the provocative tactics of the Irish Republicans is well treated in Redlich, the *Procedure of the House of Commons* (1908). For a study of filibustering, see Franklin Burdette, *Filibustering in the Senate* (1940). See also R. J. Dangerfield, *In Defense of the Senate* (1933). The study by Gilbert Y. Steiner, *The Congressional Conference Committee* (1951), compares the relative effectiveness of the House and Senate conferees.

For source material on voting, the *Congressional Record* as well as the *Journals* of the House and Senate are official; information on committee voting is difficult to acquire but some votes may be unearthed from committee reports. The *Congressional Quarterly* classifies roll call votes by subject, party identification, state (and district for Representatives), and attitude, but regrettably the voting tabulation is not always accurate and must be used with caution. Studies of various types of voting alignments include the following: David Truman, "The State Delegations and the Structure of Party Voting in the House of Representatives," *American Political Science Review,* December, 1956, pp. 1023 ff.; V. O. Key, *Southern Politics* (1949), Chaps. 16 and 17; my own volume, *Congressional Politics in the Second World War* (1956), contains charts in the appendix on partisan alignments during the war period; George L. Grassmuck, *Sectional Biases in Congress on Foreign Policy* (1951); Julius Turner,

Party and Constituency: Pressures on Congress (1951); H. Bradford Westerfield, *Foreign Policy and Party Politics: Pearl Harbor to Korea* (1955); and T. R. Amlie, *Let's Look at the Record* (1950).

CASE: PASSAGE OF LEGISLATION

This assignment encompasses the passage of a single piece of legislation, with pertinent questions raised concerning the various steps of the process and some overall considerations given to the process as a whole. A list of bills is found at the end of this case.

Hearings. Read the hearings of one committee and then answer the following questions: What functions do the hearings seem to perform? Develop several categories of witnesses, indicating the role they seemed to play in the hearings. What types of questions were asked? Why were they asked? Was there any difficulty in establishing communications between the questioners and the witnesses?

The Report. How would you evaluate the report: (1) as a document which would be informative to a member of Congress not on the committee; (2) as a guide for administrative action; (3) as a vehicle for informing the intelligent layman of the content of the legislation?

The Debate. How was the debate "structured"? Who participated? What was the content of the debate? Did the debaters seem to be interested in: (1) justifying their actions; (2) securing partisan advantage; (3) seeking favor with their supporters; (4) developing an understanding of the type of policy which would be developed from the legislation?

The Final Act. Did the Act seem to give the bureaucracy considerable freedom of action? Were the instructions clear? What provisions were made for personnel to administer the Act? What provisions were made regarding the internal structure of the agency and the supply of funds? Were there any opportunities for court review of the administrative action or the legality of the legislation itself? What provisions, if any, were made for establishing future congressional control over the policy?

The Process as a Whole. In the enactment of the legislation, what functional role was played by the following groups or individuals: the representatives of pressure groups; the committee chairmen; the representatives of executive agencies; the President? Was there a continual narrowing of disputed issues during the deliberations? Were the "important" issues discussed? Can you think of any steps which might usefully be added to the process? For what purpose? In what regard might the process be shortened? For what purpose? So far as control over the legislative process is concerned, what were the important decisions which were made and who made them?

Veterans Emergency Housing Act, 60 Stat. 207 (1946), H. R. 4761. Hearings: Senate Banking and Currency

Foreign Assistance Act of 1948, 62 Stat. 137 (1948), S. 2202
  Hearings: Senate Foreign Relations

Mutual Security Act of 1951, 65 Stat. 373 (1951), H. R. 5113
    Hearings: House Foreign Affairs; jointly, Senate Foreign Relations and Armed Services

State Fair-Trade Law Amendment, 66 Stat. 631 (1952), H. R. 5767
    Hearings: House Interstate and Foreign Commerce; Senate Interstate and Foreign Commerce

Armed Forces Reserve Act, 66 Stat. 481 (1952) H. R. 5426
    Hearings: Senate Armed Services

Veterans' Readjustment Assistance Act, 66 Stat. 663 (1952), H. R. 7656
    Hearings: Senate Labor and Public Welfare

Farm Credit Act of 1953, 67 Stat. 390 H. R. 4352 (S. 1505)
    Hearings: House Agriculture; Senate Agriculture and Forestry

Atomic Energy Act of 1953, 68 Stat. 919 (1954), H. R. 9757 (S. 3690)
    Hearings: Joint Atomic Energy (on H. R. 8862 and S. 3323)

Mutual Security Act of 1953, 67 Stat. 152 (1953), H. R. 5719 (S. 2128)
    Hearings: House Foreign Affairs; Senate Foreign Relations

St. Lawrence Seaway Development Corporation, 68 Stat. 92 (1954), S. 2150 (S. 589)

 Hearings: House Public Works (in 1953 on H. J. Res. 104); Senate Foreign Relations (in 1953 on S. 589)

Submerged Lands Act, 67 Stat. 29 (1953), H. R. 5198 (S. J. Res. 13)

 Hearings: Senate Interior and Insular

Administrative Procedure Act, 60 Stat. 237 (1946), S. 7

 Hearings: House Judiciary (held in June, 1945)

Strategic and Critical Materials Stock Piling Act, 60 Stat. 596 (1946), S. 752

 Hearings: House Military Affairs; Senate Military Affairs (in 1945)

Portal-to-Portal Act of 1947, 61 Stat. 84 (1947), H. R. 2157 (S. 70)

 Hearings: House Judiciary; Senate Judiciary

National Security Act of 1947, 61 Stat. 495 (1947), S. 758 (H. R. 4214)

 Hearings: House Expenditures

Selective Service Act of 1948, 62 Stat. 604 (1948), S. 2655 (H. R. 6401)

 Hearings: House Armed Services

Labor Management Relations Act (Taft-Hartley), 61 Stat. 136 (1947), H. R. 3020

 Hearings: House Education and Labor: Senate Labor and Public Welfare (on S. 55)

Defense Production Act of 1950, 64 Stat. 798 (1950), H. R. 9176 (S. 3936)

 Hearings: House Banking and Currency; Senate Banking and Currency

CASE: CONTROL OF DEBATE: RULES COMMITTEE AND UNANIMOUS CONSENT AGREEMENTS

Make a comparative study of the method of terminating debate in the House (by special rules) and in the Senate (through unanimous consent agreements). Examine some half dozen rules reported by the Rules Committee. What kinds of limitations were imposed by the rules? Did the restrictions appear to limit the actions of the House as a deliberative body? What types of decisions were permitted and what types prohibited? Examine several instances in the Senate where debate was terminated through unanimous consent. Did the Senate appear to have had sufficient time to deliberate the subject adequately? How do you account for the fact that Senators are willing to give unanimous consent for terminating debate, even on subjects which they disapprove? Do the House procedures or the Senate procedures appear to you to be more conducive to full deliberation?

CASE: CONTROL OF DEBATE: CONTENT

Examine closely the debate in the House and Senate during a single day. Does there appear to be any wandering from the topic or any lack of germaneness in the discussions? Why is relevancy not insisted upon? How do you account for the fact that extensive interruptions in the regular order of business are allowed? Although lack of pertinency, repetition, and interruptions are all permitted, still there are types of debate and types of remarks which are not countenanced. Investigate, for instance, instances where members have been reprimanded or forced to retract their remarks. Examine some of the numerous cases cited in *Hinds'* and *Cannon's Precedents* and determine the basis on which the reprimand was justified by its proponents.

CASE: OFFICIAL OBJECTORS

One of the methods used by the House to prevent legislation from being adopted without proper consideration is that of having official objectors see to it that "unwanted" legislation does not slip through during the call of the calendar when debate is severely restricted. Make an examination of the call of the calendar during any one session to determine the part played by these objectors. Did the same group of objectors operate throughout the session? Were they members of the same party? Did they appear to protect the public interest or were they primarily obstructionistic? Did they force some type of deliberation to take place, perhaps off the floor, by compelling adjustments and explanations to be made? What is to be said for this method of considering minor legislation, in which minimal debate is balanced by the requirement that the proposal secure what amounts to unanimous consent? Can you think of any more appropriate method of handling such legislation?

CASE: VOTING PATTERNS

The study of voting patterns in Congress shows that various types of alignments are associated with different issues. Although voting studies are laborious, particularly those of the House, they may nevertheless reveal the complicated nature of partisan alignment more effectively than any other method. The maps of congressional districts found in the back pages of the *Congressional Directory* may be redrawn on a larger scale—and perhaps imposed on maps showing such additional information as political boundaries and economic or ethnographic data—and used for plotting votes. The following problems might be considered in voting analysis:

1. The deviation of members from a "norm," such as that determined, say, by the party majority, or the position of the President, or the "liberal" position, or the votes of any one man.
2. The identification of blocs, the members of which tend to vote alike on some—perhaps all—measures, such as civil rights, silver, farm supports, immigration, public power.
3. The relative homogeneity of voting of urban representatives—by parties, regions, and issues.
4. Similarly, for rural representatives.
5. The persistency of attitudes of members from certain districts (or states) toward certain issues, regardless of party affiliation.

CASE: APPEALS FOR SUPPORT

In justifying their actions, members of Congress are of course appealing for the support of the public for their own career, for the particular policy involved, and for the government itself as an institution which can resolve conflict. How do members make such appeals?

What kinds of appeals are made? Although figures may not be available for such items as the total number of reprints made of excerpts reprinted from the *Congressional Record,* other accessible information may reveal the general procedure followed in appealing for public support. This will include, say, the use of broadcasting material for domestic consumption, weekly newspaper columns, questionnaires sent to constituents, reprints, and the free distribution of government documents. What is the content of such appeals? How effective are they? Who should finance this admittedly personal and perhaps partisan explanation of political action? What additional information might the constituents find useful in order to get a more balanced, less subjective picture of the operation of Congress as an entity?

CHAPTER 7. DIRECTION AND REVIEW

The establishment of policy through the passage of an Act may not necessarily adjust the conflicting interests in a satisfactory manner. Demands for the further reintegration of purposes may still be made, and in any event Congress will wish to know, or has the responsibility for knowing, how satisfactorily the policy is meeting legislative expectations. In order to establish a continuing relationship between itself and the policy in question, Congress has created an elaborate system of controls for giving directions and for learning how the authorized policies are actually being carried out. Directions are given legally in the form of law, but they may also be given less formally and more indirectly through debates or resolutions or even through the demands made on an agency by an influential member of Congress. The fact that directions may be given in the form of law also means that courts are brought into the system of controls through their ability to interpret and enforce the law.

For a general theoretical discussion of the establishment of political responsibility, see the rewarding study by C. J. Friedrich, *Constitutional Government and Politics* (rev. ed., 1950), where the theme of constitutional restraint runs through the entire book. The essay by J. Roland Pennock, "Responsiveness, Responsibility, and Majority Rule," *American Political Science Review,* September, 1952, pp. 790

ff., is a thoughtful attempt to clarify several concepts which are often loosely used.

There is no great abundance of literature on the establishment of responsibility for particular types of action through particular types of institutions, except so far as judicial and fiscal controls are concerned. The subject of judicial review is somewhat beyond the scope of this assignment, but the material here is of course pertinent for a complete understanding of institutional devices for establishing responsibility. Judicial statements of the boundaries imposed on Congress in delegating authority are found in *Yakus v. United States,* 321 US 414 (1955); *Schechter v. United States,* 295 US 495 (1935); *Panama Refining Co. v. Ryan,* 293 US 388 (1935); and *Hampton v. United States,* 276 US 394 (1928). The *Decisions of the Attorney General,* while concerned for the most part with administrative matters, occasionally contain interpretations of legislative Acts. On the content of statutes, see Ernst Freund, *Standards of American Legislation* (1917). See also C. T. Carr, *Delegated Legislation* (1921).

The work of C. S. Hyneman, *Bureaucracy in a Democracy* (1950), has as its general theme the ability of the legislative branch to establish and integrate political ends. For controls over international affairs, see Robert Dahl, *Congress and Foreign Policy* (1950), and over atomic policy, Robert Dahl and Ralph S. Brown, *Domestic Control of Atomic Energy* (1951). The volume by Lindsay Rogers, *The American Senate* (1926), argues for the free flow of information from the executive branch in order that the Senate can perform its function as critic.

CASE: REVIEW OF PLANS FOR GOVERNMENT REORGANIZATION

A practice has developed in recent years of permitting Congress to review plans for government reorganization before they come into effect. A number of issues are raised by this new procedural device for extending congressional control. Examine one, or several, of the reorganization plans listed below as a basis for developing some criteria on the efficacy of this type of control. Why is Congress reluctant to permit the President to reorganize administrative agencies? Is the right to consolidate or abolish functions equivalent to the right to make law? What is the relationship between the structure of administrative agencies and the structure of influence and pressure which may be brought to bear on the agencies?

1954—Foreign Claims Settlement Commission, H. Res. 594
        Department of Agriculture, H. R. 6944
1953—Agriculture, S. Res. 100; H. Res. 236
        Airline Subsidy, H. Res. 264
        Federal Security Agency, H. J. Res. 223
        Foreign Aid, H. Res. 261; H. Res. 281
        Foreign Information, H. Res. 262; H. Res. 282
1952—Internal Revenue, H. Res. 292; S. Res. 295
        Post Office, S. Res. 317
        Bureau of Customs, S. Res. 331
        Justice, S. Res. 330
1951—RFC, H. Res. 142; S. Res. 76
1950—Comptroller of Currency, S. Res. 246
        Agriculture, S. Res. 263; H. Res. 546
        Labor, H. Res. 522
        Interstate Commerce Commission, H. Res. 545; S. Res. 253
        Federal Trade Commission, S. Res. 254
1949—Reorganization Plan No. 1, S. Res. 147
        Reorganization Plan No. 2, S. Res. 151

CASE: DEPARTMENTAL REPORTING

Select for examination the annual report of a government department or agency. Does the report seem to be fully informative? What kind of information was not included which you would have wished to have seen? If you were in some fashion responsible for government policy (but not a member of the department concerned), would you feel satisfied from the information given in the report that everything was going well?

CASE: THE QUESTION PERIOD

Proposals are continually being made that Congress emulate the British parliamentary practice of having a daily question period, in which administrators would answer questions previously submitted by members of Congress. Congress has considered the feasibility of the plan from time to time, although some of the functions of the question hour are in fact performed by having administrators testify before committee hearings. (In a committee hearing, the number of participating members is limited, but the questions may range more widely and are less restricted than in the British question period.) For comparative purposes, examine several question periods in debates of the House of Commons (they occur daily at the beginning of a session); examine also the proposals for establishing such procedures in the House of Representatives. (See the intermittent debate on H. Res. 327, introduced by the then Representative Estes Kefauver: *Congressional Record,* November 12, 1943, pp. 9458–63; November 26, 1943, pp. 10038–46; March 23, 1944, pp. 2976–77; March 29, 1944, pp. 3271–74.) What would be the organizational considerations in establishing a question period in Congress? What would be the advantage of questioning administrative officials in Congress as opposed to questioning them in committee hearings? Would it be advisable to ask questions directly of the President (a privilege already extended to the press)?

CASE: THE DISMISSAL OF GENERAL MACARTHUR

The hearings conducted jointly by the Senate Foreign Relations Committee and Armed Services Committee in 1951 produced a comprehensive survey of the policy preceding the Korean War and of the conduct of the war itself. Examine these hearings carefully. Did Congress appear to be the proper institution to conduct an inquiry of this kind? Did it appear that vital, perhaps secret, information was revealed, an act which might have been harmful to the country. Was Congress entitled to have this information? Were the hearings conducted in a partisan manner? What sanctions did Congress have if it were dissatisfied with the policy being pursued?

CHAPTER 8. CONTROLS OVER PERSONNEL

The literature on government personnel frequently has an executive bias, with congressional controls over appointments often considered to be synonymous with senatorial courtesy, and dismissals being considered the exclusive prerogative of the President. Some of the disputes concerning legislative or executive jurisdiction tend to avoid the essentially political questions involved in determining personnel policy, and they may also ignore the fact that, constitutionally, many of the issues regarding personnel policy must be resolved by Congress. These issues relate to the development of standards of competence, to providing methods of recruitment, and to establishing administrative structures in order to create a hierarchy of officials competent to exercise governmental authority. A subsidiary problem also arises in determining the controls over personnel which Congress does have, or should have, when officials fail to reintegrate purposes in a manner satisfactory to Congress.

The Hyneman volume, already mentioned, discusses these issues in the chapter, "Choosing Men for Jobs," (Chap. 10), and Arthur Macmahon has written a perspicacious article, "Senatorial Confirmation," *Public Administration Review,* Vol. 3, 1943, pp. 281 ff. The study by Joseph Harris, *The Advice and Consent of the Senate* (1953) gives a historical survey of senatorial practice which is often less than flattering. *The Executive Journal of the Senate* contains a vast amount of basic information on executive nominations, including names and disposition. The volume by Grace M. Kammerer, *Congressional Committee Staffing Since 1946* (1951) gives a general account of staffing developments over a brief period, but additional analytical studies are needed of the personnel of Congress, including those in the offices of members, the staffs of committees, and the officials and staffs of the House and Senate.

CASE: THE CLASSIFICATION ACT OF 1923

The basic legislative provision for recruiting personnel is found in the Classification Act of 1923 (42 Stat. 1488). A study of the legislative deliberations leading to the enactment of this law reveals the purposes which Congress attempted to accomplish in establishing permanent policy concerning government personnel. See particularly the report of the Joint Commission on Reclassification of Salaries,

March 12, 1920 (H. Doc. 686, 66/2, 1919–1920); the debates on H. R. 8928 in the 67th Congress (1921–1923); and the reports of the committees, H. Rept. 461 (67/1) and S. Rept. 486 (67/2).

CASE: IMPEACHMENT OF PRESIDENT JOHNSON

In the impeachment trial of President Johnson, Congress attempted to punish the President for failing to be governed by the Tenure of Office Act. The Senate proceedings are found in the *Congressional Globe,* February 25, 1868, to May 26, 1868. Did the standards contained in the Tenure of Office Act seem reasonable? What was Johnson's defense for disobeying the law? Was the punishment proposed more excessive than the offense warranted? In a case where the President clearly goes beyond the bounds of the Constitution, or of legislation, what recourse is available to Congress?

CASE: THE PROMOTION OF CAPTAIN HYMAN G. RICKOVER

Nominations of military officials are ordinarily approved without controversy, but occasionally Congress raises a disturbing question. Such was the case when the name of Captain Rickover, an expert in developing the atomically propelled submarine, failed to appear in the list of promotions to rear admiral. Congress wanted to know, "Why?" See the debate in the *Congressional Record* in 1953 and 1954. What conclusions can be reached regarding the efficacy of or the need for congressional control from a study of this controversy?

CASE: THE NOMINATION AND CONFIRMATION OF CHARLES E. WILSON

What constitutes a conflict of interest? This perennial question was at the heart of the conflict over dollar-a-year men during the war, and it comes up whenever the projected role in official life seems to conflict with other interests. These other interests are mainly economic but they are sometimes ideologic, as is implied in the legal provision that personnel employed by the Tennessee Valley Authority must be in sympathy with the purposes of the agency. The possible conflict of interest between Mr. Wilson, as a stockholder and former official of General Motors, and Mr. Wilson, as Secretary-designate of

Defense, was discussed in congressional hearings before Mr. Wilson was confirmed. The fact that Mr. Wilson was first compelled to sell his stock in General Motors led one wit to comment that Mr. Wilson had been confirmed "lock and barrel." Another humorist suggested that Mr. Wilson should not be forced to dispose of his stock of General Motors but, rather, that he be compelled to buy commensurate shares of the stock of the Ford and Chrysler Motor Companies. Examine the hearings before the Senate Committee on the Armed Services, Parts I and II, January, 1953, as well as the debates in Congress (found in the Index under "Executive Nominations and Confirmations").

CHAPTER 9. CONTROLS OVER FEDERAL FINANCE

Many of the studies of budgeting, as of personnel, which are written from the administrative point of view, may be unsympathetic with legislative participation or "legislative interference," as it may be called, in the budgetary process. There are relatively few studies of budgeting which are concerned primarily with the establishment of legislative controls. In this area also there is need for research— for research directed toward the construction of useful theories of the legislative function in the budgetary process and in determining fiscal policy. The part that can best be played by Congress in making the annual budget is incompletely understood and often unsatisfactorily performed; the present system of legislative controls over spending is quite inadequate; and the controls exercised by the legislature over total fiscal policy are applied differentially, by the piecemeal method, with the problem rarely raised to a conceptual level where it can be examined in its entirety.

For a general treatment of the budget, see Arthur Smithies, *The Budgetary Process in the United States* (1955). The series of articles by Arthur Macmahon, "Oversight of Administration: The Power of the Purse," *Political Science Quarterly,* June, 1943, *et seq.,* are illuminating studies of legislative control. The publication edited by Catheryn Seckler-Hudson, *Budgeting, an Instrument of Planning and Management* (1944) contains reprints of many excellent articles on budgeting which appeared initially in other publications. See also Vincent J. Brown, *The Control of the Public Budget* (1949); George B. Galloway, *Reform of the Federal Budget* (1950); Ernest S. Griffith, *Congress* (2d rev., 1956) Chap. 7; C. S. Hyneman, *Bureaucracy in a Democracy* (1950), Chaps. 7, 13, 17, 18; Elias Huzar, *The Purse and the Sword* (1950); Lucius Wilmerding, Jr., *The Spending Power, A History of the Efforts of Congress to Control Expenditures* (1943).

For a study of the General Accounting Office, see Harvey Mansfield, *The Comptroller General* (1939); the picture described by Mr. Mansfield has been somewhat modified by amendatory legislation, a change of officials, and a softening of attitudes. See also *Budgeting and Accounting, A Report to the Congress,* prepared by the Hoover Commission—the Commission on Organization of the Executive Branch of the Government.

CASE: PASSAGE OF APPROPRIATION BILLS

The consideration by Congress of appropriation bills can be studied in much the same fashion that legislative bills were studied. Evaluate the congressional process from the following points of view: its effectiveness in controlling administrative behavior; its effectiveness in determining overall fiscal policy; its effectiveness for making decisions on allocating funds. Do you have any procedural changes to suggest which would assist Congress in performing these functions?

Labor-Federal Security Appropriation, 1953. 66 Stat. 358 (1952), H. R. 7151
    Hearings: House Appropriations and Senate Appropriations
Departments of State, Justice, Commerce, and the Judiciary Appropriations Act, 1947. 60 Stat. 446 (1946), H. R. 6056
    Hearings: House Appropriations
Civil Functions Appropriation Act, 1955. 68 Stat. 330 (1954), H. R. 8367
    Hearings: House Appropriations and Senate Appropriations
Interior Department Appropriation Act, 1952. 65 Stat. 248 (1951), H. R. 3790
    Hearings: House Appropriations and Senate Appropriations

Independent Offices Appropriations Act, 1950. 63 Stat. 631 (1949),
H. R. 4177
Hearings: House Appropriations and Senate Appropriations
Treasury and Post Office Departments Appropriations Act, 1948. 61 Stat.
216 (1947), H. R. 2436
Hearings: House Appropriations and Senate Appropriations
Legislative Branch Appropriations Act, 1949. 62 Stat. 423 (1948). H. R.
6500
Hearings: House Appropriations and Senate Appropriations
Deficiency Appropriations Act, 1950. 64 Stat. 275 (1950). H. R. 8567
Hearings: House Appropriations and Senate Appropriations
District of Columbia Appropriations Act, 1954. 67 Stat. 278 (1953),
H. R. 5471
Hearings: House Appropriations and Senate Appropriations

CASE: BUDGET ESTIMATES AND APPROPRIATIONS

Make a study of the instrumentalities for requesting funds and for
appropriating funds, found in two basic documents: *The Budget of
the United States Government,* prepared annually by the Bureau of
the Budget, and *Appropriations, Budget Estimates, Etc.,* prepared
annually by the Appropriations Committees of Congress. Do the
appropriation estimates appear to be sufficiently clear to give Congress
an intelligent grasp of the major issues? Can control more readily be
established over small items than over large items? In your examination of the text of appropriation bills, do you find any case where
legislative instructions were given on how money should be spent?
Do instructions of this sort appear to be a legitimate use of congressional authority?

CASE: COMPTROLLER GENERAL

Select a case from the volume of decisions of the Comptroller
General where there is a dispute over interpretation of the Appropriations Act. What was the issue involved? Did the Comptroller General's decision seem to you to be meritorious? Do you think that
there should be any legislative survey over these decisions? Are there
other procedural devices which you can suggest which would increase

the information received by Congress on the purposes for which money has been spent?

CASE: COURT OF CLAIMS

Select a case from the volume of decisions of the Court of Claims. What was the issue involved? Did the decision in the case seem to you to be fair? Does this procedure seem to you to provide an adequate method for resolving fiscal disputes? What roles does Congress play in the process?

CHAPTER 10. INVESTIGATIONS

The investigations carried on by Congress raise a host of issues, extending from the protection of individual rights, which is frequently stressed in articles critical of investigating committees, to the adequacy of the information available to Congress in making policy decisions. A number of studies of investigations have been undertaken from a legal point of view, but few of them relate investigations to a general theory of fact-finding, necessary for making decisions, or of control, necessary for making certain how in fact the laws are being administered. How is the function of investigating committees related to a broader theory of control? What are the limitations over their action (who guards the guardians)? What is the dilemma posed if facts necessary for making policy are not forthcoming? What are the areas of permissive secrecy?

Of the several studies of congressional investigating committees, see, especially, the following: M. E. Dimock, *Congressional Investigation Committees* (1929); E. J. Eberling, *Congressional Investigations* (1928); J. E. Johnson, *Investigating Powers of Congress* (1951); M. N. McGeary, *The Developments of Congressional Investigative Power* (1940). For a comprehensive annotation of legal cases, see the article, "Contempt of Congress or Congressional Committee," 97 L. Ed., pp. 782–821.

CASE: SCOPE OF INVESTIGATIONS

Make a comprehensive survey of the scope of investigations during a single session of Congress, including in the survey the following

material: (1) proposals for investigations (as indicated by the introduction of special resolutions); (2) investigations authorized or
existing (as indicated by the *Congressional Record* or *Congressional
Directory*); (3) investigations carried out (as indicated by the
Monthly Catalog of the Government Printing Office); (4) contempt
citations voted (as indicated by the *Congressional Record* or the
House or Senate *Journal*). What was the nature of the proposals for
investigation? Did they appear to you to have a partisan bias? Who
made the decisions whether or not to permit the investigation to go
forward? Did the majority appear to choke off investigations? Or did
the minority appear to be able to create investigations too readily?
Does the extent of investigations indicate that Congress is diligent
in exercising oversight over matters of public concern? On the other
hand, does the extent of investigations indicate that other methods
of control are not adequate?

CASE: NATURE OF INVESTIGATIVE INQUIRY

Select for inquiry any volume of testimony from some active investigations committee, such as that of the House Committee on Un-
American Activities (Dies; Wood; Velde); the Senate Judiciary
Subcommittee on Internal Security (Jenner); the Permanent Investigations Subcommittee of the Senate Committee on Government
Operations (McCarthy); the wartime Truman Committee; the Kefauver Committee (on crime); the Daniel Committee (on narcotics);
or the Special Committee to Investigate Pearl Harbor. Did the committee appear to have prepared its material carefully, or were the
questions raised at random, without order or relevance? How much
of the questioning was undertaken by members of the staff? Were the
witnesses coöperative and informative, or did they appear to be
reticent and obstructionist? Was the information elicited of a kind
which might assist Congress in developing public policy? Were you
satisfied with the method of conduct of the hearing you studied?
If not, what remedy would you propose?

CASE: CONTEMPT

Examine an instance where Congress voted to bring contempt charges against a witness. The following references may facilitate research:

House Un-American Activities,   1954, H. Res. 664–681, 704
                                   1952, H. Res. 517, 602, 717, 718
                                   1950, H. Res. 749–804
                                   1947, H. Res. 190, 192–193
                                   1946, H. Res. 573
House Education and Labor, 1954, H. Res. 693–694
House Lobbying, 1950, H. Res. 834–836
Senate Government Operations,   1954, S. Res. 280–282, 306–307
                                   1953, S. Res. 103, 147
Senate Interstate and Foreign Commerce, 1953, S. Res. 139
Senate District of Columbia, 1952, S. Res. 281–282
Senate Judiciary, 1952, S. Res. 283, 295
Senate Crime, 1951, S. Res. 43–48, 50, 66–70, 78–85, 109–120, 159–161,
               180–184, 211–214
               1950, S. Res. 358
Senate Foreign Relations, 1950, S. Res. 349–351

What was the nature of the offense? Did the action about which there was complaint appear to you to be contemptuous? Was the witness acting in good faith and attempting to be helpful? Do you think any constitutional rights of the witness were violated by the contempt citation? Was there any debate in the proceedings? Do you think that this method of protecting congressional proceedings is adequate? What other methods might be utilized?

CHAPTER 11. CONCLUSIONS

There are unattractive alternatives to a type of constitutional government where the legislature is at the heart of the process for developing policy and securing responsible action on the part of government officials. It is well known, however, that the legislatures of some countries have not proved strong enough to resist the threat of dictators and in other countries their vitality may have been sapped by the overwhelming influence of the executive and the bureaucracy. Given the goals of and the belief in constitutional government, the problem then is to strengthen legislatures in such a fashion that their function is clearly defined and understood, their authority respected, their policy wisely developed, and their influence not motivated primarily by partisan and personal advantage.

The argument has been advanced that irritations in the American system resulting from the separation of powers could be lessened by strengthening the position of the President, or by building a more durable bridge between the President and Congress. This point of view is supported by W. Y. Elliott in *The Need for Constitutional Reform* (1935); by Thomas Finletter in *Can Representative Government Do the Job?* (1945); and by Henry Hazlitt in *A New Constitution Now* (1942).

The argument has also been advanced that Congress could add to its stature by reforming its own internal organization, a point of view which found expression in the Congressional Reorganization Act of 1946. The argument for such reform is made by George Galloway in *Congress at the Crossroads* (1946), especially in the last two chapters.

Pertinent though various reform proposals may be, there is still more to be known, more thinking to be done, and more theories to be developed, before the nature and function of the legislative process can be fully comprehended and, perhaps, before reform proposals can be offered with any confidence that they will produce desirable results. Purposeful and thoughtful research is needed in many areas, not only to reveal how Congress works, or to develop plans by which it might be made to work better, but to provide a depth of understanding of the institutional and political requirements for creating wise and just policy within a constitutional framework of government. This Research Guide points up some of the areas where further research would be useful in gathering and interpreting facts. This should help to provide a groundwork of understanding, but it can only hint at, without prescribing, that which is perhaps most needed—a synthesizing, theory-building approach to legislative studies which will relate Congress more clearly to the whole intellectual process of selecting alternatives in formulating public policy and of providing standards of accountability for the control of governmental authority.

INDEX